Transforming Paradise

How Franklin D. Roosevelt and Thousands of Unemployed Americans Created Today's Yosemite National Park

JOHN BROESAMLE

The Press at California State University, Fresno
Fresno, CA 93740-8042, press@csufresno.edu

Design by Joel MaHarry, MaHarry.work

Publisher's Cataloging-in-Publication
(Provided by Cassidy Cataloguing Services, Inc.).

Name:	Broesamle, John J., author.
Title:	Transforming Paradise : how Franklin D. Roosevelt and thousands of unemployed Americans created today's Yosemite National Park / John Broesamle.
Description:	Fresno, CA : The Press at California State University, Fresno, [2024] | Includes bibliographical references and index.
Identifiers:	ISBN: 978-1-959274-02-5 (paperback) | 978-1-959274-03-2 (kindle) | LCCN: 2024937513
Subjects:	LCSH: Yosemite National Park (Calif.)--History. | Roosevelt, Franklin D. (Franklin Delano), 1882-1945. | National parks and reserves--United States--History. | New Deal, 1933-1939-- History. | Civilian Conservation Corps (U.S.)--History. | Depressions--1929--United States. | United States--Economic conditions--1918-1945. | United States--Social conditions--1933-1945.
Classification:	LCC: F868.Y6 B76 2024 | DDC: 979.4/47--dc23k

LCCN 2024937513
ISBN 978-1-959274-02-5

For my family

CONTENTS

FOREWORD

This is a special book, for many reasons.

Yosemite is arguably America's most famous, popular, and spectacular National Park, and its early days have been thoroughly charted by historians. Its transition from a pristine Native American homeland in the mid 19th century, to an international attraction and symbol of environmental preservation in the 20th, has been equally well documented. These accounts, we now acknowledge, must be viewed with a substantial caveat: Most narratives about the settling of the American West, seen through the lens of the values of Manifest Destiny, fail to reckon with the tragic destruction this visited on our continent's vital indigenous cultures. That failure is at last, in more recent works, beginning to be rectified.

Yosemite's transformation, in the 1920s and '30s, from an untamed wilderness embodying the lofty conservationist ideals of John Muir and Teddy Roosevelt, into the modern preserve and accessible wonder of the world it is today, is the other key piece of narrative we've been missing.

Until now.

John Broesamle, an acclaimed historian and author of many academic and popular works, has brought this untold chapter of Yosemite's evolution during FDR's New Deal to stirring and vivid life. You won't find much about John's personal journey to this book's creation in these pages, but it's worth recounting and bearing in mind, before entering the world he's conjured up within.

The milestones of John's years are inextricably entwined with Yosemite. As a young boy he and his parents spent every summer roughing it in the park. Later, while still a student, he began his working life there, which led to John meeting his future wife Kathy, who has her own deep ties to this paradise. Five generations of the family have now made the park their spiritual home. While earning a PhD from historian heavyweights at Columbia, John decided against advancing his promising academic future in the Ivy League. The Sierras spoke so strongly to him he chose to return home to California to keep them within reach.

After retiring from his celebrated teaching career at Cal State Northridge, John amassed a peerless record as a dedicated conservationist and leader of nonprofit environmental organizations. In the spring of 2018, at the height of success in his commendable second act, he drew a terrible hand: A diagnosis of pancreatic cancer.

With characteristic stoic resolve, and extraordinary medical care, he beat the odds, surviving to live another five years that John later called the most important and satisfying of his life. The presence of mortality, he said, has a marvelous way of focusing one's heart and mind. Dedicating these precious weeks and months to his family and friends, he decided to capstone his life's work with this saga of Yosemite's forgotten decades. As a living link to that period, he brought together his personal and professional passions in this elegiac tale of a vanishing era that would have, without him, passed into time's shadows.

When John's cancer returned in the spring of 2023, he had just secured The Press at California State University, Fresno as publisher for the book, and *Transforming Paradise* had entered its final editorial stages. (In a lovely bit of synchronicity, one of the Civilian Conservation Corps volunteers profiled in the book later became a distinguished member of Fresno State's History faculty.) With the help of his family, John's final days were spent refining its finishing touches.

I've been fortunate to count John among the closest handful of true friends this life has ever brought me. This book is not only an act of personal courage, but evidence of his profound dedication to the principles and ideals that made him the man so many who knew him loved and admired.

I'll be forever grateful for the years I knew John. His legacy of kindness, dignity, passion, joy, and idealism lives on in everyone who knew him well.

This book is his final gift, and I hope you'll find it as rich and rewarding an experience as his friendship was to me.

Ojai, California

PREFACE

It had never occurred to me to write this book, even though the subject stood out in plain sight. I just failed to see it, which is a little odd. I am both a professional historian and a lifelong denizen of Yosemite National Park. I first visited Yosemite as an infant in the summer of 1942, when the New Deal's great transformation of the park was winding up. At some point in recent years, I looked to see what had been published about that transformation as a whole and encountered a virtual void. The New Deal years – 1933-1942 – were the period when the park we know today emerged; they account for *why* it emerged. Having stumbled into this untold story, I became fascinated by it.

The story tells how the great changes came about. It profiles many of the people who carried them out, from President Franklin D. Roosevelt down to park rangers and crews on the ground. Extraordinary individuals cross the stage, many of them forgotten and a few unknown until now. We will explore a Yosemite that we readily recognize today – and another Yosemite, from the 1930s, that we have trouble recognizing at all.

The past, it is said, is like a different country; people do things differently there. Some of what this book discloses has genuinely startled me. Though not an age of innocence, the decade of the 1930s was more innocent than today. It preceded the nuclear age. It also preceded the hardened negativism that later curdled the sense of possibility in American political life. That abundant sense of possibility inspired a boldness in the New Deal that now strikes us as remarkable. Just as the Roosevelt Administration was responsible for national programs of immense ambition – from Social Security to the Tennessee Valley Authority to the wartime GI Bill – the same ambition characterized its approach to Yosemite. Proceeding with a truly stunning sense of assurance, Roosevelt's New Deal transformed the park. To carry out the work, Washington mobilized thousands of the unemployed and impoverished. Programs primarily intended to give jobs to people dispossessed by the Great Depression left a permanent imprint on Yosemite, and, in turn, Yosemite left its mark on them. The unfolding story will continually remind us that the past does indeed resemble a different country.

ACKNOWLEDGMENTS

I owe a debt of gratitude to so many that it is very hard to know where to begin.

Let me start by thanking my doctors. A whole group of cancer specialists kept me going while writing this book, and two went far beyond their professional obligations – Doctors Joshua Rosenberg of UCLA and Susanne Warner of City of Hope (now of the Mayo Clinic).

Over the years, my debts have also mounted to ophthalmologists – two in particular, because on separate occasions each brought me out of blindness. They are Doctors David A. Lee, who now holds a chair in ophthalmology at the University of Texas Health Science Center at Houston, and Anthony J. Aldave of the UCLA Stein Eye Institute.

Tom Bopp, the longtime pianist and raconteur at the Wawona Hotel, is a Yosemite institution. He is a leading authority on the history of the Wawona region of the park. Tom's generosity in sharing his knowledge and research files has known no limits.

My daughter, Carolyn Vondriska, took photos for the book of the park as it is today. She also had the inspiration to reach out on my behalf to the families of men who served in the Civilian Conservation Corps in and around Yosemite. This helped break the project free of the COVID-19 constrictions that shuttered research archives across the country while the pandemic raged.

Carolyn's inspiration connected me with the daughter of Al Monteverde, Nona Monteverde Rafferty. She and her husband, Gary, provided a painstaking transcription of her father's invaluable memoir; his correspondence from his time in the CCC; and his contemporary photos. Nona's and Gary's personal reminiscences of Al and his family have been invaluable.

Others responded with remarkable generosity of time and effort. Jack Ricci shared images and memories of his father, John. Sue Fouke furnished information and photos for the portrait of her father, Joe Bryan. And Andrea Miller provided recollections of her father, Alf Bergly, together with a trove of photographs.

One of the most stirring interviews I had for the book was with the CCC veteran Carl "Mel" Melvin. While he served in Iowa not Yosemite, his personal experience spoke to the broader picture. It is detailed in his memoir, *The Journey: From Farm Boy to World War II Pilot to Los Angeles Cabbie* (privately published, c. 2010).

At the Yosemite Archives, Paul Rogers and Samantha Goza were superb in providing information and photographs. Virginia Sanchez of the Yosemite Research Library was likewise of steadfast assistance. My thanks are all the deeper because they helped me navigate around COVID-19, which closed their own facilities.

Other current or retired park professionals provided critical assistance and ready responses to my questions. Margaret Julson, the Park Forester, sat for a long interview orienting me toward today's forestry practices. Jim Snyder, a leading Yosemite historian as well as an expert on trails, filled in key details. Shelton Johnson, a Yosemite legend who as a ranger brings the park to the people, helped unearth the story of African Americans in the CCC. Stephen Shackelton, now director of the National Parks Institute at UC Merced, shared a wealth of knowledge and insights drawn from a career during which, in the early 2000s, he served as Yosemite's Chief Ranger. Laura Goforth, the park's education director, offered excellent advice and help. The interpretive park ranger Eric Smith proved that the great tradition of the ranger naturalists still endures. Rob Grasso, an aquatic ecologist, briefed me on current thinking about non-native fish in the park. Moose Mutlow, Yosemite Senior Projects Director for NatureBridge, provided valuable guidance and information.

In the midst of the COVID-19 pandemic, Michael Constandy, Director of Westmoreland Research, moved heaven and earth to get access to archival materials that I needed in the National Museum of American History, Smithsonian Institution. It required months, but eventually he succeeded.

The critiques of my readers improved the book in many ways. My wife, Kathy, went over each page with the same devotion she has given to my prior books for the past half-century. The renowned author, screenwriter, and producer Mark Frost pointed out ways to make the story more vivid. Peter Cantle brought to the project the eyes of a fine prose critic who is also a professional ecologist. Richard Walker, professor emeritus of Geography at UC Berkeley and Director of The Living New Deal, gave the manuscript an extraordinarily insightful reading. Retired Yosemite National Park Ranger Dean Shenk's review offered clarity unique to a park insider. Carolyn Vondriska and her husband, Gil Vondriska, provided both Carolyn's sure touch with language and Gil's perspectives as a retired military officer (very helpful in my treatment of the army's role managing the CCC).

I owe a debt of gratitude as well to Bryant Baker, Robert Buckingham, M.D., the Center for Research Libraries, Ivan R. Dee, Susan Ives, the James F. Justin Civilian Conservation Corps Museum, Susan Kinkella, Terri Laine, Philip Murphy and the Seibel-Murphy Archives, Karla Olson, and Leon G. Partamian, M.D.

Finally, this story could not have been told without The Press at California State University, Fresno, including the tremendous support of Dr. Sergio La Porta, Co-Director of The Press, and Brenna Barks, Administrative Analyst/Specialist, Office of the Dean. Graphic designer Joel MaHarry made it come to life.

My heartfelt thanks to all.

INTRODUCTION

If you know where to hunt for it near the base of El Capitan, you will discover one of Yosemite's most obscure monuments. It is a stone fireplace whose chimney looms up in the woods. Set in the middle of the fireplace, above the ruined mantel, is a heart-shaped rock. The building that the fireplace once heated disappeared a long time ago. On any evening in the late 1930s, though, it would have been filled with noisy young men who had joined the Civilian Conservation Corps – the CCC. This was their mess hall. After their hitch ended, they went on with their lives. What they achieved in Yosemite remained, and much of it, like the fireplace, still does.

The Civilian Conservation Corps has been accurately characterized by Yosemite historian Linda Wedel Greene as quite simply "the largest conservation movement in history."[1] All around the United States, prominent monuments to the Corps have gone up; but not in Yosemite. No fitting memorial signifies the work accomplished by the thousands of men who belonged. The legacies of other federal programs from that era go similarly unacknowledged. Instead, you must know to look for the monuments built by the workers themselves – roads, buildings, trails. Once you do, you see them everywhere.

The story of all that took place in Yosemite during the 1930s makes for a fascinating tale – but why should it matter to us today? The simple answer is that, since Yosemite is one of the greatest natural wonders of the world, anything important which has ever happened there remains important now. Yosemite symbolizes to us as a society, and to the world at large, that there are places on the planet that are simply too precious to destroy. Recognizing this, the Abraham Lincoln Administration gave Yosemite permanent protection in 1864, at the height of the Civil War. Never had the federal government done such a thing – set aside a place forever because it was unique.

There are less obvious, more specific reasons why the story of the 1930s matters now. During the early twentieth century, Washington regarded Yosemite as the crown jewel of the national park system. As such, Yosemite became a focus for addressing the question: *What actually is a national park?* Yosemite was a proving ground for concepts that could be applied to the other national parks. It also became a proving ground for whole new theories about what government owed to the people during an economic catastrophe. Finally, Yosemite was a crucible of environmental and physical transformation on a concentrated and very rapid scale – everything from a forest pandemic to shrinking glaciers to a disastrous flood. During the 1930s, Yosemite National Park was a vast laboratory of interacting environmental and social change.

From time to time in the book, I reminisce. Yosemite has significantly shaped my life and most of my values. I belong to a generation that links the New Deal era to today. Where a personal experience or sense of a particular place bears in some way on the larger story, I share it. For example, the book recounts some of the deaths and injuries that occurred in the park during the New Deal era. I believe it has helped in relating these events that I have had somewhat parallel experiences myself. As a small child in Yosemite, I tipped off a chair into a campfire. I was nearly killed at age eight or nine by a small boulder that brushed my scalp on its plunge down a cliff. I have hiked with smashed ribs, nearly had my legs amputated by a falling tree, experienced a couple of memorable car crashes, raked the ashes of a family cabin in Wawona after it burned to the ground . . . and so on. I do not consider myself particularly accident-prone. Where people are concerned, though, Yosemite can be a fickle place.

Perhaps I should add a bit more about my relationship to Yosemite. Like countless others, I have a passion for the park. My parents were teachers, and while they did not have a lot of money, they did have abundant free time for going camping during the summers. In the 1940s and 1950s, a couple of days after the school year ended, our family would leave suburban Southern California for Tuolumne Meadows. We camped there all summer, returning just before school commenced again. I grew up spending a quarter or more of the year living in a tent, keeping warm in front of a campfire, and reading by the light of a kerosene lantern. I had a corps of summer friends my own age, and, in my teens, devoted myself to hiking and fly-fishing. At the end of each summer season, like many other campers, our family would stow a lot of gear in a cavity under a boulder, where it would be waiting for us the next year. (Nearly every family we knew had its own cache.) It was in many ways a Huckleberry Finn sort of childhood, filled with adventures and unforgettable characters; but, unlike Mark Twain's novel, it was practically free of care or conflict.[2]

I have taken the liberty of dwelling on a few subjects at greater length than a reader might expect – for instance, bears. These little digressions sometimes reflect a personal predilection (bears interest me). More basically, though, I believe the digressions help to illustrate some general themes of the book. Few stories better convey the tension between people and the Yosemite environment than bears did during the 1930s.

Before we begin the story of Yosemite and the New Deal, I would like to say a bit about the unusual challenges I faced with research; to register a point about gender; and to clarify a few terms.

I wish I had written this book decades ago, because the passage of time has made it difficult to locate living veterans of the Civilian Conservation Corps and other New Deal programs in Yosemite. I have been exceedingly fortunate that, in response to an outreach on social media, members of some of their families have volunteered rich biographical information and photographs. Those who have helped are thanked in the Acknowledgments.

I also wish I had begun the book earlier for personal reasons. Although I was able to complete much of the primary research before the COVID-19 pandemic hit, that crisis then shuttered all of the relevant archives through most of 2020-2021. A pancreatic cancer diagnosis, though, suggested that if I was going to finish the book, I had to maintain momentum. I had written under plenty of deadlines before, but never a deadline from the great beyond. An unexpected remission bought more time. I decided to begin writing with only about half of the necessary research completed; explored unconventional ways of conducting research outside of archives; and incorporated the final manuscript research after the initial waves of COVID-19 abated and the archives finally reopened.

One additional obstacle deserves mention. In sixty years of historical research, I have never come across a subject where the sources were so opaque; so frequently disagreed about basic facts; or, with astonishing frequency, were completely missing. A lot that is described in the literature about Yosemite as settled fact is actually wrong or incomplete. It has been said that historical research is half detective work, and researching this book has made me feel like a private eye. After much weighing and sifting, I have done my best to tell the story accurately. Any errors of fact or judgment are entirely mine.

Some readers may take surprise in the fact that the great majority of the figures depicted in this book were men. While limited numbers of women did find their way into New Deal programs in Yosemite – I have been at pains to identify as many as possible – the overwhelming majority were male. The 1930s was far removed from today's fluid understanding of sexuality, gender identity, and gender expression. It was a world in which, as the cliché went, men were men and women were women. Gay, lesbian, and transgender people were under tremendous pressure to conform to socially prescribed binary norms. One of the most important norms was that men were breadwinners and women were housewives. The New Deal never fundamentally questioned that paradigm, but it did provide public employment and positions of prominence to a good many women. The most prominent of all was the First Lady, Eleanor Roosevelt, who challenged gender conventions constantly. We will see how, on one of her visits to Yosemite, the rangers (all men) had trouble keeping up with her. But the last place an expansion of gender roles would ever have materialized during the 1930s was a place like Yosemite, where the great bulk of the work that transformed the park involved gender-identified jobs like forestry, construction, and roadbuilding. That should not surprise us, because today what is truly astonishing about the gender distribution in these same jobs is not how much has changed, but how little. As of 2018, of all the frontline field workers in the construction and extraction industries, just 3.4 percent were women.[3]

Readers may also wonder why so little in this book pertains to American Indians. The Indigenous population of California had earlier been decimated by diseases introduced from Europe, by the mission system, by invasive gold rush miners, and by outright slaughter. Yosemite's Ahwahneechee were driven out in the middle of the nineteenth century. During the early twentieth century, only a few Indigenous people lived permanently in Yosemite Valley, typically working for whites or selling baskets to tourists. The Roosevelt Administration instituted dramatic new policies for American Indians, what was called an "Indian New Deal." But the program bypassed Yosemite, which had become an object of federal natural resource protection and a mecca for tourists. The book relates a quite painful account of Indigenous dispossession that began in Yosemite during the 1920s, but in relation to building New Deal Yosemite, it has more to say about African Americans and Hispanics.[4]

Now to clarify the use of a few terms. Members of the Civilian Conservation Corps were most commonly called "boys." Their formal title was "enrollees." Informally, they went by "civies" or "juniors" or "men in green" or "peavies." (A peavey is a hooked tool used by lumberjacks to maneuver logs.) Countless enrollees later attested – as CCC veteran Carl "Mel" Melvin has said of himself – that he "became a man from a boy" in the Corps.[5] In other words, he grew up. But the word "boy" got a lot of general application in the 1930s, including to mature enrollees. In my view, neither then nor now should a person eighteen to twenty-five years of age be termed a "boy." Visiting a CCC camp in 1933, President Roosevelt referred to the enrollees as "men."[6] We will do the same. The ones we get to know best we will call by their first names.

During the 1930s more commonly than now, middle names or initials were used. Except in rare cases where the initial goes indelibly with the person (Franklin D. Roosevelt, for example), I have deleted middle names and initials. Roosevelt is also readily evoked as FDR. In common with other writers today, I often identify his wife, Eleanor, as ER.

I have chosen not to modify quotations by silently correcting spelling or punctuation, nor have I inserted a nagging "[*sic*]" after any slips. People wrote the way they wrote. Editing their words, even in a conventionally allowable scholarly way, would, I think, have diminished and distorted what they wrote when they were conveying their meaning perfectly well.

Tree and plant citations follow Calflora format.[7]

And now we begin the story of how Yosemite was transformed in the 1930s. We will start with a tour across Yosemite around the middle of that decade – what you might have seen at the time, what it would have felt like. The book then provides a broader tour ranging geographically back and forth across the park, and chronologically from the early twentieth century through the New Deal years. At the end, we will look at what remains from the 1930s, and what has changed.

DRIVING ACROSS THE PARK IN THE MID-1930s

Imagine you are taking a drive through Yosemite National Park on a summer day in the middle of the 1930s. You may have driven from Southern California through the San Joaquin Valley, up Highway 99. When you hit Fresno, you know not to turn north toward the park. Getting to Yosemite from Fresno takes forever, along winding old roads and through construction zones. Instead, you keep on driving another sixty miles to Merced, where you pick up the new All Year Highway (State Route 140) northeast toward the Sierra. You twist and turn your way up the Merced River canyon until you reach the park entrance at Arch Rock.

Descending toward Yosemite Valley, traffic is thick; you inch along. Circling the valley floor, you see that the campgrounds are clogged with cars and tents. Bordering one of the camps, you notice a lot of young men dressed in baggy blue denim who are planting small trees. They're members of the Civilian Conservation Corps. Proceeding at the pace of a funeral cortege, you get to Camp Curry, where the parking has overflowed. After buying a few lunch items back down the valley at the Village Store, you decide to leave the crowds behind and head for the high country. Crossing over Yosemite Creek, you see a lot more men in baggy blues. What is that, a re-sloping job they're doing along the banks?

You wait at a traffic control stop near the El Capitan ranger station for forty-five minutes, until the hour turns over: up-traffic on the even, down-traffic on the odd. You grind your way up, cramping the steering wheel and downshifting to navigate a wicked hairpin turn called the Zig-Zag. To your left you catch a flashing glimpse of Bridalveil Fall,[1] but you're focused on avoiding a cliff that drops into space. At Crane Flat you spot a CCC camp, with nobody around. Now you're headed where you want to go, in the direction of Tenaya Lake and Tuolumne Meadows. But the road is a mess. Some of it twists and turns along a nineteenth-century wagon route; some of it is newly realigned but dusty. Heavy equipment rumbles around, and you pass through clusters of workers wearing dirty fedoras. You finally reach Tenaya Lake, noticing a campground on your right.

Beyond the lake, you crawl up the stiff grade behind a line of cars – old ones belching smoke, a newer model or two dragging a trailer. The needle on your heat gauge starts to climb. The radiator boils. You pull over at the side of the road to let it cool down. You top off the radiator out of a water bag you have strapped to your hood ornament.

Eventually you reach Tuolumne. You see more men in blue outfits, cutting down saplings that have invaded the meadow. Suddenly you're on a brand-new asphalt highway that, after endless gravel and dust, feels as smooth as a bowling lane. For the first time in recent memory, you shift into high gear. You relax and take in dazzling views of the great meadow bordered by granite domes, with background peaks that inspired people to name them after cathedrals and pinnacles and unicorns.

The easy drive lasts for a dozen miles, until you reach the eastern park entrance on Tioga Pass. Here, at nearly ten thousand feet, you see a new rustic rock-and-timber ranger cabin, together with a similar-looking public restroom. Leaving the park puts you on rough road again, though, and once you pass Ellery Lake you're staring out into space for the second time today. The Lee Vining Grade you've just started down is single-lane at the top, with turnouts spaced a long distance apart (or do they only *seem* like a long distance?). On your right, it's almost straight down for a couple thousand feet. You notice the car ahead of you clinging to the inside of the road, as far away from the cliff as possible. But now a car is coming up, and, by law, down-drivers – you included – have to find a turnout fast or else back up. The driver ahead stops dead in the road, opposite a turnout to his right. The climbing car has to navigate its way around on the wrong side, through the turnout and back onto the road. Now it is confronting you. Clenching the steering wheel, you back up ever so slowly until the climbing driver can inch by. Three hairpin turns later and now on two-lane road, you pull into a turnout to let your overheated brakes cool off before they start to fade. Three more hairpins, and you finally make it to the bottom of Lee Vining Grade.

This is the way it would have felt to cross Yosemite at the height of the New Deal in the mid-1930s. By that point, New Deal programs were well along toward transforming the park (including its roads). Yosemite's unique beauty and geology did not change, of course. They were why the park existed. But the *human-made* park as we experience it today was taking shape.

If the car on the drive I've just described happened to be a new 1937 Plymouth sedan, my parents could have been making this trip. They first camped in Tuolumne Meadows that year. Previously, my mother's parents had camped in Yosemite Valley, possibly as far back as the 1920s. Born in 1941, I would become the family's third generation in the park. Until my parents bought a new car in 1950, the three of us would crowd together in the front seat of the aging sedan. As a child, I straddled the floor-mounted gearshift. Seat belts lay years into the future. Heavy camping gear jammed every remaining nook of the car, badly overburdening its eighty-two-horsepower engine. The motor liked to overheat. I recall the smell of the Plymouth's brakes to this day.

[1]
YOSEMITE TAKES OFF IN THE 1920s

The sheer scale of Yosemite's transformation in the 1930s became possible because the park had been primed for it during the first three decades of the twentieth century, climaxing in the 1920s. Working in tandem, the National Park Service and the park's concessioners struggled to attract as many tourists as possible to Yosemite. New roads were constructed to ease access, and Yosemite Valley was turned into an entertainment zone. But more visitors put more stress on natural resources, raising the question of how to balance preservation against unprecedented human impact. Everything the New Deal would later do raised the stakes.

From the end of the 1920s through most of the 1930s, the key front-line figure contending with these issues was the superintendent of Yosemite National Park, Charles Goff Thomson. Born in 1883 in central New York State, Thomson earned a veterinary degree from Cornell in 1907. He went on to direct the Alabang Serum Laboratory in the Philippines. After a stint stateside heading army remount depots that provided horses to American units in Europe during World War I, Thomson ended the war as a lieutenant colonel commanding troops in France. Park Service personnel addressed him as Colonel Thomson. Almost forgotten today – the shared fate of Yosemite superintendents – Thomson was an exceptionally interesting person.

A prolific author of magazine articles, Thomson wrote two adventure novels during the 1920s – *Terry: A Tale of the Hill People* and *Time Is A Gentleman* – both released by the celebrated publisher Macmillan.[1] *Terry* is the one that interests us here. The book drew on Asian experiences that went well beyond those of a laboratory administrator in the Philippines. Thomson had also served as assistant prison director for the Philippine government, then under U.S. colonial control. The hero, a young American officer named Dick Terry, is captured by a dangerous, isolated stone-age Philippine tribe, the Hill People. Through a series of clever plot twists, Terry persuades them to end their isolation and join the wider world of the early twentieth century. In taking over the Philippines from Spain rather than granting independence following the end of the Spanish-American War of 1898, President William McKinley had declared that America's role was to "uplift and civilize and Christianize" the Filipinos. Thomson's novel is full of that sort of thing, providing today's reader with some eye-opening passages. If one can get past those, which isn't easy, what remains is a tale of the rip-roaring kind, with some genuinely compelling passages – and, for its time, some fairly erotic ones. The book is still available in the twenty-first century, and the casual reader who may expect to simply skim through it is likely instead to get drawn in.

Something about the plot may hint at one of the reasons why, eventually, Thomson's official reports to Washington about the Civilian Conservation Corps in Yosemite would be so enthusiastic. Dick Terry comes from a comfortable old New England family, but his pinched, traditionalistic Vermont hometown – symbolically named Crampville – contains a ghetto of struggling new immigrants from Italy and the Balkans. They are Emma Lazarus's huddled masses, memorialized on the Statue of Liberty. Thomson describes them as "a frugal, law-abiding lot" who "furnished the brawn needed" by the town. But along with physical isolation, the immigrants are socially ostracized – except by Terry, who passes comfortably between the old Anglo establishment and the newcomers. The novel's long, sympathetic passages about a particular Italian family could have been describing the families of a good many CCC men in Yosemite. We will follow one of these men throughout this book.

Dynamic and energetic, Thomson confronted enormous challenges in Yosemite. One of the biggest involved striking a balance between public demands on the park and protecting its unparalleled natural resources. What the right balance was seemed different then than it does today. Thomson, for example, issued kill-on-sight orders against rattlesnakes. Rattlers might be native, but they threatened people. When a lounge called the El Dorado Room opened on the second floor of the new, luxurious Ahwahnee Hotel, decked out in a forty-niner motif, Thomson recoiled, declaring Gold Rush decor "out of place in a national park."[2] He could do nothing about it, though, because – although in full charge of the park – the National Park Service (NPS) lacked authority over the interior of a concessioner's hotel. These kinds of dilemmas and choices came up continually.

***

Meanwhile, Yosemite's boundaries kept changing. If you hike through the woods inside the park's western edge today, you may come across rotting railroad ties, tumbledown trestles, or random hunks of iron. This seems surprising. Yosemite is a national park, isn't it? Yes, but not always.

The legislation establishing the Yosemite Grant in 1864 entrusted Yosemite Valley and the Mariposa Grove of Giant Sequoias to the State of California, to be preserved "for all time."[3] In 1890, Yosemite became a national park. Since no agency existed for administering national parks, the army wound up running it during the next quarter-century. Because the State of California retained its original hand as grantee, though, the actual national park excluded the valley and the grove. Eventually, the great naturalist John Muir – the first president of the Sierra Club (founded in 1892) – persuaded President Theodore Roosevelt to consolidate everything under federal control. Roosevelt followed through in 1906. But the creation of an administrative agency to run the national parks still lagged. The federal government of that era bore only a small fraction of the responsibilities that it does today. It took on new ones with a certain caution, even reluctance. And so, in the national parks, the army carried on. If you visited Yosemite well into the twentieth century, you were going to encounter soldiers.

Finally, in 1916, President Woodrow Wilson – whose administration (1913-1921) expanded the role of the federal government in significant and permanent ways – signed legislation creating the National Park Service. Meantime, though, his administration had compromised Yosemite in a striking way. In 1913, Wilson approved a measure granting San Francisco access to Yosemite National Park in order to dam the Hetch Hetchy Valley and pipe its water across California to the City by the Bay. Hetch Hetchy was another, smaller Yosemite Valley located twenty miles to the north. A fight over whether or not to dam Hetch Hetchy had gone on for years, growing into the greatest environmental battle of its time. John Muir called the outcome "damn-dam-damnation."[4] During the 1920s, San Francisco completed its dam. Hetch Hetchy's spectacular waterfalls now plummeted into an artificial lake. The city next set its sights on raising the dam to trap yet more water while flooding more of the once-spectacular valley.

As it originated in 1890, Yosemite National Park was about a third larger than it is today. The third amounted to hundreds of square miles. Numerous tracts – totaling some 60,000 acres – had been purchased for logging, mining, grazing, and speculation before the 1890 boundaries folded them in.[5] Now these tracts sat inside a national park whose administration had no authority to prevent resource extraction from going forward. The inholders wanted to exercise their rights. It seemed best, Congress decided, that the properties in question devolve to national forest status, with its "land of many uses" latitude for exploitation but where some level of regulation would still apply, at least in theory.

The private claims on the western side of the park included some of the finest timber on the planet. The logging of giant old-growth Sugar and Yellow pine that followed, by firms like the tauntingly-named Yosemite Lumber Company, appalled preservationists. The pace of cutting only escalated during the 1920s. Demand arose to save at least some key stands. In the nick of time, the national parks' preeminent philanthropist, John D. Rockefeller, Jr., opened his wallet, with a match from Congress. The Rockefeller Purchase of 1930 saved 12,000 acres north of Crane Flat, and the park boundary was adjusted to take it in. Between 1937 and 1939, the Carl Inn Tract, next to the Rockefeller Purchase, was annexed as well. By now vast timber acreage had been lost, but at least a portion of it was rescued.

In August 1932, following a proclamation by President Herbert Hoover, the 8,785-acre Wawona Basin was officially added to the park. The basin's boundaries included an entire unincorporated historic community, which remained in private hands. The federal government acquired the venerable Wawona Hotel. The annexation also included a long stretch of the South Fork of the Merced River[6] and the expansive Wawona Meadow.

***

While the 1864 legislation setting Yosemite aside had provided for preservation, it contained another key provision – that the preserved land "shall be held for public use, resort, and recreation."[7] Finding a proper, sustainable balance between preservation and use has presented the central, perennial question for the entire national park system – its classic conundrum. The National Park Service Organic Act that set up the system in 1916 did not settle the issue. Under the act, the park service would both "conserve the scenery and the natural and historic objects and the wild life therein and to provide for the enjoyment of the same in such manner and by such means as will leave them unimpaired for the enjoyment of future generations."[8] The debate over preservation versus public use has gone on longer in Yosemite than in any other park because Yosemite was the first to be set aside for preservation and, of course, for public use.

How to balance preservation with visitation in Yosemite had begun to present challenges in the late nineteenth and very early twentieth centuries, when only a handful of people visited the park; but by the late 1920s, Yosemite was attracting hundreds of thousands a year. A promotional travel brochure from 1926 urged that no one come to Yosemite Valley without confirmed reservations, "as the congestion is very great during the summer months."[9] Charles Michael, the park's assistant postmaster, grumbled in 1927 that "Yosemite Valley is getting to be an awful place," overrun by crowds, the air "filled with smoke, dust, and the smell of gasoline."[10] At the time, one could pitch a tent in more places than today, which helped absorb some of the numbers. The Ahwahnee opened in 1927 to serve an elite clientele. Other hostelries and commercial camps existed too. Yet summertime demand kept shooting ahead of capacity.[11]

The NPS wanted tourists to visit Yosemite and the other national parks, and was doing everything it could to attract more visitors. Numbers provided a useful metric of public appreciation. Numbers built a political constituency for the parks. And, since the park service lacked a predictable ongoing funding base, numbers mattered every time Congress voted on annual appropriations: "Say, how many visitors did Yosemite have last year?" Early on, securing funds had presented a struggle. During the 1920s, though, Congress became more generous as the park service stressed the necessity of providing specifically for better access – trails, roads inside the parks, and (beginning in 1932) approach roads from major highways to the parks.[12]

In trying to draw more visitors to Yosemite, the NPS ran neck-and-neck with the park's multiple concessioners. The two most powerful of these were the Yosemite National Park Company and the Curry Camping Company. They competed fiercely until, in 1925, the Secretary of the Interior made them merge into a near-monopoly called the Yosemite Park and Curry Company. (Acronyms varied; YP&CCo for our purposes.) Before the merger, the concessioners thought of the valley as a venue to fill, like a stadium. After 1925, the objectives remained the same: get the customers here, keep them entertained, keep them renting rooms and buying sundries, keep them coming back, and hope they'll spread the word.

So Yosemite Valley turned into a theme park, whose unique raw beauty was the theme. If you somehow got bored with the scenery, you could easily find plenty more to do.

As the twentieth century opened, Yosemite's master of ceremonies was David Curry, a profit-driven entrepreneur of extraordinary focus and determination. In 1899, he and his wife Jennie – both restless educators-turned-hosts – strategically positioned a tent camp concession at the foot of Glacier Point. If the NPS wanted more visitors to the park, the Currys naturally wanted every single one of those they could attract. They succeeded spectacularly. The spirit of Camp Curry was self-consciously democratic – just plain folks, affordable prices. Its tents cost half what a hotel room did. The Currys threw up a permanent dining room, restrooms, and a bathhouse. On one occasion, when the camp became overwhelmed with guests, they boosted their carrying capacity by separating husbands from wives and packing them into unisex tent dorms.[13] Couples didn't *have* to put up with this deprivation of connubial bliss. It was a tolerable annoyance because, in every other way its proprietors could think of, Camp Curry gave people what they wanted. David Curry himself was a legendary host, impresario, and vocal entertainer.

Unfortunately, Curry also distinguished himself offstage by being spectacularly ill-tempered, belligerent, stubborn, and generally obnoxious. Army Major H.C. Benson, the park's acting superintendent from 1905 to 1908, wanted the Currys gone.[14] The Currys dug in, and it was Benson who eventually moved on.

Camp Curry's most dazzling draw was the firefall. Indeed, it has been said that, apart from Half Dome, the firefall – a fully human invention – was Yosemite

Valley's most famous feature.[15] At night, the very opposite of Yosemite Falls would plunge off Glacier Point – not cascades of water, but cascades of glowing embers. The Currys did not invent the firefall (the first one occurred in the 1870s), but they did make it their own production. Camp Curry had an unsurpassed location for observing the spectacle. The ceremony featured David Curry's voice, universally described then and since as "stentorian." His sobriquet, in fact, was The Stentor of the Yosemite, a stentor being a person with conspicuous vocal capacity. "Let the fire fall!" Curry would boom to the top of Glacier Point, over three thousand feet above. (An early version was, "Let'er go, Gallagher!") Down below, crowds that had gathered around the Camp Curry campfire would crane their necks. Originally an event reserved for special occasions, the firefall eventually turned into a nightly feature.

The firefall brought David Curry both tragedy and triumph. When in 1913 he insistently demanded a government contract to operate his camp that ran longer than the accustomed year-to-year permit, he thoroughly offended the Assistant Secretary of the Interior. As a punitive measure for Curry's various offenses, Washington cancelled the firefall altogether. Nothing if not persistent, and backed by tourists who clamored for it, Curry got the firefall reinstated four years later. Along with that success came a new five-year lease. Not merely a seasonal event anymore, the firefall became a year-round one too. During the 1930s, YP&CCo stationed employees at Glacier Point even in the dead of winter to host hotel guests and to push off the firefall's regulation glowing red fir bark. In the late 'thirties, snowplows labored to keep the road open all the way, with guests' cars following behind.[16]

Camp Curry offered more than the firefall, a lot more. It featured paid professional entertainment, a swimming pool, a bowling alley, a dance pavilion (with live bands during the New Deal-big band era), tennis and croquet courts, and a pool hall. Camp Curry's children's park, the Kiddie Kamp, offered miniature train rides. In winter, there was an ice rink and an "ash can" run (for sliding down snow on anything from a trash can lid with the handle removed to a food tray.) The camp later built a four-track, half-mile toboggan run, with speeds reportedly reaching up to sixty miles an hour.[17]

Down-valley at the Old Village, other attractions beckoned. Since very early in the century, the Village – located just south of the Merced River, barely west of Sentinel Bridge – had served as Yosemite's governmental and commercial hub. Nothing remains of it today except a famous chapel; but in its heyday visitors flocked there for everything from lodging to groceries to getting advice at park service headquarters. At the Village you could take in a movie. Prior to prohibition, you even had your choice of saloons. Not far away, at the Yosemite Lodge, you could play tennis or jump in the pool. Over at The Ahwahnee, a pitch and putt golf course beckoned. It is not hard to imagine a number of park visitors viewing Yosemite's scenery as basically a backdrop for all the available activities, or as throwing off an irritating glare while nursing a hangover.

***

A lot of Yosemite's attractions involved animals. From the 'teens through the 'twenties, for example, the valley drew visitors with a full-scale rodeo called Indian Field Days (because it had an Indigenous American theme). The valley also featured a zoo. When it opened in 1918, the zoo only had on display three orphaned mountain lion cubs, but it quickly expanded. Elsewhere, a paddock went in for a couple dozen Tule elk, not native to Yosemite. The zoo caused a lot of soul-searching – a zoo in a national park? Toward the end of 1932, a start was made toward removing the animals, pens, and cages. California's officially designated state cougar hunter – Jay Bruce, of Wawona – dispatched the lions and collected his bounty. The elk were transported to the Owens Valley (where they weren't native either).

No animal show, though, came close to rivaling the bears.[18] Today one looks with surprise at photos of early National Park Service directors feeding bears, even showing children how it was done. This calls back memories of my own childhood. I never fed a bear by hand, but when camping in Tuolumne Meadows during the 'forties and 'fifties, bears were present every day and especially every night. It never for a moment occurred to me that seeing bears all the time was the slightest bit unnatural.

Bears were simply one of Yosemite's biggest attractions. The park service and concessioners wanted visitors, and the visitors wanted bears. While bear feeding in Yosemite (and Yellowstone) did set off a debate within the park service, to its leadership the issue was settled because bears enthralled people. The valley and Tuolumne Meadows belonged to Yosemite's "bear feeding program," through which campers' garbage was deposited daily in "bear pits." At night in Tuolumne, cars would line up at the pit and, after dark set in, shine their headlights on the piles. Bears would dine, cavort, and often misbehave. In particular, I recall, they showed a disregard for monogamy that caught the attention of a seven or eight year-old – me.

In the valley, the old Yosemite National Park Company erected a feeding platform along the bank of the Merced River. Right after the 9:00 firefall, visitors would pour down the valley for the bear show. Excursion buses from The Ahwahnee, Camp Curry, and the Yosemite Lodge joined the parade of cars, which might line up by the hundreds. On one July night in 1929, some two thousand people turned out. Rangers would direct traffic using flashlights.

Carl Sharsmith

At the right moment, flood lights would switch on, illuminating as many as twenty, forty, or even more bears dining on garbage across the river. A ranger would deliver a talk. One night, a young ranger named Carl Sharsmith took his turn at it. Fundamentally a botanist, Sharsmith was not well versed in bears, so he had to do some cramming. Colonel Thomson – who had a way of turning up unexpectedly anywhere around the park at any time – materialized the night of Sharsmith's bear talk. Afterwards, in his gravelly voice, Thomson told Sharsmith that his maiden effort had been "lousy."

The human-bear attraction proved mutual. Once scarce and seldom seen, the bears multiplied. They became a problem. If campers did not suspend their food from a tree limb out of reach of a bear – and bears have an impressive reach – they risked having their food-filled cars ripped open. Hungry bears invaded tents and inspected suitcases. Visitors got scratched and bitten. Some people cut their stays short and fled.

What to do? One solution had already been arrived at – the bear feeding program was intended not just to entertain but also to divert the bruins away from the visitors, simply by keeping them fed. There were, though, the aggressive problem bears. The idea of shooting large numbers of offending animals repelled Charles Thomson, though he did make exceptions. The solution that emerged was the bear trap – a big piece of corrugated pipe mounted on automobile wheels, with one end sealed shut, a trap door at the other, and a hunk of meat in between. The captured bear would be towed to a less populated part of the park and released into the wild. It was highly prudent of the bear to remain there and not return to civilization, because repeat offenders were dealt with in a more permanent way.

Meanwhile, public bear feeding went on. In the valley, a recycling operation occurred every day, where edible garbage would be separated from the inedible kind, then transported to the feeding platform. In time, as the valley's bear population continued to swell, new platforms were erected at Gin Flat, near Crane Flat. Surplus valley bruins were trapped and relocated there. When members of the subcommittee of the House of Representatives overseeing appropriations to the Interior Department (and therefore also the Park Service) visited Yosemite in 1937, one of the designated excursions, right along with the valley floor and the Mariposa Grove, was to the bear show. Their guide was the park naturalist.

***

When Herbert Hoover arrived in Yosemite in August 1934, he brought his fishing gear. In fact, fishing was reportedly the favorite park sport of visiting celebrities at the time.[19] During the early twentieth century, Yosemite became a fishing mecca. Though devoted to angling, Hoover had actually passed up the opportunity to play a landmark role in Yosemite's fishing history. In 1922, when Hoover was Secretary of Commerce, three guests – Horace Albright, Arno Cammerer, and Washington Lewis – visited his office in the nation's capital to request a fish hatchery for Yosemite. Yellowstone already had one; Yosemite wanted one. Albright, and in turn Cammerer, would eventually become the second and third directors of the National Park Service; Lewis was the Yosemite park superintendent. Hoover's often-chilly temperament was especially cold that day. "It ought to be done," he told his important visitors, and that was all he said. They made a quick exit. Nothing happened. Instead, the State of California, which had been running a temporary hatchery in the park for several years, opened a permanent one at Happy Isles in 1926. From then on, half a million to over a million fish were planted annually.[20]

The state hatchery got its eggs from Frog Creek, near Lake Eleanor in the Hetch Hetchy area. The eggs were stripped from live trout, then hatched at Happy Isles by the millions. Rainbow trout are native to the overall region of the park, but now they had a lot of new company – nonnative Brown and Brook,[21] along with a few other varieties in smaller numbers. One-inch fish (fingerlings) were jostled to lakes and streams in large cans strapped aboard mules. A remarkable number of lakes took the names of army troopers and rangers who served during the park's early history, including, on occasion, the person who first planted them. Fish materialized in myriad places they had never existed before, all the way up to glacial lakes suspended beneath the highest pinnacles of the Sierra. In a single timberline lake over the years, I have seen Rainbow, Brown, Brook, and Cutthroat caught.

Put into high relief: The park service was introducing nonnative predators into as many bodies of water as possible. The overriding aim, as the superintendent reported in 1938, was "to maintain the best possible fishing for visitors."[22]

This drew so many fishers (then and often still called fisher*men*) that the planting program could scarcely keep pace. By the 1950s, one heard the quip that Yosemite had more anglers than trout. Before World War II, though, the fishing was spectacular. Around a million fish were planted annually. The monthly report of the park superintendent included meticulously detailed accounts of catches, such as these from 1934:

> Mr. Wojick, E. E Adams and A. Oakum, Merced, caught 23 Eastern Brook 12 to 15 inches in length in May Lake. . . . Sam Kuffman, North Hollywood, caught 6 Rainbow and 19 Eastern Brook in Harden Lake and Middle Fork [of the Tuolumne]. . . . Mr. McCanless, Mr. Taylor, and Mt. Frei, Merced, caught 43 fine ones in Tenaya Canyon using spinners and flies.

As of 1937, the bag limit in the park was an astounding twenty-five trout (or ten pounds) per person per day. In 1938 it dropped to twenty.[23]

In Tuolumne Meadows, which offered some of the best fishing in Yosemite, two angling cultures emerged: those who used flies, and those who used bait and/or spinners. They were friendly rivals, but had a contrasting view of fishing that reflected different perspectives on the park, and, I believe, on life in general. The fly-fishers tended to take only the number of trout they wanted to eat, catching and releasing the rest. In response to all the efforts extended by the National Park Service and the State of California to provide outstanding fishing experiences, the bait fishers (not all, but many) would gleefully fish a lake bare, returning day after day to clean it out. The bait fishers (not all, but many) would leave behind cans, jars, Kleenex, and other junk; the fly-fishers carried home their trash. Observing what really amounted to different worldviews deeply impressed me as a boy, and has ever since – a life lesson in sociology and ecology. Both fishing clans loved being in the mountains, but one group loved the mountains enough to show them respect.

***

Don Tresidder

However many visitors that fishing or bears or the firefall may have helped attract to the park, the concessioner and the park service wanted more. After David Curry died in 1917, his family dominated the consolidated Yosemite Park and Curry Company. During the Depression, its president and general manager was the Currys' son-in-law, Donald (Don) Tresidder. A handsome Stanford graduate and a nonpracticing medical doctor, Tresidder possessed the polish that David Curry had lacked. Charming and enthusiastic, he was at the same time aggressive and opportunistic in the earlier tradition. Determined to advance the interests of the company, Tresidder left major imprints on Yosemite. The Ahwahnee was one, although the park service pushed YP&CCo to build it. Another was the Christmastime Bracebridge Dinner at The Ahwahnee. Still another was winter sports, and along with them the development of a winter travel season in Yosemite.

Prior to completion of the All Year Highway in 1926, Yosemite hardly had any winter visitors at all. A great deal of pressure had built, though, to open the park year-round, and on this Tresidder and the park service fully agreed. Stephen Mather – the first head of the NPS, and its guiding light from 1917 to 1929 – wanted to spur year-round travel to every possible national park, including Yosemite for winter sports. When Mather thought about Yosemite, it was not just with the detached long-distance perspective of a Washington agency chief. He had camped in it. "There is no question that Yosemite was his favorite of all the parks, and he spent time there every year," recalled his deputy, Horace Albright. "It was the place where he launched his newest programs, tried out his ideas, and worked to enlarge and improve the concessions."[24]

Mather was an extraordinary human being. His role in getting the national park system founded in the first place, and then leading it, was so critical that one historian of Yosemite, Dayton Duncan, has compared his importance to John Muir's.[25] Earlier in life, Mather had made a fortune in the borax industry. He struggled with a mental disability, likely bipolar disorder, which from time to time led to shattering breakdowns. That Mather had to fight such inner demons made his achievements all the more remarkable. Many national parks contain a memorial plaque to Mather that states: "There will never come an end to the good that he has done."

Once active in the Sierra Club, Mather embodied and epitomized the club's philosophy of how to build a constituency for the parks. Put simply, more park visitors (cars included) would lead to added public support, which would garner higher budgets for the park service, thereby funding added protection for natural resources – a circle.[26] In short, on this bedrock proposition the park service agreed with the Sierra Club and with YP&CCo: growth was good.

As its name implied, the new All Year Highway – whose construction the park service had strongly backed – made a winter season possible; and the park service enthusiastically joined forces with Don Tresidder and YP&CCo in creating one. In 1927, the year after the highway opened, park visitation jumped, much of it for winter sports. Whatever park officials would approve, Tresidder would promote, be it a skiing event or a college hockey game or an ice pageant. He created the Yosemite Winter Club. A ski school materialized. The ice rink at Camp Curry was billed as the biggest on the entire North American continent. Even if not, it may well have been the biggest outdoor rink in the west. Unlike today's smaller affair, the rink covered acres – the whole Curry parking lot. With park service support, Tresidder even launched a failing bid for the 1932 Winter Olympics. One is left to wonder whether Yosemite, instead of Lake Placid, might have hosted that year's Winter Olympics had the Badger Pass ski complex and its full array of downhill runs existed yet. Very soon those, too, would become legacies of his.[27]

Like his late father-in-law, even if less abrasively, Tresidder had a way of overreaching even with a park service that shared his broader promotional goals. In 1929, he advanced the idea of a cable car system running from the floor of the valley to Glacier Point, and to YP&CCo's money-losing Glacier Point Hotel. Actually, the idea of a tramway was not as farfetched as it seemed. For one thing, the road to Glacier Point was terrible. YP&CCo wanted it shut down, which would make its proposed cable car system a monopoly apart from trail access. And there were precedents. Europe had plenty of tram systems. One had been considered by the State of California (under the Yosemite Grant) as far back as the 1880s. In 1913, a San Francisco developer applied to the Interior Department for a green light to build one, but he never got permission.[28]

Like Tresidder, Mather envisioned the Glacier Point Hotel and its environs as a year-round destination, comparing the wintertime potential to Switzerland's St. Moritz. The park service itself had induced construction of the hotel back in 1917. But Mather rejected the tramway idea as an affront to the aesthetics of the park. Cable cars running up and down in full view were out as far as he was concerned. He did think, though, that a vertical shaft could be drilled *inside* Glacier Point that would provide an invisible route up and down, similar to the elevators in a skyscraper.[29]

Ignoring Mather's idea, YP&CCo company directors took the cable car proposal straight to President Hoover at the White House. Their overture was just barely mistimed. The park now had a brand-new Advisory Board, which was oriented toward protecting natural values and toward landscape design.[30] The board turned thumbs-down on the project. Horace Albright, as NPS director, came out in utter and absolute opposition to cable cars. So did the Sierra Club. And Charles Thomson, with his writer's flair, denounced the idea as "a longitudinal merry-go-round," completely unsuited to a national park – "a bizarre distraction from the supreme dignity of the spectacle."[31]

The proposal stalled – without ever quite disappearing. The tramway idea was still being debated as late as the 1970s. By this time, Yosemite Park and Curry Company had sold out to the Music Corporation of America, an entertainment giant. The Glacier Point Hotel had burned to the ground in 1969, but even without it, the thrill ride business remained to be tapped. And who knew what else the park service might approve at the Point?

***

Starting in 1929, the Great Depression took a huge bite out of annual visitation to Yosemite. In just one year – from 1932 to 1933 – it plunged, in round numbers, from five hundred thousand to three hundred thousand as the economic collapse hit bottom.[32] After that, though, visitation began to rebound. During the single month of August 1934, the park welcomed not only Herbert Hoover but also the Hollywood stars Jean Harlow, William Powell, Otto Kruger, and Adolphe Menjou. The creator of Tarzan, Edgar Rice Burroughs, paid a visit. The 1935 travel season set new records, with July the biggest month.

And records kept on falling. July 1936 set another, with people arriving from every state in the union. July 1937 marked still another – nearly 121,000 came, by far the most for any single month to date in park history. In 1937 all prior records fell for the summer travel season, just shy of half a million. With the San Francisco Exposition on, August 1939 established a record for that month, including a spectacular jump in visitors from out of state. The summer record set in 1937 fell in 1940, when for the first time Yosemite topped half a million. That July, yet another monthly record-breaker, 124,587 people and 37,576 cars arrived.[33]

The tide of visitors during the 1930s sometimes overwhelmed Yosemite Valley. If you could make it to the park and pay the $2.00 fee to drive in, living was cheap during the Depression. Concessioner prices for food and gas might be high, but campgrounds were free and stays were unlimited. As Fernando Peñalosa wrote years later: "It was something we as a modestly living lower-middle class family could do without straining the family budget."[34] Yosemite's public campgrounds were models of democracy. In my own experience, professionals mixed with wage earners, farmers with schoolteachers, and well-heeled retired businesspeople with down-at-the-heels pensioners. Democracy went unstated, but it was one of the great givens of the camping experience in the park.

Jammed campground in Yosemite Valley

And so the campers came. Even over the July 4 holiday of 1933 – at the bottom of the Depression – close to ten thousand campers packed the valley floor. Cramming tents and equipment and cars together, they generated a feeling of density which Charles Thomson described as "tenement-like."[35] That summer, with valley campgrounds often jammed, rangers directed hundreds of people to other places to camp – Wawona, the Mariposa Grove, Glacier Point, Tenaya Lake, and elsewhere. In 1935, a thirty-day limit was imposed on camping in Yosemite Valley. This spelled the end of summer-long stays in favorite annual sites. The limit was soon extended to Wawona as well.

While growth prevailed as the commanding Yosemite philosophy through the early Depression years, the Advisory Board's ethic of natural values presented an alternative point of view that had influential supporters in the academic world, including the University of California. Over time, the argument found ears. A new type of orientation toward the environment reached the visiting public by way of a new kind of park service employee – the ranger naturalist.[36] Popular though they might be, attractions like the zoo and the firefall gave naturalists pause. Outdoor education about the park's truly *natural* wonders underwent a revolution during the 1930s. Ranger-led nature walks, hikes, and campfire programs became staples of the Yosemite experience. Naturalists introduced the traveling public to the geology, flora, and fauna of the park. During the summer season, Tuolumne Meadows, possibly more than anywhere else, attracted ranger naturalists who possessed genuine gifts as teachers.

The foremost among them was Carl Sharsmith, a man of complex brilliance. If Sharsmith's maiden bear talk did misfire, as Charles Thomson contended, it would have been one of the few times that happened during Sharsmith's long career in a ranger uniform. Sharsmith became one of the nation's first ranger naturalists. In 1931 he was posted to Tuolumne Meadows for his first season in the job. He returned nearly every summer after that, driving up in a 1936 Ford convertible that he never found cause to trade in. He and the car simply aged together. (I recall riding in the Ford's rumble seat; my closest summertime friend was Carl's son John, named for John Muir.) With a doctorate in botany from UC Berkeley, Sharsmith held a professorship at San Jose State, where he taught and did research; but his overriding love always remained Tuolumne Meadows. An outdoor teacher of genuine greatness and charisma, he became one of Yosemite's human legends.

"Regular" rangers and the naturalists had a touchy relationship during the 1930s. The regulars tended to think of the naturalists as bogus rangers, calling them "posy pickers." A person like Sharsmith was unusual, idiosyncratic – a research botanist-college professor doing seasonal outdoor education and leading rounds of "Row, Row, Row Your Boat" at campfire programs.[37] Conventional rangers fought fires, wrote speeding tickets, and recovered the occasional dead body.

Sharsmith had an absolute passion for nature and wilderness. Some of the regulars once used one of Sharsmith's wildflower displays for target practice. Charles Thomson, the consummate professional ranger, puffed on cigars and a pipe. Sharsmith strictly adhered to his professorial pipe. Whatever his relationship with the other regulars, though, Sharsmith genuinely admired Thomson.[38] One reason must have been Thomson's concern for Yosemite's natural resources, including its meadows. Meadows were a passion of Sharsmith's; over time he did much to preserve and restore them. And what act of restoration in Tuolumne could rival Thomson's ban on meadow camping? Another reason for Sharsmith's admiration may have had to do with Thomson's sympathy for immigrants. Born in 1903 to Swiss parents, Carl Sharsmith was christened Karl Wilhelm Schaarschmidt II, a name he later anglicized.

The overriding question at the outset of the 1930s was which set of values would prevail – those of rangers like Thomson and Sharsmith, who prized the natural setting; values focused on concessioner profits; or some set of values in between? The final answer could not be decided in Yosemite alone. It would have to come from Washington.

***

While Yosemite Valley became a great entertainment zone by the 1920s, with a full array of attractions for visitors, the prominence of the valley's Indigenous people as a tourist draw actually diminished thanks to Charles Thomson.[39] Recall that the plot of his novel, *Terry,* revolves around a young American officer ushering an isolated tribe into the modern world. Thomson's attitude toward stone-age Filipinos resembled his attitude toward the park's Indigenous community. He considered it an assemblage of "backward peoples," in his own words, and he wanted to dissolve them "as a racial unit and, in time, diffuse[e] . . . their blood with the great American mass." Especially from a man so sympathetic toward downtrodden European immigrants, these words shock and sting.

Of all the national parks, just one – Yosemite – contained an active, still-functioning American Indian community. Comprised of elements of multiple regional tribes, these people had grouped together following the dispersal of the (likewise heterogenous) Ahwahneechee in the 1850s. They became a major tourist attraction. The revival of the community, in fact, was keyed to tourism –

working for park concessioners, for example, or selling services and objects, notably fine baskets, to tourists. In 1929, Indian Field Days – the rodeo and its accompanying activities – drew only 169 Indigenous Americans but a full crowd of 4,300 park visitors. Other visitors, though – lovers of "pure" nature – subscribed to the mythic ideal of Yosemite as a never-inhabited wilderness. For them, an Indigenous people in Eden was a contradiction in terms. In truth, Yosemite had been occupied and altered by humans for thousands of years before Europeans arrived. But Yosemite National Park was never a tribal reservation. Its Native Americans had no treaties with the federal government, which did not recognize them as a tribe. This made them terribly vulnerable.

During the 1920s, plans materialized to relocate the village where Indigenous families had congregated over the decades in order to make room for a new hospital and store. When Thomson arrived in 1929, he inherited these plans. He seized on them as a means for exercising authority and control. He told the villagers that living in the valley amounted to "a privilege, and not a vested right," and that the privilege was "dependent upon proper deportment" as evaluated by the park service. Supported by his new boss in Washington, Horace Albright, Thomson instituted a goal of gradually, and without publicity, removing Indigenous residents from the park. Countering an otherwise-universal emphasis on making Yosemite the biggest tourist magnet possible, the replacement Indian Village was built farther from tourist routes. The new housing, which began to open in 1931, was cramped and inadequate – as of 1938, fifteen cabins of scarcely more than four hundred square feet for fifty-seven people. Their landlord was the NPS. They could lose their housing under a variety of pretexts, including lack of steady year-round work – extremely difficult or impossible to sustain out of tourist season.

Thomson's long-term goal was achieved. Gradually, Indigenous residents departed or died. Following eviction of the final handful of tenants, the last of the cabins in the 1930s Indian Village were burned in a practice firefighting exercise in 1969 – around the peak of the national civil rights era.

How could a man like Charles Thomson – some of whose ideas about the environment anticipated twenty-first century thinking – be so stunningly rooted in nineteenth-century attitudes toward Indigenous people? In insisting that they join "the great American mass," he was advocating the *opposite* of the racial segregation that was then at its height. Instead, he insisted that American Indians embrace the twentieth-century industrialized world and *blend in*. This was conventional late nineteenth and early twentieth century thinking. Cultural assimilation – the ideal of the melting pot – was the official policy of the federal government. It was as coercive as segregation because American Indian feelings about blending in were ignored. Indigenous families were driven to send their children to boarding schools that suppressed tribal cultures, religions, and languages. The New Deal's Indian Reorganization Act of 1934 would substitute a focus on renewing and restoring tribal cultures and lands. But for the small community of Yosemite, the die was already cast.

Thomson's reference to "deportment" suggests that he had immediate concerns that went beyond abstractions about the melting pot. Certain Indigenous practices were hard for the park service to ban or regulate the way it would monitor a park concessioner, or were just "different" – gambling, say, or charging tourists to pose for photos. Ultimately, Thomson did agree to an ongoing public exhibition involving one or two Indigenous families displaying traditional practices during the summer months. But the overall tendency was to view the original inhabitants of Yosemite with a patronizing kind of ambivalence and as a burdensome problem that required solving. Looking ahead to the 1960s, a long conflict would break out between the NPS and Yosemite's rock climbers, legendary countercultural nonconformists, that lasted for decades. A direct comparison between the Indigenous of Yosemite and the climbers would be misleading, but the situations are at least analogous, reflecting a narrowly tailored standard of acceptable, regulated conduct within a carefully tended national park.

Charles Thomson's hand lies on Yosemite to this very day. His decisions, some of the most important ever made in shaping the park as we know it, were often models of foresight and wisdom. By contrast, it is impossible to imagine anything resembling his policy on removing Native Americans occurring today. The past really *is* like a different country. In visiting it, we must weigh our assessments of people – their motives, decisions, legacies – very carefully. The story of Yosemite in the 1920s has compelled us to do that repeatedly. The longer story of the 1930s will continue to test us.

[2]

FDR AND THE NEW DEAL

The transformation that would forever change Yosemite National Park actually began on Wall Street. During the fall of 1929, the stock market underwent a sickening crash. By 1932, some seventy-five billion dollars in the market value of listed stocks had vanished – well over a trillion dollars in today's money. The rest of the economy went down like an avalanche. In four years, industrial production plunged by half. A third of the nation's banks failed. A quarter of the labor force could not find jobs at all, while innumerable more workers scrambled after full-time employment. By 1933, thirty million people worldwide were jobless. Of those, half lived in the United States. Middle-class Americans fell into poverty. Already-impoverished Americans dropped toward destitution. Lines stretched in front of soup kitchens. Hunger marches wound through New York and Chicago. A million people, perhaps two million, many of them young, cut loose from conventional society and simply drifted, hopping freight cars or thumbing rides.

Meanwhile, encampments of the dispossessed spread across public parks and vacant lots. These scrap and cardboard shantytowns were named for the sitting President of the United States – Hoovervilles. A thousand World War I veterans descended on Washington to appeal for relief, throwing together their own Hoovervilles. Having been promised a bonus for their wartime service that would become payable in full in 1945, this Bonus Army wanted lump-sum payments immediately. Still more veterans arrived from across the country – perhaps seventeen thousand eventually converged, with more than twice that number counting family members and sympathizers. Their shacks, lean-tos, and tents stood just a short distance from the Capitol. When their bonus appeal died in the Senate, most of the veterans left Washington, but two thousand refused to go. After police failed to drive them away, Hoover ordered in the army, which finished the job using tanks, cavalry, and tear gas. The army chief of staff, General Douglas MacArthur, oversaw the operation. This occurred in late July 1932. The presidential election was just four months away.

Hoover would wind up with time on his hands for fishing trips in Yosemite because Franklin D. Roosevelt defeated him in a landslide. In his nomination acceptance speech, Roosevelt promised to confront the Depression with "a new deal for the American people." Among many points of emphasis, this would quickly come to include a focus on Yosemite National Park. FDR considered Yosemite to be the showplace of the national park system. New Dealers designated Yosemite as a model for other parks, including Shenandoah and Great Smoky Mountains, both established during the 1930s.[1]

Historians today rank FDR, along with Washington and Lincoln, as one of the three authentically great American presidents. By transforming the country, Roosevelt's became the pivotal administration of the twentieth century. But it might not have happened at all.

A tall, vibrant, active man, Roosevelt's life changed forever on August 10, 1921, when he was thirty-nine. He spent that day running, sailing, and swimming with his children, but he felt strange. Two weeks later, his doctors pronounced that he had infantile paralysis – the polio diagnosis that then caused universal dread. For the rest of his life, Roosevelt would depend on leg braces, wheelchairs, crutches, canes, and friendly arms. It was an era when families hid disabled children from view or institutionalized them because disabilities were considered signs of shame. Roosevelt did everything possible to play down and conceal the fact that he could not walk.

Polio practically extinguished Roosevelt's role in politics for the next seven years. He relied on his wife, Eleanor, with whom he had a strained and conditional relationship,[2] to keep his name before the public. Then, in 1928, he narrowly won the governorship of New York. Four years later, at the bottom of the Great Depression, Americans elected him president.

Running for the White House, Roosevelt portrayed the New Deal in fairly gauzy terms. He did call for "bold, persistent experimentation," but what did that imply? The first hundred days filled in a lot of the blanks, including a start on getting people back to work. With one of every four American workers out of a job, the private sector had no means of employing them in the near term; and who knew when the Depression would end? The only solution involved "relief," which conventionally meant a straight welfare check, the "dole." Roosevelt recoiled, terming the dole "a narcotic, a subtle destroyer of the human spirit."[3] The alternative he favored was *work relief* – jobs provided and paid for by the federal government.

***

The sheer scale of New Deal work relief programs staggers the imagination. Their ambition has never been repeated. In round numbers, the U.S. population in 1930 was one hundred twenty-three million; in 1940, one hundred thirty-two million. The Works Progress Administration (WPA)[4] provided a total of 8.5 million Americans with employment between 1935 and 1943. WPA strategy emphasized labor-intensive projects intended to create as many jobs as possible. At its peak in 1936, 3.4 million people were on WPA rolls, paid directly by the federal government.

The Public Works Administration (PWA) took a contrasting approach during its lifespan from 1933 to 1939. It administered grants and loans to state and local governments as well as to other federal agencies. These recipients in turn hired private contractors to carry out big projects that emphasized not mass labor so much as large scale, expertise, heavy equipment, and permanence – in today's term, *infrastructure.* PWA projects included such monuments as Grand Coulee Dam, New York's Triborough Bridge, highways, schools, subways, sewage treatment plants, and naval vessels (including aircraft carriers later critical to turning the tide of World War II in the Pacific). In all, the PWA undertook some thirty-four thousand individual projects.

In Yosemite, too, the PWA carried through with its trademark large-scale, permanent approach. The WPA played a much more peripheral role (for example, producing dioramas for the museum). In parallel, another federal agency, the less famous Bureau of Public Roads (BPR), completed most of the park's modern road infrastructure. By elevating their priority and pumping in resources, the Roosevelt Administration transformed older federal agencies like the BPR into New Deal agencies. The BPR illustrates how this worked in practice. The administration raised roadbuilding to top priority. Thousands of miles of BPR projects got partial funding from the PWA and WPA. Everything was circular. The same with the preexisting National Park Service. Its priority went up and resources poured in, producing constant interaction between new Roosevelt-era agencies and the NPS.

The program that epitomized New Deal Yosemite, though, was the Civilian Conservation Corps. It was the American public's favorite New Deal program. (Even my family, rather conservative at the time, had a soft spot for the CCC.) The Corps was FDR's own favorite too. Its origins went all the way back to his early life, and help to explain how Roosevelt became one of America's foremost champions of the outdoors – among the greatest conservationists the country has ever produced.

Roosevelt grew up on the family's Hudson River estate in Hyde Park, New York, where tree climbing was a favorite activity of his childhood. On his European honeymoon with Eleanor in 1905, he developed an admiration for German forests and forestry practices. The Germans emphasized that forests belonged to communities, not just to individuals, and their forests were managed for long-term sustainability. FDR's distant cousin, Theodore, then the president, was laying the groundwork for an American system of more sustainable forestry, capped by the creation of the United States Forest Service in 1905. This, though, happened long after much of the eastern U.S. had already been cut over.

FDR set out to transform the Hyde Park estate into a model tree farm. As Douglas Brinkley has noted, "trees were more than just aesthetically pleasing to Franklin Roosevelt, they were God's greatest utilitarian invention." The word "utilitarian" is important. Roosevelt's orientation toward forests involved the concept of *conservation for use* – that rather than just cutting a stand of timber and moving on to the next one, in the time-honored (and unsustainable) American fashion, trees should hereafter be harvested under a plan that included growing new trees. Hence, the Hyde Park tree farm, where ancient conifers were preserved while lesser trees were kept free of insects and disease until being cut, sold, and replaced. Roosevelt believed in *managing* – while also *modifying* – the natural world.[5]

He advanced these principles in Albany as a state senator from 1911 to 1913. He had already been encouraging New York to adopt the German model, which the state eventually did in such places as the Catskills. Roosevelt's efforts now led to pioneering legislation that protected the Adirondacks from denudation by regulating timber harvesting on private land. Following his long post-polio absence from public life, Roosevelt made conservation a priority of his governorship. Surrounding himself with forest enthusiasts and agronomists, he spirited through an amendment to the state constitution that provided for reforestation on a massive scale.

Though he governed a state boasting the nation's largest city, Roosevelt identified himself as a tree farmer from Dutchess County, New York. As one of his advisors later put it, FDR regarded cities "as rather hopeless" places, and "always did, and always would, think people better off in the country." His presidential administration would set landmark precedents in public housing; yet, given a choice between rehabilitating a slum or moving people out into the countryside, to him the answer was clear. In fact, across the political spectrum, sentiment had grown for resettling unemployed city-dwellers out in rural America. This "back-to-the-land" movement would become something of a New Deal priority, one in which Eleanor Roosevelt directly participated. It followed naturally, then, that the best place for needy young urban men was not in the streets, but on the land.[6]

FDR's long affiliation with the Boy Scouts of America provides an important example of his strong belief in introducing urban youth to outdoor life. Scouting has always been grounded in the belief that getting boys into the woods builds character, self-reliance, and a capacity for teamwork. During the first summer of his presidency, Roosevelt's open car rolled into a Boy Scout camp in the Catskills, Secret Service agents balanced on the running boards. A throng of Scouts cheered as Roosevelt donned an American Indian headdress, becoming the first and only president ever inducted into the Order of the Arrow.

In 1931, as governor, Roosevelt established the Temporary Emergency Relief Administration to provide work relief in the State of New York. The TERA was the first comprehensive relief agency created by any state during the Depression. One of its main objectives involved planting trees; before 1932 was over, more than ten thousand destitute young men were putting trees into the ground.

On March 15, 1933 – eleven days after his inauguration – Roosevelt held a press conference where he laid out the problems that the nation's forests faced and positioned the issue as a core New Deal priority. He wanted, he said, to put two hundred thousand men to work in the woods as soon as possible. That very day, wheels began turning to create the Civilian Conservation Corps under an overarching official rubric termed Emergency Conservation Work.[7] In later years, New Deal veterans would argue about how much of the New Deal was planned and how much was improvised. With the CCC, no question at all exists.

Roosevelt already had the TERA model at hand, and he was very specific about its new national counterpart. Naturally, he emphasized work relief. He talked about flood control, which he had long tied together with good forestry. He stressed building national wealth through forestry practices that would produce more commercial timber. But he wanted it understood that wealth was secondary. "More important . . . than the material gains," Roosevelt declared, "will be the moral and spiritual value of such work." "It is my belief," he said in a message to CCC enrollees as the program was rolling out, "that what is being accomplished will conserve our natural resources, create future national wealth and prove of moral and spiritual value not only to those of you who are taking part, but to the rest of the country as well."[8]

In essence, Roosevelt's primary objective was to get unemployed young men out of the nation's cities and onto the land; treat them respectfully and humanely, with a deep focus on their individual well-being; restore their morale ("moral and spiritual value"); make them healthier; and help rebuild the national economy in the short term through work relief. Conservation provided the means by which these things would happen. Conservation meant restoring forests, together with other kinds of environmental work, and also meant projects to improve recreational opportunities for the general public. The overriding objectives – *human* conservation and *outdoor* conservation – were explicitly, inextricably linked and given urgent priority. "We are killing two birds with one stone," Roosevelt said of the CCC in a fireside chat. "We are conserving not only our natural resources, but our human resources."[9] Though it had a precursor in the TERA, the whole idea, like much of the rest of the New Deal, was experimental.

To anyone accustomed to American society and politics in the late twentieth and early twenty-first centuries – an era that has been called the New Gilded Age – such ideas may seem almost bizarre. The New Gilded Age focused on globalism, markets, entrepreneurialism, and education (conspicuously, on attending the "right" university). This value system resided in the notion that a meritocracy existed – that "you can always make it if you try." If you didn't make it, that was your fault; your talents fell short, or else you didn't try hard enough. These notions were bipartisan. Although it lingered in the DNA of the Democratic Party, a focus like Roosevelt's on *labor* and *youth* did not even register when it could have been summoned back to life during the Great Recession of 2007-2009. It was as if the dignity and value of work – work as such – had been completely forgotten. The CCC was precisely about the dignity and value of work, however ordinary, and the importance of work to the nation. Work meant serving the common good, and service in itself was considered patriotic.

The CCC, though, also stood out against the value system of the *original* Gilded Age. It was that Gilded Age of the late-nineteenth-century, still in memory in the 1930s, that was the point of reference for the New Deal. During the 1880s or 1890s, the idea of mounting a government program to provide meaningful work for millions of unemployed, starving people (of whatever age) was alien to both major political parties. In the matter-of-fact words of Grover Cleveland, the only Democratic president elected during the whole era, "while the people should patriotically and cheerfully support their Government, its functions do not include the support of the people."[10] This logic remained powerful enough as late as the 1920s that it helped destroy the Hoover presidency. Casting it aside was one of the New Deal's greatest departures from rigid inherited orthodoxy.

Hoover did more than any prior president had to battle a depression. He drew the line, though, in refusing to provide direct federal relief to the unemployed and impoverished. Hoover refused to cross that line out of fear that it would lead to socialism. His White House repeatedly promised that things would work out in the long run. To that, Harry Hopkins – who ran New York's Temporary Emergency Relief Administration, and who would play a central role in the New Deal – timelessly retorted: "People don't eat in the long run, they eat every day."[11]

During the New Deal era, and carrying on into the postwar years, the United

States passed through a period when small-d democracy received more than a routine nod of approval; it was genuinely exalted. Small-d democracy favored social equality. It favored making the good things of life available to everyone. It favored inclusivity as opposed to exclusivity. Vice President Henry Wallace captured the spirit when he famously declared that the century ahead must be "the century of the common man." The composer Aaron Copland wrote a Fanfare for the Common Man. In the wake of the Great Depression, gilt went out of fashion, and wealth was displayed in more subdued ways. Compensation differences between CEOs and shop floor workers were incomparably narrower than they are today. The sentiment of the time was captured in a two-page ad spread that appeared in a 1941 issue of *Life* magazine. The ad, for Schlitz beer, read: "In mill hand's home or millionaire's mansion – at the country club or in the farmer's cottage – the beer that made Milwaukee famous graces any table. Not everyone can own the finest pearl, or drive the costliest car. But America's most distinguished beer is within the reach of everybody. Here, indeed, is democracy in a bottle! That famous flavor found only in Schlitz knows no class distinction."[12]

To jump-start the Civilian Conservation Corps, the White House quickly sent a proposal to Congress, which enacted it on March 31, 1933, just twenty-seven days after FDR's inauguration. To head the program, Roosevelt appointed Robert Fechner, vice president of both the International Association of Machinists and the American Federation of Labor. A machinist by trade, Fechner had left school at sixteen. He enjoyed telling people that all his clerks had a better education than he did. As plain-looking as a potato, Fechner was an honest, hardworking man with simple tastes. Well-liked and well-respected, he proved a good organizer and administrator. He also checked the labor union box; the Roosevelt Administration wound up doing more for organized labor than any administration before or since.

The CCC program rolled out quickly. Those eligible were to be men between eighteen and twenty-five years of age. Compensation would run thirty dollars a month – a dollar a day. But the men could keep only five. The rest would go back home as a form of family support. While the characteristic recruit would always match a single profile – a young man from a needy family, typically on relief – the program offered slots as well to American Indians across a wide age span, and to unemployed foresters. CCC ranks also included Local Experienced Men – LEMs – of varying ages, who provided training to enrollees in work settings where the LEMs lived. (An enrollee in Yosemite might hail from New Jersey or North Dakota and be trained by a LEM from Oakhurst or Mariposa.) Finally, in dramatic contrast to Hoover's response to the Bonus Army, Roosevelt signed an executive order providing CCC employment for twenty-five thousand veterans of World War I. Over the life of the program, eight times that many would find jobs in the CCC.[13]

The Corps admitted African Americans, too – while largely hewing to the rigid racial boundaries of the 1930s. Eleanor Roosevelt and Secretary of the Interior Harold Ickes were the administration's two foremost advocates of civil rights. ER provided a fearlessly eloquent voice for racial equality. In 1933, Ickes began instituting desegregation measures throughout his own governmental domain, including the national parks.[14]

But FDR was hemmed in by the reality that the adoption of his New Deal legislative priorities depended absolutely on the support of the southern Democrats in Congress. He could have chosen to mount a frontal offensive for civil rights. It would have failed – not for another thirty years did major civil rights legislation finally make it through Congress. Or, Roosevelt could leave the South's racial caste system alone, get landmark programs like Social Security through the House and Senate, and make racial progress at the margins. That is what he did. Many Blacks appreciated even this cautious approach to such a degree that the New Deal era marked the point at which African Americans, in those places where they could actually vote, began to shift away from the Republican Party and toward the Democrats.

Operating within the hard strategic calculation that Roosevelt made, did the CCC go as far as it might have to advance racial justice? The frank answer is no. The blame for this does not rest with the young men who served in the Corps, but with the racial mores of the time and how CCC administrators coped with them. A nondiscrimination provision made it through Congress in the original legislation that authorized the program; and there developed a loose and quiet, albeit inadequate, quota system to ensure that Blacks did actually secure slots in the CCC. But while some experiments were made toward integration, by and large the Corps was segregated. There was a great deal of white community blowback – not just in the South, but in the North as well – over stationing companies of African Americans close by, even though they were nearly all led by white army officers. Black units were often housed on military reservations or in remote areas in order to isolate them from outraged locals and the Ku Klux Klan. Fechner ordered that Black CCC enrollees be kept within their own state, or at least their region, even while movement was a constant reality for everyone else.[15] At the very end of the nineteenth century and into the first years of the twentieth, units of Black troops patrolled Yosemite, and are celebrated today. But not Black CCC companies three decades later.

However, this bleak story has a better side. At various times and places outside the South, a limited number of CCC companies were integrated. This occurred in Yosemite Valley. How do we know? There is a notable absence of mention in the park's written records. The real evidence is photographic. For however long, and to whatever degree, the company stationed on the valley floor was integrated.

Integrated CCC group, Company 942, Yosemite Valley, 1934

Early on, Eleanor Roosevelt tried and failed to get women incorporated into the Civilian Conservation Corps. Robert Fechner, for one, resisted the idea. Then, she and Secretary of Labor Frances Perkins created a small shadow CCC for young women, dubbed the She-She-She. (Frances Perkins was the first woman ever to serve in a president's cabinet.) Separately administered from the CCC, the shadow program did not send women into the woods with axes and saws. They did jobs deemed more feminine. The few unemployed women who actually did affiliate with any CCC camps – female campers, they were called – were there to do housekeeping chores, and received even lower pay than the men.

The CCC was not set up in 1933 as a freestanding agency. Instead, it operated through cabinet departments – Interior, Agriculture, Labor, and War. The Labor Department would carry out the initial recruitment of candidates, working in tandem with relief agencies at the state and local levels. The job of final screening, though, would fall to the army, and the army would administer the program.

That particular fact aroused a good deal of objection throughout the 1930s. In the Civilian Conservation Corps' very name, the word *civilian* was counterbalanced by the military term *corps.* If run by the army, wouldn't the CCC be militaristic? Indoctrinating? A threat to democracy? In other words, how different was it from the Nazis' mandatory labor program for younger workers, the Reich Labor Service? It did not exactly allay suspicions when the CCC acquired the nickname, Forest Army. People to the left of the American political spectrum felt especially jittery, but so did some on the right – a shared sense of anxiety that might inspire a pacifistic socialist, say, to join hands with a New Deal-hating isolationist in opposing the program. Their only point of contention would be whether the CCC was fascistic, the prevailing theory on the far left, or Bolshevik, the prevailing theory on the far right. Subscribing to the first supposition, the U.S. Communist Party absolutely loathed the CCC.[16]

In actual fact, the War Department wanted no part of the Civilian Conservation Corps, whether in Yosemite, where the army already had a history, or anywhere else. Throughout the 1930s, the United States Army was puny, totaling some hundred forty thousand officers and men when Roosevelt took office. The army had to stretch itself just to carry out its regular, military assignments. (At decade's end in 1939 – the opening year of World War II in Europe – the U.S. Army ranked just nineteenth in the world, below the armies of Switzerland or Portugal.)[17]

Another consideration differentiating the CCC from the Reich Labor Service was the simple fact that Roosevelt was not Hitler. He despised Hitler. A central

New Deal goal was to undermine fascism and other forms of political extremism in America while strengthening the democratic system.[18] Nazi propagandists liked to stress how "superior" their labor program, which included racist and nationalist indoctrination and was part of the larger design to rebuild Germany's military, was to America's Civilian Conservation Corps.

FDR directed Robert Fechner and the army to get moving right away and put a full quarter-million men to work in the forests by July 1, 1933. Fechner thus found himself in charge of the biggest peacetime mobilization in American history. Douglas MacArthur, still the army chief of staff, issued orders to the army's nine geographic corps jurisdictions to make immediate preparations: CCC camps must be built and staffed at once. Casting aside the accustomed bureaucratic inertia involving requisitions and implementation, the army moved at top speed. Multiple candidates were applying for every CCC slot. On April 6, the first man was enrolled. By the beginning of July, more than thirteen hundred camps were up and running nationwide, and the quarter-million goal had been far exceeded.

FDR visits CCC Camp Fechner, Virginia, 1933 (Robert Fechner to FDR's right)

The initial camp setup worked this way. Each camp had a company of around two hundred men, presided over by a captain in the regular army who was referred to as the camp commander. The captain was assisted by two lieutenants and four enlisted men – first sergeant, supply sergeant, mess sergeant, and cook. An army doctor saw to the care of each thousand enrollees. The army also furnished dentists as well as part-time circuit-riding chaplains.

The doctors and dentists were no frill. Even after an initial health screening, most newly enrolled men were in bad physical shape – and they were painfully aware of it. The Depression had had four years to do its work on their bodies. An army study in 1937 found three-quarters of them to be so malnourished and underweight that they were easy targets for disease.[19] In photos, many look gaunt. The Corps had a minimum weight requirement, and the most skeletal applicants – desperately unfit, desperately in need – got rejected. One seventeen year-old applicant from New Jersey, who had been rejected the first time on account of underweight, stuffed himself with food – topping it all off with three pounds of bananas he bought with his last twelve cents – just before his second physical. He succeeded (barely), tipping the scale at one hundred five pounds.[20] A nineteen year-old from Massachusetts who also made it through screening entered the Corps weighing one hundred six pounds and already missing several teeth. For the first time in his life, in the Corps he received proper medical and dental attention.[21]

Unquestionably, there were hundreds of thousands like him. As a leading historian of the CCC, John A. Salmond has written, "for most enrollees, enlistment in the CCC had been the final act, the culmination of a long period of despair and helplessness." A scholar of measured judgment, not given at all to overstatement, Salmond adds that enlistment "proved also to be a turning point. The Corps rekindled hope for the future and faith in America and its way of life."[22]

The first CCC camp, named for FDR, opened in Virginia at the beginning of May 1933 – just a month after he had signed the legislation. During the summer, Roosevelt authorized reserve officers to run the camps, freeing the regulars to return to active duty by the start of 1934. CCC enrollees replaced the non commissioned officers.

Originally, the Corps was authorized for a total life of only six months. This was then extended for another six, and recruits who had not found private sector employment received permission to reenroll. The first enrollment period began in April 1933, and so it went, in six-month cycles, until 1942. Over that span of time, more than three million men served in the CCC – five percent of America's total male population. Roosevelt stipulated that most of the program's outlays go to paying people instead of for materials or machinery. With the multiplier effect – $22 to $25 (typically $25) of every $30 going to the men's families – millions more across the country directly benefited.

Within the national parks, CCC projects were launched in a very particular way. Often, as was at least partially true in Yosemite, they followed master plans that the NPS Landscape Division had already laid out. Landscape architects, historical experts, engineers, and foresters would scrutinize project proposals and oversee their implementation. These specialists – their vantage point ranging from faraway Washington to within the parks themselves – red-flagged any ideas that threatened damage or overdevelopment. After the Washington office signed off on a project, the park superintendent had the responsibility of carrying it out: planning, formulating work programs, hiring work supervisors, oversight, reporting.

While on the job, CCC men fell under the civilian authority of what were collectively called the Technical Services; all the rest of the time, they came under the authority of the army. Camp superintendents (later called project superintendents), who were hired civilians, would break down park projects into daily work schedules that typically involved forty to fifty men. A civilian foreman would oversee the work itself. Additional hires for a project might include heavy equipment operators, mechanics, carpenters, masons, and other skilled labor. Both foremen and skilled workers came from the available pool of Local Experienced Men.

Over time, the organizational setup would evolve; but in Yosemite it was clear that, starting almost immediately, the CCC would present unprecedented opportunities. The park service would find itself with a labor force that it could never have imagined before. The enrollees would be lucky enough to have jobs – and jobs in Yosemite instead of some dreary backwater. It was one of those rare moments when everything suddenly comes together.

First contingent of CCC en route to Wawona from Yosemite Valley

[3] THE CCC ARRIVES

In visualizing the kind of volunteers he wanted for the Civilian Conservation Corps, FDR might have pictured Al Monteverde, John Ricci, Alf Bergly, and Joe Bryan. Their stories reflect the widely varied experiences of the thousands of CCC men who passed through Yosemite, and their personal photographs throughout this book bring the stories to life.

Al Monteverde arrived in the United States at around a year old when his parents immigrated from Mexico in 1916. His father died in a car crash when Al was seven. His widowed mother could barely keep the wolf from the door. She neither spoke English nor knew how to drive. The Depression only made things worse. When he started kindergarten, Al spoke no English either. In April 1933, shortly before graduating from his Los Angeles high school and with the family in desperate

Al Monteverde

John Ricci

straits, Al joined the CCC – "a port in a storm," he later called it. "We didn't know what we were getting into," he said of himself and his fellow recruits, "but we all looked at it like it was the chance in a lifetime. Something to do at last, thank God!"[1] Al came into the Corps with a beginning knowledge of photography that he had acquired in high school. He also exhibited a fluid, witty writing style in the letters he mailed home to his family. Generally quiet, Al was calm and self-effacing. He was humble – yet also very proud, very bright, and very perceptive. When he did speak, people paid attention. His friends called him Monte.

John Ricci would have made an ideal image for a CCC recruiting poster. He looked like a budding movie star. John grew up in Jersey City. His parents had immigrated from a tiny Italian mountain village east of Naples. Theirs was a classic immigrant story of struggling to establish a new life in America at the turn of the twentieth century. John's father came over as a teenager in 1898, married in 1902 back in Italy, then struggled as a laborer in the U.S. for three more years to save enough money to pay his wife's passage to America. Seven children were born, who required a lot of room and a lot of food. John's mother made the family's bread and pasta, putting up sauce in Mason jars from what the backyard garden produced. Her husband made the wine. During Prohibition, a room in the house was turned into a speakeasy. Italian was the language the Riccis spoke at home. Once the Depression hit, family dinners featured lots of pasta but little meat. Young John joined the CCC in the spring of 1934. Stationed first in Mississippi, his company was transferred to an area north of Yosemite, from which he was deployed into the park.[2]

Alf Bergly and his fiancée Ethel at Mirror Lake, 1946

Born in 1919 into a Norwegian immigrant family, Alf Bergly grew up in a small house in Reynolds, a hamlet in eastern North Dakota. The Depression hit his family hard. As a youngster, he took jobs doing farm work. Alf also poured drinks at a bar in town, until the owner discovered that he was underage. (The bar is still in business today.) Alf's mother died when he was around twelve, leaving behind five young children. He left school after finishing the eighth grade. His formal education never went beyond that, but he had a very quick mind, and from then on mostly taught himself. Alf was a complex man with a wide emotional range. At seventeen or perhaps eighteen, he joined the Civilian Conservation Corps. He was stationed two places, in Idaho and a camp near Sequoia-Kings Canyon. This was close enough that his outfit would have gone on excursions to Yosemite, and his life was intertwined with Yosemite before and after World War II.[3]

Joe Bryan was a farm boy from Sanderson, Florida, a small unincorporated community in the northern part of the state. His parents' eighty acres were planted in cotton until boll weevil wiped it out, and after that tobacco. Born in 1923, Joe was one of six children. They lived in a log cabin. There was no plumbing, no electricity; the smell of lamp kerosene permeated the place. Cattle and hogs roamed around. The family never traveled farther than to visit an aunt who lived a short distance away, over the Georgia line. Joe joined the CCC at seventeen, and was transported off to California. As his daughter puts it, going to "California was the same as going across the world."[4] The Corps stationed him in one of the most remote and isolated corners of Yosemite. The contrast between Sanderson, whose elevation above sea level is one hundred fifty-seven feet, and Yosemite astonished Joe. An affable, outgoing person, Joe loved people, and they responded in kind. He never met a stranger, prized a good joke, had a contagious laugh. He possessed a fine work ethic, making him an excellent match for the CCC. Joe also liked things to be organized and orderly, another valuable trait. Deeply spiritual, he was a godly man.

Joe Bryan

For all their differences, Al, John, Alf, and Joe were representative CCC recruits. While the rules did change in various ways over time, the initial policies laid out in 1933 reflected the administration's intent and set the tone. Along with being eighteen to twenty-five, "junior" enrollees (as opposed to war veterans or Indigenous Americans) were to be unmarried, unemployed, U.S. citizens, in decent enough physical shape, and have dependents at home. Upper age limits were later altered, and the lower limit reduced to seventeen. (A lot of recruits had lied about their age. One has the impression that in desperate times, this detail was often simply overlooked.) The portion of each CCC check that was sent home helped support the recruit's typically large, typically on-relief family, ideally lifting it off of welfare. Since the overarching aim was to support destitute families through work relief, young men riding the rails and disconnected from their families were excluded until 1937.

One cites statistics at the risk of over-generalizing and making CCC men appear homogeneous, which – as we have just seen – they decidedly weren't. Acknowledging that risk, we can broadly summarize. Over the life of the program, 1933-42, the average junior recruit was seventeen or eighteen years old, five feet-eight inches tall, one hundred forty-five pounds. One in five, like John Ricci and Al Monteverde, had foreign-born parents. The home that the typical recruit came from was spartan, like Joe Bryan's – no indoor plumbing, no telephone. The father was likely an industrial worker, or else a farmer, who had gone a considerable time without work. His family depended on welfare checks. The average CCC recruit had gotten as far as ninth grade, but had fallen far behind in arithmetic and reading. The educational span, though, stretched widely: 3 percent could neither read nor write, while 13 percent had graduated from high school. A handful had gone to college. The typical recruit had scant work experience – 40 percent had none at all – but he hoped the CCC would teach him *how* to work.[5]

Men applied for the CCC through city, county, or state welfare agencies. If they advanced, they reported to an army recruiting station. The army made the final cut after a candidate passed a medical exam and (during the initial years of the CCC) underwent a two-week physical conditioning program in a special "conditioning camp."[6]

In April 1934, having gotten through the initial screening, Al Monteverde reported to downtown Los Angeles for a thumbs-up, or down, from the United States Army. Bussed to Fort MacArthur in San Pedro (named for Douglas's legendary father, General Arthur MacArthur), Al arrived along with young men from around Southern California. "It was very much like joining the Service," he later wrote.[7] All took the physical examination. If they passed, they took an "oath of enrollment." This oath was described in its preface as "a contract between the enrollees and the U.S. Government," and indeed it read like a contract. The key provisions committed the signer to completing his term of enrollment, obeying individuals in authority, and following the rules and regulations.[8]

Once admitted, each man was issued blue denim work clothes. He also received a modified army dress uniform for more formal occasions: starched and ironed olive drab shirt and pants, more-or-less matching overseas cap and web belt, black tie, and brown dress shoes. Initially, CCC issues came out of old army stocks. One of Al's fellow inductees got a mess kit with an engraved message on the lid: "The Hell with the Kaiser."[9] A lot of the time the clothes didn't fit well, which led to a flourish of alterations using any and all tailoring skills available. It wasn't until the Corps' final years – when he realized what a mishmash even the dress uniforms were – that FDR directed that spruce green dress uniforms designed specifically for the CCC finally replace the old army attire. By 1939, these replacement issues were being widely worn.

Whether from big city ethnic neighborhoods or isolated rural hamlets, recruits like Al, John, Alf, and Joe now entered a wider world they had never experienced before. The Corps mingled different sorts of Americans and put them in wholly unfamiliar places. Many enrollees, notably those like John from big cities, but also flatlanders like Joe, had no experience in the mountains. Nor did recruits typically have any familiarity with tools, at least the kind they would be putting to use in the woods.[10] Coming from coastal cities in California or from parts of the South, some had never experienced snow. When men arrived in Wawona, they were taken aback by the isolation of the place.[11] Ironically, the wider world of the CCC could actually seem, in Yosemite, like a narrower world.

Al Monteverde recalled that everything happened very fast at first. Conditioning camp may have been skipped completely. (His older brother, Paul, later also entering through Fort MacArthur, did go through conditioning.) Al was quickly separated from two friends. "I now was alone among a bunch of strangers, and all kinds of crazy thoughts were racing through my mind. Where are they taking us? Where, how, what, who? Then someone in authority said that we were to board a train right there at Fort McArthur, and we'd be on our way to a place called Buck Meadows near Yosemite National Park! Everyone let out a yell of relief and happiness."[12] North of Fresno, Forest Service trucks picked them up. Al was already making new friends and feeling a great sense of adventure.

Before long, word came down that, late in May, Al and some other men would move on to Crane Flat, inside Yosemite – "a dream come true." Al had only heard about the wonders of the park. "The ride up there was one revelation after another." As they ascended, the trees got taller and taller, until the vehicles reached the Tuolumne Grove of Giant sequoias. "I could not believe my eyes. They were awesome and I thanked God that He let me share His great creations."[13]

***

The original CCC camps were as improvised as the clothes. At first most of them consisted of leaky World War I army tents. As winter approached, temperatures dropped, and camps started to get uncomfortable, better housing was needed right away. Hastily constructed wooden buildings went up, each camp getting four or five barracks measuring a hundred by twenty feet. These were often designed to last for only a short while, but they might just last as long as the CCC did.

In time, though, the initial guessing game about the program's future came to an end, and building standards were improved. After 1936, pre-cut, prefabricated, mass-produced buildings became the state of the art. Identical in construction, they could easily be transported from one place to another. Yosemite, though, continued to have a wealth of summer-occupied tent camps in addition. When Al arrived at Crane Flat – which was considered the park's one perennial summer camp, and had some amenities – he moved into a tent erected on a wood frame, with bunks and a wood stove. A mess hall and showers awaited. "All the comforts of home. . . . At this point, I was really feeling good about myself, like I was part of a team."[14] In fact, the setup resembled one of today's Yosemite High Sierra camps. Smaller summer field camps – called "side," "spike," or more commonly "stub" camps, which were satellites of the main ones – also continued to rely on tents.

The buildings in a typical CCC camp were arrayed in a U-shape, with the hollow of the U used for sports and activities. Normative camps by the mid-'thirties consisted of four or five wooden barracks sleeping forty men each; a mess hall; a fully plumbed bathhouse; a recreation building; quarters for officers and supervisors; and administrative structures. Eventually, an education building went up as well, making twenty-four structures in all. Building exteriors might be creosoted, painted green or brown, or tar-papered. Heating was provided by potbellied stoves. In Yosemite Valley, two small stoves were relied on to heat a fifty-two-man barracks in the dead of winter, with the enrollees taking turns at feeding in the wood.

Men took pride in any upgrades they could add to the raw, standardized buildings, notably anything that helped to insulate them. Eventually in Wawona, plywood paneling was nailed up in the mess hall and kitchen. Linoleum flooring improved the infirmary and the officers' quarters. The latrines got interior wallboard. The camp barber shop acquired two real barber chairs. Interior lighting was upgraded, too.[15]

Camp personnel were continually in flux. Sometimes in Yosemite companies ran at full strength; at other times they fell below – a sort of seesaw. Some men would leave after a single six-month hitch, while others re-upped. Generally, companies remained at a single assigned camp, but frequently companies or individuals got transferred to other camps in the same or different states. John Ricci's move from Mississippi to California was not unusual. Joe Bryan and Al Monteverde were transferred, too. Alf Bergly's time in the Corps was split between California and Idaho. For a Wawona man, the next stop might be Alabama or Florida, while in the meantime men were being transferred to Yosemite from the South.[16]

The continual shifting could affect morale. In 1935, the company stationed at Wawona got reassigned to Glacier National Park. Glacier sounds like a fine destination, but the men, not wanting to leave, took it as a blow.[17]

However much men moved around, and wherever they landed, the daily camp routines were similar. With some variations, they ran this way. The workday began with reveille at 6:00 A.M. Calisthenics/physical training came next, then washing up before breakfast. Breakfast was followed by bunk-making, barracks and camp cleanup, roll call, and inspection. At around 7:45, the men climbed aboard trucks that took them out to the day's worksite. (A few would remain in camp, for example, clerks, cooks, or launderers.) Noon brought a break for lunch.

CCC work caravan climbing old Big Oak Flat Road, 1934 (Bridalveil Fall in background)

Work ended at 4:00. An hour or so of free time followed for sports or other recreation. The men then showered, shaved, and donned dress uniforms. Retreat and the flag-lowering took place at 5:15, followed by the evening meal at 5:30. The rest of the evening provided free time for education or recreation. Barracks lights went out at 10:00; the bugler blew taps; and the camp commander made a bed check at 11:00 to ensure that every bunk had an occupant.

At the time, the New Deal was institutionalizing the forty-hour week as the national standard, one of organized labor's hardest-fought goals. The CCC workday constituted eight hours, including transportation. Men put in a straight five-day week, with weekends off. Weekends were a busy time in camp, filled with sports, excursions, work on the camp newspaper, education, and other activities. If bad weather had impeded work during the week, though, the lost time was made up on weekends.

Some men earned promotion to roles as Leaders or Assistant Leaders. Pay rates were commensurate with rank, $45 and $36 per month, respectively, and men could keep the extra pay. The men holding these positions typically totaled twenty-six out of a company of two hundred. Over his two years in the CCC, John Ricci, for example, moved up to Assistant Leader and then to Leader.

Leaders worked with foremen running crews, or oversaw certain camp duties. Assistant Leaders served as company clerks or assistant cooks or the like.

CCC man piloting a bulldozer

***

The month Roosevelt was inaugurated, Charles Thomson, in his brisk manner, had begun immediate preparations to welcome the CCC to Yosemite. It didn't hurt that Thomson had been a senior army officer. The New Deal presented the national parks with an unprecedented torrent of resources – labor, budgets, and energy. To borrow terms from a later era, Yosemite abounded with backlogged deferred maintenance and shovel-ready projects.

Practically every member of the park service was called on to assist the army in getting the CCC camps up and running. The initial recruits arrived in the middle of May 1933; on May 15-16, the two Wawona camps – YNP 1 and 2 – opened, making them among the first camps in the West.[18] (A permanent, winterized Wawona base would not be constructed until late in 1934.) Meanwhile, preparations were under way for three more two-hundred-man camps in the park, making a total of five – one thousand recruits in all. In addition to the two in Wawona, two went up at Crane Flat and one near Chinquapin. By the end of June, as planned, well over a thousand men had materialized.

At the end of the 1933 spring-to-fall season, Yosemite's CCC camps were evacuated. Two-thirds of the members of YNP Camp 1 had re-registered for another six-month hitch; in November, they were relocated to Sequoia National Park. That same month, the men of Camp 2 were moved from Wawona to Cascade Creek, between the western edge of Yosemite Valley proper and Arch Rock. Their new, permanent, winterized installation – numbered Camp 6 – was called Camp Cascades.

Today, the site of Camp Cascades is a sprawling picnic ground along Highway 140 – and no wonder. Here the Merced River settles into a long, unbroken run of flat water. It almost resembles a lake. One can easily imagine it in the 1930s as an immense swimming hole full of young men coming off a day's work. Immediately adjacent, Cascade Creek makes its final plunge down a spectacular five hundred-foot waterfall before emptying into the river. If one were looking for a perfect site anywhere in the park for a CCC camp, nothing could have surpassed this big, level, sandy expanse of land. That is, unless the river rose – because the land is a floodplain.

Remnants of old Camp Cascades at river's edge

Civilian foremen provided continual oversight in getting the camps erected and with other projects. Traveling from place to place, Howard Cox filled that role in Yellowstone, Yosemite, and other CCC camps in California. A photo shows Cox as a rangy man wearing boots and smoking a pipe. Typically, he would arrive at a site ahead of the other staff or enrollees. Assigned to Yosemite in 1933-1934, he oversaw work on roads and public campsites. At the time of his death in 1994, he was still designing and planning parks for the State of Arizona.[19] Foremen like Cox were critical. As Al Monteverde observed at the time: "A good boss is a fellow that can get the work out of his crew without being harsh to them. In other words treat them right & they will work willingly!!"[20]

***

Besides setting up and occupying the camps, during its first weeks in the park the CCC began removing debris in sequoia groves, cleaning up the residual mess from former logging operations, felling snags, and working on fire suppression projects. Thomson commended the "vim and vigor" the recruits brought to their work, and how quickly they were toughening up. He recorded improvements in weight, strength, and outlook on life. Visitors, too, were impressed. By August, all of the straight forestry work in the park was being done by the CCC, under the guidance of some fifty foremen.[21]

Fire suppression crew

The original concept of the Civilian Conservation Corps had focused on tree planting, and in Yosemite the men went right to work at it. Around the country, CCC men shinnied up trees to gather seeds. These went to government nurseries, where they germinated into seedlings (much like the egg-to-fry cycle in a fish hatchery). At six to eight inches, the seedlings were ready to plant. The men would form teams of two. One man would dig the hole, the other would insert the seedling. From time to time they would switch jobs. A forester would specify where the trees should go and oversee the process generally. In the right conditions, the work could move fast. Teams might plant as many as five hundred trees a day.

In Yosemite, planting took on a far wider scope than trees alone. During the summer of 1933, CCC men began collecting seeds from literally thousands of the most beautiful flowering plants, including ceanothus, Mariposa lily, lupine, buckwheat, and Indian paintbrush. They did this by tying paper sacks to a plant to catch the seeds. One man would eventually gather seeds from high-elevation plants at the base of the Lyell Glacier. During the summer of 1934, under the supervision of Frederick Clements, a park service plant ecologist who possessed a doctorate, men carried out extensive planting along roadsides. Clements's strategy favored harvesting and distributing the seeds of flowering plants that deer avoided grazing. Research was carried out, too. The CCC fenced off a patch of the valley floor to keep deer out, which allowed for an impact study of grazing on plant life.[22]

In 1938, a dense protective belt of small native trees and shrubs was planted around the Mariposa Grove's Grizzly Giant, one of the largest Giant sequoias in the world. The belt was intended to protect the soil surrounding the tree's shallow root system from trampling and compaction by the thousands of tourists who annually came to stare in wonder. There had been a problem, too, with vandals – including visitors who courted immortality by carving their initials into the great ancient tree. Ever since 1912, efforts had been made to keep people at a distance from the Giant. In 1930, Charles Thomson came up with a novel solution that drew on his experience on the Western Front in World War I: barbed wire. He directed that the tree be surrounded by a barbed wire maze, screened by shrubs and ferns. Thomson thought the treatment was "splendid," but at some point the barbed wire came out.[23] Later, the CCC also endeavored to make its own barrier look as natural as possible. The men added oiled paths and low guard rails to guide visitors along the appropriate routes.[24]

Together with tree planting went tree thinning. In 1934, CCC men cleared out trees to improve the view of Yosemite Falls. Although that may seem counterintuitive, it wasn't at all. Decades later, infiltrating trees made it harder and harder to see Vernal Fall from the bridge below. Had that occurred in the 1930s, the CCC would undoubtedly have been ordered to carry up saws and cut down the offending trees.

Because of the great concern the park service took for how things looked in general, and how well specific sites presented themselves to visitors, the CCC was directed to strip the Mariposa Grove of live non-sequoias – largely white fir – along with snags, down timber, and undergrowth. This dramatically improved the view of the big trees, placing them into even higher relief and creating, in the words of one senior ranger, a "park-like" effect.[25] Forestry practices often involve thinning and removal, and the CCC did plenty of both. It eliminated debris, snags, and dead limbs that detracted from a view or posed a hazard. It cleared out "suppressed" conifers that clogged the forest floor with no prospect of receiving direct sunlight. In campgrounds, it felled dangerous and dead trees by the thousands, and limbed dead wood from live trees. Campers must have been delighted to find firewood waiting for them, pre-cut to the proper length and stacked by the CCC. Crews took down mistletoe. At points along the major roads, driftwood was hauled out of the Merced River and logjams were removed to make the river more appealing to the eye. Beyond removing tree hazards and enhancing aesthetics, though, all this cutting and trimming was also intended to reduce the fuel load for forest fires.[26]

Tree felling, then, went on continuously. Chain saws existed at the time but were not put to use by the CCC in Yosemite. Instead, men would take up position on either end of an eight-foot (or longer) two-person crosscut saw. At Crane Flat in 1934, an African American logger called "Tiny" – who of course was huge – would do the preliminary axe work, cutting a notch into the side of a tree's direction of fall. (One wishes more were known about him.) Years later, Al Monteverde recalled "the romance of the solid sound of a felling axe hitting its mark with a cadence that the lumberjack of today would be hard pressed to imitate." Al also remembered the particular challenge of cutting stumps off right at ground level.

The reason for that was aesthetic, so that travelers in cars passing by would not have to see any stumps sticking out of the ground.[27]

Along the main roads, besides cutting down trees to open up views, the CCC planted trees in order to screen things off. On the valley floor, for instance, hundreds of trees were planted so as to screen campgrounds from these same main roads. All of this planting, clearing, pruning, and removal reminds one of a dentist working on a mouthful of teeth.

Park administrators took concern over what was deemed the "intrusion" of small trees into open meadows, threatening to turn the grassy open viewsheds into forests. In Yosemite Valley, meadow-invading trees were transplanted to campgrounds as part of the overall screening project. From its beginning, the CCC also received assignments to remove harmful non-native invasive species along major roads and elsewhere in the park. The men tore out various non-native trees and shrubs (along with tall wire fencing) around the old twenty-eight acre tule elk paddock in the valley once the non-native elk themselves were removed.[28]

***

Meanwhile, fighting another kind of invader became a big, labor-intensive routine for the CCC every single year. The invader was blister rust, a disease that attacked White pines. Originating in Asia, blister rust appeared in North America as early as 1908, conveyed from Europe in shipments of nursery stock. By the 1930s, it had spread to every significant White pine region across the United States from coast to coast. The realistic fear arose that blister rust might drive White pines to extinction in America.

The disease spread this way: an infected tree would throw off orange-colored spores. The spores would settle on leaves of bushes of the genus Ribes – currant and gooseberry – then produce an even more deadly generation of spores. From the bushes, these hyper-spores would spread on the wind throughout the forest. The cycle would then repeat. Infected trees sprouted blisters around their trunks and branches, and eventually died or (at the least) suffered damage. In Yosemite, the natives that blister rust attacked were western White pine, Sugar pine, and Whitebark pine.

The direct threat of blister rust to America's forests came as an enormous shock, right behind two comparable previous shocks. Both of these, like blister rust, involved an invasion by foreign pathogens. They led to true pandemics – like the influenza pandemic of the early twentieth century or the COVID-19 pandemic of the early twenty-first – except that instead of people these pandemics killed trees.

The first invader was the American chestnut blight. Called a "perfect tree," producing both superb wood and bounties of nuts, the American chestnut was an iconic native with a range across the eastern United States from Maine to northern Florida, and west to the Mississippi. Chestnuts made up a quarter of the eastern hardwood forest. With a height exceeding a hundred feet, the chestnut was the giant of the eastern woods. Arriving from Asia, the chestnut blight, a fungal pathogen, first attracted attention in the U.S. in 1904. It killed some *four billion* chestnuts during the first half of the twentieth century. The American chestnut was practically wiped out. This has been called the greatest single ecological forest catastrophe in world history.[29]

The next invader was Dutch elm disease, a tree fungus spread by bark beetles. Probably carried from Asia to Europe during World War I, and from there to America, the disease was first reported in the U.S. around 1930 (accounts vary). The American elm, like the chestnut, was an archetypal native tree, with a range spreading halfway across the continental United States. Like the chestnut, the American elm was big; a mature tree's canopy covered a quarter-acre. Despite a major battle to halt it during the New Deal era, by the 1980s the disease had wiped out three-quarters of all American elms.[30]

Now came White pine blister rust, threatening the nation's conifers. Blister rust challenged the entire notion of Yosemite as a stable, parklike environment. It called up the question, is nature ever really in balance, or is it constantly in flux? If the latter, then what if flux leads to depletion or devastation? Biologists and conservationists debated these questions not just for Yosemite but in a world context. With blister rust, the New Deal inevitably came down on the side of balance over devastation. Fighting this tree plague became a focus of the CCC from Maine to California, wherever the disease intruded into the woods, whether the trees were protected in a national park or commercially logged in national forests.

Spores from a blister rust-infected tree could travel up to two hundred miles before landing on a Ribes host currant or gooseberry, but spores from infected bushes could spread only as far as a thousand feet to infect a tree.[31] Obviously, the most effective way to stop blister rust was to go after the host bushes. Two techniques existed. Either the plants could be sprayed, or else men could take on the very hard work of uprooting the gooseberry and currant bushes out of the ground. Charles Thomson opposed both ways. The science around blister rust was still tentative.[32] Thomson thought that destroying currant and gooseberry, even to save stately old forests from an invasive pathogen, risked damaging the overall ecosystem of Yosemite. Subscribing to the premise of first do no harm, he recommended research into how the host species interacted with the park's other plant and animal communities.[33]

Thomson's reservations, as things turned out, were exceedingly prescient. In fact, by the mid-1930s, NPS wildlife biologists assigned to monitor CCC projects in the national parks were raising alarms about the CCC's broader campaign against forest diseases and insects. A number of biologists, at least, argued for leaving the forests alone. The issue became big enough to generate national press.[34] In retrospect, Thomson had some sort of sixth sense.

At first, though, as the campaign against Ribes rolled out, reservations did not matter. From the vantage point of Washington, park service director Arno Cammerer regarded blister rust as one of the greatest single threats the national parks faced. This represented plain common sense. The natural response was to fight the threat based on the current state of scientific knowledge and by using whatever means were at hand.

So, especially before its funding began to slacken in 1939, the Corps went after blister rust tooth and nail nationwide; and men kept right on fighting it in Yosemite until the CCC itself came to an end in the early 1940s. One camp, Crane Flat, was entirely dedicated to blister rust eradication work. For Yosemite, uprooting (as opposed to spraying) became the method of choice. At the start of the workday, string lines would be laid out demarking sections of, say, four hundred feet by fifty feet. A crew of ten or so would go about examining every square foot for Ribes. They would grub any target bushes they found using pickaxes, hoes, or McLeods – heavy wooden-handled tools with a thick-tined rake on one side and a hoe on the other. In some areas, the Ribes bushes grew underneath a thicket of buckbrush or ceanothus; men had to bushwhack their way in or crawl underneath to find them, keeping a sharp eye out for rattlesnakes. It wasn't enough just to chop off a plant at the ground; the root system must also be dug out. Even then, Ribes would stubbornly sprout again, so CCC men would have to return.

In Yosemite, statistics were maintained on all this massive effort. In 1934, an area of some four hundred acres yielded more than seventeen thousand Ribes bushes. Multiplying this gives a sense of the sheer scale of it all. During 1934 alone, Ribes crews swept some eighty-five thousand acres. In the summer of 1938, men from four Yosemite CCC camps uprooted 1,634,500 individual Ribes plants from roughly seven thousand acres. During the single month of May 1940, 329,990 bushes were tallied. In 1941, the year before the Corps' demise, the CCC was obtaining permits from dozens of private landowners in Wawona to grub their property for Ribes. Fighting blister rust might seem like trying to check gravity, but in fact the nationwide struggle during the New Deal years slowed the spread of the disease dramatically in some locales, while actually halting its advance in others.[35]

Together with Ribes, the private property permits in Wawona authorized the CCC to battle insects. Use of crews to control tree-destroying insects in the park went back many years. During the early 1930s, an upturn in pine beetle infestations reached the epidemic point. Eradication efforts accelerated in 1932. The following year, the lion's share of combating beetles was assigned to the CCC. What the Forest Army brought to the battle was numbers, not to mention energy.

Starting in 1933, the CCC attacked infestations of mountain pine and bark beetles that killed Sugar pines and Ponderosas. "Bug crews" would cut down and limb infected trees in the early spring, peel off the bark that housed the insects, and spray it with oil to prevent adult beetles from escaping. They would then burn the bark. Because of fire hazard, in the summer the routine changed: the stripped-off bark would be laid out flat in the sun, which proved nearly as effective as flame. By 1935, Sugar and Ponderosa pines looked their healthiest in years, to the point that natural predators were holding new beetle infestations in check. CCC maintenance crews continued to keep watch.[36] The focus now turned to needle-miner, an onslaught of moths and larvae that was increasingly afflicting a variety of conifers throughout the park and leaving behind particularly grim-appearing "ghost forests" of dead Lodgepole pines. In 1935, a cooperative field laboratory and insectary building went up on a site along the Wawona Road. Here entomologists could methodically study threats to the park's forests.

Pest control, whether done by the CCC or other agencies, routinely involved chemicals. Crews controlled pesky rodents using carbon disulfide or cyanide gas. A stub camp stationed at Illilouette Creek to do insect work also sprayed fuel oil on Puncturevine, a noxious weed. Mosquito larvae were killed by applying oil or kerosene to ponds. Later, an organic insecticide, pyrethrum, was sprayed on the pools. Mosquito-harboring water was sometimes drained. In 1934, the CCC dug ditches to bleed off water close to Happy Isles, while filling in other mosquito ponds near El Capitan and the valley chapel.[37]

Arsenic and lead arsenate featured conspicuously. In 1935, a thousand gallons of an arsenic compound were sprayed on alders in the Mariposa Grove to eradicate the alder flea beetles which had been defoliating the trees. Non-native elms in the Old Village were sprayed using the same mixture. Lead arsenate was sprayed on alders around Arch Rock. A thousand more gallons of lead arsenate went onto elms in the Old Village to knock out elm leaf beetle. And fourteen hundred gallons were sprayed on the two hundred seventy-five very old non-native apple and pear trees at Camp Curry to exterminate codling moths and their fruit-devouring larvae.[38]

***

Among all the multiple priorities for protecting Yosemite's forests, fire suppression occupied a unique place. Fire presented the greatest single threat to the national parks in general. Perennially lacking sufficient crews, the parks never had adequate firefighting capacity prior to the New Deal.[39] Yosemite did not even have a fire truck until at some point it finally received a (possibly new, possibly used) 1925 model.[40] By 1928, though, the park did have a fire prevention plan, and, beginning in 1931 at Crane Flat, a network of fire lookouts.

Yosemite was cooler then. Long-range data confirm an ongoing temperature rise throughout the twentieth century and into the twenty-first. Since 1895, the park has warmed at a rate of 1.6 degrees Fahrenheit per century. The rate has accelerated – since 1950, at 3.4 degrees per century.[41] Data aside, anyone who has spent time in the park over the span of just a few decades can attest from personal experience that it has gotten warmer. Measurements of the park's glaciers as far back as the mid-1930s showed that they had retreated dramatically. John Muir had described glaciers in the nineteenth century that by the 'thirties no longer existed. "Accurate yearly measurements confirm the belief of scientists that glaciers are disappearing in the Sierra," the park superintendent's report noted in 1935 with a tone of alarm.[42] During the 1930s, though, climate change remained an obscure theoretical issue for the scientific community to bat around. And – even though it was cooler then – Yosemite and its environs still experienced some hellacious fires.

Yosemite's first five CCC camps in 1933 were erected right inside the park's most dangerous fire zones. This made for quick reaction time.[43] But most of the firefighting occurred not inside, but outside, the park. Stationed outside at Buck Meadows, as well as inside at Merced Grove, enrollee Clair Nelsen later recalled that the men accepted firefighting "as relatively brief bursts of grueling work interspersed with long periods of more mundane, sometimes boring labor."[44] Battling blazes became a recurring annual ritual. With snow all around, the Wawona camp newspaper remarked in January 1935: "At least we may be sure it will provide a refreshing memory when we are fighting forest fires next August."[45]

One of the first national firefighting priorities undertaken by the CCC involved essential training. Starting in 1937, this meant one full day of training a month during the fire season, The following year, the Corps stepped things up by instituting nationwide firefighting "schools." While every enrollee in Yosemite received training, specific teams were singled out to specialize in firefighting, like elite troops. (Al Monteverde was assigned to a team while stationed outside the park, where he drove a fire truck.) To prevent fires, men throughout the national parks cleared firebreaks, removed dead wood and underbrush, and strung telephone lines to fire towers. In 1937, the Yosemite CCC got new purpose-built firefighting trucks.

Given the sheer number of CCC men and the rising level of training, it comes as no surprise that the National Park Service began to positively rely on the Corps to prevent and battle fires. It had never even remotely had such assets to call on before. The way the park service's outlays for fire suppression in Yosemite plummeted tells a story in itself. In 1931, the cost averaged $360 per fire. In 1933, it averaged $7.40.[46] The prominent contemporary park ranger John Bingaman summarized the change in a single sentence: "The CCC Boys were a Godsend when it came to fighting forest fires."[47]

Even with training, of all the CCC's many risky activities firefighting remained the most dangerous. During the lifespan of the Corps, around the country forty-seven men died fighting fires.[48] When a fire hit, men would roar off in trucks to take it on. From any available pond or stream, they would fill their thirty-five-pound hand pumping units. In the case of real infernos, crews of thirty men or so would clear firebreaks using axes and rakes. Backfiring helped too. CCC crews from inside Yosemite routinely fought fires outside the park. In 1934, big fires broke out in forests across the western states. That summer, an inferno roared across thousands of acres of Forest Service land near Yosemite, traveling seven miles in a single day and threatening the Merced Grove of Giant sequoias inside the park. When the Forest Service issued a call, the CCC rolled out of the park to take on the fire.[49] John Newcomb, who was serving in Wawona at the time, may have been referring to this fire when, as he later recalled, his crew went one hundred-two hours without sleep.[50] Battling a fire in 1935 just west of the Hetch Hetchy dam, crews alternated in shifts of sixteen hours on and sixteen hours off.[51]

Assigned to another huge blaze just west of the park that was devouring stands of Sugar pine, Al Monteverde had a close call while approaching by truck. The driver plowed into flames that were "licking at the road," but quickly yanked the crew back out again. Crown fires, bursting from tree to tree, mimicked "the sound of a giant draft furnace."[52] Though battled by hundreds of firefighters, the flames roared on for weeks. Enrollee Darrell Stover recalled a similar scare along the Tuolumne River near Hetch Hetchy. High winds sent burning pinecones sailing through the air, setting off spot fires like incendiary bombs. The men were overwhelmed. Some fled to an area that had already burned over; others went right into the river. No one was killed or injured.[53]

The CCC's biggest single project in California was a mammoth firebreak, the Ponderosa Way. It stretched some eight hundred continuous miles along the western Cascades and Sierra Nevada. The intent was to separate the foothills, where fires often broke out, from the conifer forests at higher elevations. The Ponderosa Way ran along the line where chaparral yielded to timber, and varied in width from fifty to two hundred feet. In 1935, nearly five thousand CCC men were at work on the project.[54] It amounted, in effect, to a fire prevention highway. The story of the Civilian Conservation Corps in Yosemite began as FDR had intended, with forestry. In itself, forestry presented a remarkable array of tasks – tree planting, tree removal, debris cleanup, disease and pest eradication, and firefighting. The administration poured so many men and resources into the park that, early on, the CCC could be assigned additional projects that had little or nothing at all to do with trees. Very soon, enrollees by the hundreds would be at work on jobs that required T squares or jackhammers instead of axes and saws. Because they do not change in the way that forests inevitably do, it is these projects we recognize today as the legacy of the CCC in Yosemite.

[4]
TWISTING ROADS

Yosemite's remarkable modern road system began to emerge before the 1930s, but it is primarily a creation of the New Deal. Easily taken for granted today, as though they had simply dropped from the sky, these roads required a tremendous investment of planning, money, and labor. They stand as landmarks of national park infrastructure. Their story is complex, and its telling threatens to divert us onto all sorts of byways. We will stick to the main routes, which have twists and turns enough.

The landscape is where the story begins, because everything revolved around it. Yosemite, especially the valley, resists road construction as if it had some inner urge not to be scarred. Ice Age glaciers, going back millions of years, carved Yosemite Valley into a U-shaped trough. When the glaciers retreated – they had largely melted off by around ten thousand years ago – they left behind granite walls thousands of feet high. Roads had to be engineered to run beneath the walls, above them, through them, or right up the sides. Elsewhere in the park, roads must pass around granite formations including cliffs and domes. The challenge that road engineers and crews confronted was genuinely astonishing.

Franklin D. Roosevelt's life transcended the early auto era. Despite his disability, he was able to drive a car of his own, modified with special controls that he operated by hand. The customized automobile was a 1936 Ford phaeton which, like Carl Sharsmith's 1936 Ford convertible, was designed for the open air. Roosevelt loved viewing the country, and especially the countryside, from behind the wheel. He wanted as many more Americans as possible to enjoy the same opportunity to see America's great natural wonders by car.

Therefore, Roosevelt endorsed well-designed, high-quality roads that would welcome more people to their national parks. He would have agreed with John Muir, who wrote that "thousands of tired, nerve-shaken, over-civilized people are beginning to find out that going to the mountains is going home; that wilderness is a necessity, and mountain parks and reservations are useful not only as fountains of timber and irrigating rivers, but as foundations of life."[1] The New Deal opened a spigot of money for road construction in Yosemite, and park administration welcomed the inflow for very good reasons. The perennial story of tourist travel to Yosemite could be summarized in three words – expensive, dirty, and scary.

***

Most of Yosemite's relatively few visitors during the latter half of the nineteenth century had been wealthy easterners or Europeans, with the money and discretionary time to make the trip. One writer in 1873 advised that a traveler should allocate at least ten days and $150 to experience Yosemite properly.[2] That sum would equal well over $3,000 today. As of 1890, annual earnings in America merely averaged a bit over $400.

The first routes to Yosemite Valley were nothing more than primitive trails. The traveler might descend, for instance, from Tamarack Flat across a plunging slope of granite talus, eventually winding up on the valley floor. One slip along the talus stretch, and a horse and rider would drop two thousand feet. Despite assurances that this had never happened, visitors felt a terror of becoming the first. "It is impossible to repress fear," one of them reported in the 1870s. The famous feminist Elizabeth Cady Stanton refused to trust a horse, opting to hike the trail instead.[3]

There was another risk as well. Yosemite was part of the late nineteenth century Wild West, and robbers would often hold up stages coming or going. During the early twentieth century, they updated their techniques by holding up tourists traveling by car along the Big Oak Flat and Wawona roads.

Besides the risks, another universal complaint involved the dust. The historian Richard H. Quin has remarked that travelers experienced dust in the way they experienced Bridalveil Fall or El Capitan, as "one of the great wonders of Yosemite."[4] David Curry called dust "pulverized scenery."[5] Tourists would arrive outfitted in long protective overgarments – "dusters" – but those did not save their eyes or lungs. Dust clouds followed horses like ghosts, and enveloped bouncing, rocking stagecoaches hour after hour in palls of grit. Inches deep on rudimentary, unpaved roads, dust coated foliage anywhere nearby. Tourists arrived at their destinations feeling exhausted, battered, and filthy. Before shedding their dusters, they first had to be swept off – with feather dusters.

Roads within and approaching Yosemite materialized and dematerialized helter-skelter in reaction to the whims of private investors. During the late nineteenth century, constant angling went on to build new roads toward the park. For reasons of trade and speculation, surrounding hamlets – today called gateway communities – all wanted one. Galen Clark, Yosemite's legendary first Guardian (in effect, superintendent), offered lodging to travelers in Wawona. Accordingly, during the 1870s he promoted the construction of a route that would pass through Wawona on its way to Yosemite Valley. Eventually, in 1875, a new turnpike from Wawona to the valley did become the precursor of today's Wawona Road.

Sometimes competing schemes for road construction took on an almost comic dimension of rivalries and feuds. One company got a franchise from the state to build a toll road from Chinese Camp and Big Oak Flat, two mining towns to the west of Yosemite. A small army of Chinese immigrant laborers had pushed this wagon road as far as Crane Flat by 1870. From there, travelers still had to take the saddle trail down the last seven miles and across the notorious talus slope before they reached the valley floor. A new, hotly competing road from Coulterville came to a similar halt, requiring visitors to mount up for the final stretch.

Going anywhere involved forking over money for tolls. After all, tolls on roads that were constructed as private monopolies (turnpikes) provided the incentive to build these routes in the first place. The Yosemite traveler of that era constantly encountered toll collectors calling out for payment. The Four Mile Trail connecting the valley floor with Glacier Point started out as a toll *trail.* Then, in the 1880s, with state funding, the board of commissioners that administered Yosemite bought out the toll roads and trails inside the boundaries of the Yosemite Grant, and made them free to the public.

Meanwhile, at the outset of the 1880s, the Great Sierra Consolidated Silver Mining Company threw up the town of Bennettville inside the Tioga Mining

District. The company bored a deep tunnel for extracting ore. To ship supplies in and ore out, with the help of Chinese labor, Great Sierra constructed a wagon road that connected to the west with the Big Oak Flat Road. This Tioga Road, as it came to be called, was the highest route across the Sierra. Its modern counterpart still is. Astonishingly, crews completed the fifty-six-mile road in under six months. They made heavy use of dynamite. Along the edge of Tenaya Lake, for instance, they blew a roadbed out of the granite shelf that fringes the lake's north side. (Today's modern highway rests on it.) The mine proved a disastrous failure. But the tunnel and the remnants of Bennettville remained, and so did the road, deteriorating decade by decade as the years passed. During the first decade of the twentieth century, the State of California built a road from the east, an engineering marvel running up Lee Vining Canyon.

Great Sierra Mine at Bennettville

Roads multiplied in Yosemite. During the late 1870s and early 1880s, the first ones were built to the Mariposa Grove and Glacier Point. During the quarter-century that the army administered the park, beginning in 1891, various road and trail improvements occurred. In 1906, the State of California ceded Yosemite Valley and the Mariposa Grove back to the federal government, as John Muir had strongly urged. The Sierra Club advocated construction or reconstruction of roads in and around Yosemite to boost tourism – in turn boosting the number of people who would become advocates for the park and its preservation.[6]

It was not hard to recognize pent-up demand to visit Yosemite. In 1913, Secretary of the Interior Franklin K. Lane remarked: "Before we know it, they will be dropping into the Yosemite by airship."[7] But Muir knew that automobiles – which he called "mechanical beetles" – were the real wave of the future. The trend began in 1900, when a steam-powered Locomobile made it to Wawona, then to Yosemite Valley, and finally out onto the jutting overhang at Glacier Point. The Locomobile was the first car ever driven into a national park.[8] Yosemite's administration put a ban on cars in 1907 because some drivers were flouting the rules of the road, but lifted it after six years. Lifted it, that is, subject to sixty-five separate driving regulations – maximum speed was set at fifteen miles per hour, for instance, and a driver had to stop to avoid scaring horses.[9] At the time, most visitors approached the park by train, typically riding the final leg in a stagecoach. By 1916, though, for the first time more visitors came by car than rail.

The Sierra Club wanted roads of a kind that harmonized with the environment, optimized the scenic experience, protected wilderness, and had as little physical impact as possible on the natural landscape. In 1907, Muir and the club submitted a plan to the Interior Department calling for a new road network on the valley floor, designed by a landscape architect to replace the existing "haphazard dust, sand & mud ruts."[10] This Sierra Club document, and the philosophy behind it, foretold the strategy that would guide the New Deal's approach to building roads in Yosemite decades later.

Road improvements in the valley, including relocating, widening, and hard surfacing or oiling, began to occur before the U.S. entered World War I in 1917. Considering that existing routes had been developed for the stagecoach era, a tremendous amount needed doing to accommodate cars – not just because they were faster, but because they would bring far more visitors flocking to the park. Progress inched along, though. As late as 1916, the founding year of the National Park Service, Yosemite had one hundred-three miles of government roads, of which just one mile was soundly paved.[11]

Having camped in Yosemite himself, the park service's Stephen Mather looked forward to the day when Yosemite would welcome more people with "camping outfits packed on their cars." Mather's vision of campers in cars came true. The increasing affordability of mass-produced automobiles quickly democratized Yosemite. In dramatic contrast with the nineteenth century, it became a destination for the middle class. State of California highway planners and the Automobile Club of Southern California cheered on more highways and more cars. By 1920, two-thirds of visitors arrived by automobile – over one hundred thousand cars a year.[12] During the following decade, principal roads in the valley were finally paved. The Yosemite Park and Curry Company built gas stations and a garage.

Roads aside, Stephen Mather wanted Yosemite to have better visitor facilities in general, but facilities of the right kind. In 1918, Mather and assistant director Horace Albright issued a policy statement declaring that any kind of development inside the national parks had to be planned so as to harmonize with the natural surroundings. A park service landscape engineering bureau was set up to help design buildings and other projects, including roads and bridges. In Yosemite, the pace of work stepped up.

In 1917, the federal government acquired the Wawona Road, together with its side routes to the Mariposa Grove and Glacier Point. These roads now became free to the public, and so the curtain fell on the toll road era. In 1919, the California Highway Association (an alliance of civic and commercial interests, including car dealers) began advocating construction of a new All Year Highway into Yosemite. The proposal had the full backing of the park service, with Albright directly lobbying for it in his capacity as assistant director. (In 1927, Albright would move to Yosemite for a brief time as acting superintendent, where he advanced additional big transitions.) The State of California committed to building the All Year route up the Merced River Canyon. Finished in 1926, this long state stretch became the first of the modern, paved highways to Yosemite that we know today. At the time, in fact, it was the most modern highway approaching any national park in the country.[13] Important to a motoring era before automatic transmissions, the new route was, in the contemporary language of road engineering, a high-gear highway, designed to minimize having to hand-shift the prevailing manual transmissions.

Meanwhile, Mather had long since entertained a particular desire to acquire the crumbling Tioga Road. Not only would this open the park's magnificent upper region to travelers; it would provide the only route across the Sierra within an expanse of two hundred-seventy miles. After grinding congressional budget processes stalled quick action, Mather set out to simply buy the road outright and *give* it to the federal government. No provision existed for Washington to accept a donation like this; Congress actually had to authorize it, which it did in 1915. Mather personally raised half of the $15,500 it took to purchase the road, and – in a sterling act of generosity – contributed the other half himself for the benefit of the American people. The Sierra Club and the Modesto Chamber of Commerce also donated generously.[14]

Horace Albright took over the National Park Service from Mather in 1929, sharing Mather's priority on roads – not just roads inside the national parks, but roads running from major highways to the park gateways. The fiscal 1932 congressional appropriation was the first to provide for these approach roads – $1,500,000, alongside $6,000,000 for road and trail work within the parks.[15]

***

A major question remained at issue as the 1920s yielded to the 1930s – where to build roads, and where not to. Ideas for more abounded. John Muir had proposed a circle route through Little Yosemite Valley and back by way of Hetch Hetchy (before it was flooded).[16] One of the biggest prods for roadbuilding by the 1920s was the congestion in Yosemite Valley, which might be alleviated by dispersing visitors throughout the reaches of the park. Yosemite's superintendent from 1916 to 1928, Washington Lewis, promoted a route from Happy Isles to Tuolumne Meadows by way of the upper Merced River Canyon, with a side road branching off to Glacier Point.[17] Where roads were concerned, the NPS and the Sierra Club maintained a close, if sometimes prickly, collaborative relationship.[18] In 1927, the Club urged a new, direct road to Tuolumne by way of Tenaya Canyon. The Tenaya Canyon route presented possibilities for winter sports in the high country.[19] The Sierra Club also called for roads along both rims of Yosemite Valley, with viewpoints on El Capitan and Taft Point.[20] The available knowhow and technology made any of these proposals entirely feasible. The real question was where to stop – or whether to stop at all.

An idea of Herbert Hoover's brought that question into high relief. Not for nothing was his sobriquet The Great Engineer. A geology major at Stanford,

Hoover had earned an illustrious reputation as an international mining engineer. Vacationing in Yosemite sometime before his presidency, Hoover rode a horse down the famously vertical zigzag trail between Tenaya Lake and the valley floor. The trip inspired him to recommend that a system of automatic elevators be constructed next to Snow Creek Falls for hoisting automobiles up and down. He surmised that the required electricity might be produced by waterwheels. The project would, Hoover thought, provide a big tourist draw.[21] It was never built.

In the middle of the 1920s, the park service reached an agreement by which roads throughout all the national parks would be constructed by the Bureau of Public Roads, an agency of the Department of Agriculture.[22] The NPS would determine where roads ran and how they were designed, and would sign off on the final plans. In particular, the park service wanted minimal impact on the landscape; it specifically prohibited rampant blasting, or the unnecessary destruction of rock outcrops or vegetation. By park service design, roads in the national parks were intended to "lie lightly on the land." Following natural contours, they optimized the visitor's encounters with the scenery – sightseeing as opposed to speed. Every new road represented some degree of compromise between providing access on one hand, and resource preservation on the other. Impact being unavoidable, the disruptions that did occur would be softened under the direction of NPS landscape architects. Crews would flatten or round off roadcuts, replant vegetation, and open out natural viewsheds. The whole process, from design to execution, would prove painstaking in the extreme.[23]

From the mid-'twenties on, road construction proceeded rapidly in Yosemite. The BPR either hired contractors or, if need be, did the work itself. Taking the baton from the State of California at El Portal, in 1926 the bureau completed the final leg of the All Year Highway into the park. The roads on the valley floor were being paved, or at least oiled, to suppress the dust. The BPR constructed new bridges as well, in rustic style with natural granite facings.

Redoing the Wawona Road came next. Park service landscape architects and the BPR put the plan under a veritable microscope, including its impact on granite cliff faces along the approach to Yosemite Valley. One way to spare the cliffs was to bore a tunnel through the solid granite. Early in 1932, Charles Thomson drove the inaugural automobile through the 4,233-foot Wawona Tunnel. A parade signified its formal dedication in June 1933, just weeks after FDR's inauguration. It was then the longest motor vehicle tunnel in the western United States, and remains to this day the longest highway tunnel in California. By the end of 1933, after eight years of work, the rest of the Wawona Road, including a branch to the Mariposa Grove, had been finished except for surfacing.

***

Meanwhile, with crews felling trees out ahead, tractors were grading a new Tioga Road in 1933. The park service and the Sierra Club agreed that this was preferable to building scenic but incredibly destructive routes that had been proposed up Tenaya Canyon or through Little Yosemite Valley.[24] Charles Thomson had taken up the possibility of redoing the Tioga Road with the BPR, and in 1931 surveying began. That year, a new park entrance and ranger station were built in the rustic style atop Tioga Pass. Right at the head of the Tuolumne River, where its tributaries converge, crews labored on abutments, piers, and the temporary framing necessary for erecting a new bridge. Grading started in July 1933, and, by the spring of 1934, the entire twelve-mile stretch from the Tioga Pass entrance through Tuolumne Meadows, as far as Cathedral Creek, was under construction. The contractor, C. G. Willis and Sons, of Los Angeles, employed a crew ranging to well over one hundred-fifty men. The second phase – White Wolf to Crane Flat – was expected to take two years. By 1938 the entire Tioga Road project across the Sierra should be completed.[25] While the Sierra Club approved the project overall, it cautioned that for the sake of preserving wilderness, it wanted the new road constructed along the alignment of the old one – in other words, road improvements, not a realigned new highway.[26] This caveat – a huge caveat – proved prescient.

Glacier Point also came in for its share of attention. Terrible access had provided one of the rationales for cable cars. Over a hundred thousand visitors reached Glacier Point each summer, but 90 percent of them made it there by *trail.*[27] During the early 'thirties, crews graded and oiled the old road each year, but it was like trimming the locks on a corpse. With its hairpin turns and steep grades, drivers were justly leery of the treacherous one-way route. The park service had decided that a new road would have to be built. Between 1932 and 1934, a paved, sixteen foot-wide stretch was constructed from Chinquapin as far as Bridalveil

Creek, where a new bridge went in.

Meanwhile, Granite Construction Company had a fleet of some three dozen trucks hauling rock from a big crushing plant in Wawona to lay the base course for surfacing the new Wawona Road. Even in its current state, travel on the road had dramatically increased. The spectacular view from the Wawona Tunnel's eastern portal was a tourist mecca. Traffic volume also increased to the Mariposa Grove. For the first time, the big trees became accessible to drivers in midwinter.

Now the Civilian Conservation Corps arrived. Overseen by an ecologist from the Carnegie Institution, and following guidelines from the park service's landscape division, CCC men went to work along the Wawona Road. Together with planting native species up and down the new route, crews rounded off or flattened down cut banks. More than that, they stained naked exposures of blasted granite "for the purpose," as Thomson reported, "of artificially aging them."[28] The most prominent granite scar was just outside the western mouth of the new tunnel. Using a compressor, paint gun, and ropes, a crew sprayed a combination of lampblack and oil or mineral spirits onto a thousand square yards of granite. They achieved a shade of gray that matched the weathered faces of the surrounding natural outcrops. As Albert Gordon, a fourth-generation Wawonan, later observed, "to the casual eye, it appeared nature had benevolently regenerated the torn earth, but she did so only after the CCC gave her a sharp nudge."[29]

The new Civil Works Administration (CWA) joined in on some of the road work. The CWA was purely temporary. A fear had developed that over the winter of 1933-1934, the nation could well see widespread starvation unless Washington acted fast. In and around Yosemite, unemployment tended to worsen during the winter, in part because work had to be cut back. The CWA emerged in November 1933 as a means of providing short-term jobs to the unemployed on a massive scale. Its chief was Harry Hopkins, who had pithily observed that people eat every day.

Hopkins had devoted his entire career to advancing the well-being and rights of the poor. An Iowan transplanted to New York, he had served as President of the National Association of Social Workers. After tapping Hopkins to head New York's Temporary Emergency Relief Administration, Roosevelt brought him to Washington as the Federal Emergency Relief Administrator. In that role, Hopkins ran the Civil Works Administration, and later the Works Progress

Administration. Hopkins was a man of paradoxes – idealistic, sentimental, cynical, and tough all at once. He possessed a biting wit.

The CWA relied for funding on a portion of the monies already allocated to the Public Works Administration, and on the army for tools, mostly pickaxes and shovels. It paid minimum wage (forty to sixty cents an hour, depending on the region of the country). By January 1934, the CWA had provided work-relief jobs to well over four million people. The nature of the work was based on what could be initiated quickly, particularly maintenance jobs and light construction.

Starting in early December 1933, tents and a shower building were installed to house CWA workers in Yosemite. As they arrived, they went right into road sanding and snow removal. The CWA did erosion control work; removed snags and stumps; undertook minor building improvements (such as varnishing, landscaping, rockwork, and structural repairs); and repaired and maintained vehicles as well as machinery. CWA employees labored on roads and trails; water, sewer, and electrical systems; light road construction; and myriad other duties. They built hundreds of campground tables. They painted the interior of the museum. They ground their axes using an electric motor confiscated by prohibition agents from a moonshiner's still.

Like the CCC, the CWA preferred using hand labor over heavy equipment because it stretched out the number of jobs. Also, handwork had a less brutal impact on Yosemite's natural resources. A lot of CWA efforts overlapped those of the CCC, but many did not. A few CCC men would do technical work of, say, a historical or biological nature. CWA employees catalogued whole collections of the museum; a CWA-employed botanist produced displays of trees and flowers; and a taxidermist catalogued collections of mammals and birds. Ferdinand Burgdorff, an artist employed by the CWA, painted backgrounds for exhibit cases in the museum.

Charles Thomson termed the CWA program "a boon to Yosemite." By the end of December 1933, Thomson credited the CWA and other New Deal programs with having "solved" the problem of unemployment in the park and its nearby surrounding communities.[30] Compared to other locales, the counties adjoining Yosemite were extremely fortunate, because the park became a job-generating machine.

March 1934, though, saw Civil Works Administration employees laid off week by week. By the end of April, all CWA projects in the park had come to an end. In its inclusion of a wide range of projects and skills, and especially in spreading work to the maximum possible number of people, the Civil Works Administration had anticipated the far better-known Works Progress Administration. It also set precedent for the WPA by hiring both women and men. The CWA did a solid job, but a brief one – never more than a stopgap intended to provide work through the harsh months of winter. After it was terminated, the unemployment rate in Mariposa County skyrocketed again, to the highest level in a year.[31] And when the WPA eventually superseded the CWA on the national scene in 1935, it barely made an imprint on Yosemite.

What did carry forward, though, was the road construction in which CWA workers had briefly taken part. The Bureau of Public Roads did not miss a beat. The Bureau and its contractors continued hiring day laborers and construction crews to keep new roads advancing throughout the park, generating jobs with every mile.

[5]
THE PIVOTAL YEAR: 1934

Looking back from the perspective of the twenty-first century, 1934 was a pivotal year in the history of Yosemite National Park. New Deal agencies undertook diverse, ambitious new projects. Extending itself far beyond its original forestry mission, the Civilian Conservation Corps branched into construction. The Bureau of Public Roads continued rolling out mile after mile of asphalt. Massive Public Works Administration projects upgraded the infrastructure of the park. National Park Service planners found themselves racing to keep ahead of it all – place this building *here,* construct that bridge *there.*

At the same time, both at the federal level and inside Yosemite itself, the mission of the NPS came in for reevaluation. The question arose, what is a national park for? And, how do new projects serve or threaten that mission? These issues have not been fully resolved to this day.

Compounding these concerns, in June 1933, FDR had signed an executive order that more than doubled the size of the national park system by transferring over military parks and battlefields, national monuments, and other federal property. This, in turn, automatically doubled the environmental stakes to the system as a whole.

***

We cannot begin to get a grasp on the importance of 1934 to Yosemite without introducing another of the key New Dealers, Harold Ickes (briefly mentioned before for battling racism). As FDR's Secretary of the Interior, Ickes oversaw the National Park Service. Within the national parks, the Interior Department had overall charge of the CCC (subject to army administration of the camps). Ickes also ran the Public Works Administration. He visited Yosemite in July 1934, wearing a rumpled business suit that contrasted with Charles Thomson's formal ranger attire. Although Ickes looked utterly ordinary – like an aging small-town newspaper publisher, perhaps, or the president of a middling bank – he was anything but. In fact, his biographer required no fewer than a thousand pages to tell his story.[1]

Charles Thomson (to left) and Harold Ickes in the Mariposa Grove, 1934

A progressive Republican rather than a Democrat, Ickes started off as a municipal reformer in Chicago, backed Theodore Roosevelt's insurgent Bull Moose presidential bid in 1912, then crossed party lines again to support FDR in 1932.

In all of this, he displayed a fierce independence; Ickes almost gave a new meaning to the word. He was curmudgeonly, cantankerous, volatile, prone to tantrums, and loved a fight. Yet he also had a cautious streak. Nicknamed Honest Harold, his generalized suspiciousness, his horror at any hint of corruption, and his perfectionism got in the way of using the PWA to re-prime the American economy by promptly launching big projects with big payrolls. He would study – minutely – every project proposal and contract before approving or rejecting it.

The 1934 Yosemite stamp

FDR and Ickes comprised one of the closest, most effective teams in the history of American conservation. As interior secretary, Ickes brought a constant environmental voice into Roosevelt's inner circle. He wanted, in fact, to transform the Department of the Interior into the Department of Conservation. In the 1930s, Ickes's views on preservation were cutting-edge. As he declared on NBC radio: "I think we ought to keep as much wilderness area in this country as we can."[2]

Together with wilderness, Ickes also advocated an outdoor aesthetic. This took forms from the gargantuan down to the miniature. Sharing a passion for philately, Ickes and FDR worked together on a series of stamps commemorating 1934 as the Year of the National Park. The idea for both the Year and the stamp was Ickes's. Roosevelt offered his own artistic suggestion for the first issue in the series – the one-cent Yosemite stamp. It featured a rendering of El Capitan above the Merced River.

Ickes's passions for the wildness and sensations of the great outdoors came together in what he said about the national park system. "Our National Parks," he declared,

> so far as possible, ought to be kept in their natural state. . . . I am not in favor of building any more roads in the National Parks than we have to build; I am not in favor of doing anything along the lines of so-called improvements that we do not have to do. This is an automobile age. But I do not have a great deal of patience with people whose idea of enjoying

> nature is dashing along the hard road at fifty or sixty miles an hour. I am not willing that our beautiful areas should be opened up to people who are either too old to walk, as I am, or too lazy to walk, as a great many young people are who ought to be ashamed of themselves. I do not happen to favor the scarring of the wonderful mountainside just so that we can say we have a skyline drive. It sounds poetical, but it may be creating a natural atrocity. . . . So long as I am Secretary of the Interior and have anything to say about the parks, I am going to use all of the influence I have to keep parks just as far as possible in their natural state.[3]

In his diary, Ickes carefully recorded his impressions during a visit to Yosemite in July 1934 – his first. With a discerning PWA-CCC eye, he looked at the campground layout and took note that Yosemite Valley had a power plant and sewage system. The Mariposa Grove left him awestruck. He wrote that the "wonderful trees . . . made a great impression on my imagination with their strength and endurance and majesty. . . . They appear to be as irresistible as time." He visited the Rockefeller grove of Sugar pines, another species of conifer he had never seen before. "I found them to be truly magnificent trees," he wrote, "second only to the sequoias." He also noted that they were threatened by beetles. Ickes mused about how insignificant the woods made him feel, yet also about how being in nature restored "peace to the mind."[4] From the spirituality of nature to the practicality of power plants and sewage systems, Harold Ickes was a man of many parts.

Before leaving the park, Ickes had lunch with the late David Curry's wife and collaborator, Jennie. Her son-in-law, Don Tresidder, drove Ickes to Merced, then flew him to San Francisco in his private plane. Ickes paid tribute to Tresidder in his diary.[5] But Ickes was always on guard, and with reason.

At the time, Tresidder had his back to the wall. The Yosemite Park and Curry Company's founding board included powerful figures like Harry Chandler, publisher of the *Los Angeles Times* and the city's surpassing promoter-developer-speculator. But at the bottom of the Depression in 1933, YP&CCo barely turned a net profit.[6] Tresidder had stockholders to satisfy, not to mention commitments to put up buildings under YP&CCo's long-term contract with the park service. The pressure undoubtedly honed Tresidder's business edge, and edginess.

In June 1935, Tresidder's friend Ansel Adams, the great photographer, gathered together in Yosemite what he titled a Conservation Forum.[7] It was sponsored by a who's who of conservation organizations, universities, federal and state agencies, and the Director of the National Park Service, Arno Cammerer. Adams hoped that the forum would produce a new, overarching consensus among public agencies and conservation organizations about how to protect what remained of California's natural heritage. Those in attendance included Charles Thomson, who viewed the whole kumbaya theme skeptically and started out the gathering openly, jocosely dismissive of some of the conservationists' remarks. Also on hand was Don Tresidder.

What ensued is described by Adams's biographer and collaborator, Nancy Newhall:

> [Tresidder] declared that the 'intangible values' of wilderness were not only negligible, since they could by appreciated only by a few thousand nature lovers and mountaineers, but actually negative, since insistence upon them barred the Sierra to millions who wanted more tangible pleasures when on holiday. Consider also, he urged, the plight of the operators of such public service companies as his own; hedged in by government restrictions on one side and barred by 'intangible values' on the other, the operators could not expand or improve their facilities.

So, Tresidder went on, the companies were stuck between the choice of operating as philanthropies or risking bankruptcy. Roads were not necessarily bad. Why not welcome the whole world to take in the splendor of America's national parks? Tresidder had a few more things to add, about lodgings with views and ski slopes surpassing those of the Alps.

Adams regarded Tresidder (in Newhall's words) as "a warm personal friend," and had expected him to talk about the harmony between conservation and commerce. Adams took in Tresidder's remarks with "shock," and in fact "was aghast." He even entertained the thought that Tresidder might be kidding. Charles Thomson, whose lighthearted cynicism had already started things off badly, was, in Newhall's telling, "furious" at Tresidder.

Just eight months earlier, in November 1934, at a meeting of national park superintendents in Washington, Harold Ickes had pinpointed what he saw as a fundamental error in the prevailing ideas about park development: "We lie awake nights wondering whether we are giving the customers all of the entertainment and all of the modern improvements that they think they ought to have." He viewed that approach as a wrong turn onto a highway without end. As between The Ahwahnee and the public campgrounds, Ickes preferred the campgrounds. Big luxury hotels were a mistake. Fanciful (even though feasible) road ideas, like the one up Tenaya Canyon, were a mistake. Ickes laid out his own vision for the parks: "I do not want any Coney Island. I want as much wilderness, as much nature preserved and maintained as possible." He declared that the parks were for people who longed to have "a renewed communion with Nature," such as he had had in Yosemite. He sympathized with concessioners like YP&CCo, he said – but he wished the federal government had the ability to buy them out and run the concessions itself. Since it did not, "we must not yield to their pressure" to satisfy tourists' every fancy. The national parks constituted America's "great outdoor temple. And we ought not to desecrate them or permit them to be desecrated."[8]

Don Tresidder knew all about Ickes's conviction that, as a policy objective, private concessions in the national parks ought to be eliminated in favor of public ones. Tresidder heard it from Ickes firsthand. Government concessions would directly reverse Stephen Mather's policy, on which YP&CCo was premised. Before the U.S. entered World War II, YP&CCo began to consider selling out – either to a private buyer or else to the federal government.[9]

At least in broad intent, Ickes was decisively departing from Mather's master strategy in more ways than one. He was crossing the bridge between early conservationism and modern environmentalism. Indeed, Ickes gave voice to ideas that were not just ahead of their own time, but – having been incompletely achieved in the national parks even today – also ahead of *our* time.

In Washington, Ickes was not alone in his concern about protecting wilderness as wilderness or about overdeveloping the national parks. Early on, from his vantage point as park service director when the CCC program launched, Horace Albright saw the risk that – by focusing the energy of thousands of young men on Yosemite and the other parks – things might go too far. If excessive brush and ground cover got removed, for example, it would threaten the habitat of small mammals and birds. CCC director Robert Fechner dismissed concerns like these, but Albright and Ickes were thinking broadly in parallel.

It was all the more unfortunate, then, that, instead of Albright, Ickes found himself resentfully working with Arno Cammerer, a new park service director whom he did not want in the position at all. In August 1933, Albright – already a park service legend – resigned to become the vice president and general manager of the United States Potash Company. Mather had arisen from gypsum; Albright descended to potash. Cammerer now succeeded him. A career civil service employee, Cammerer had climbed the National Park Service ladder as far as associate director prior to his new promotion. Ickes didn't like Cammerer and accepted him reluctantly, after looking around for alternatives. Ickes regarded Cammerer as a stodgy, uninspired bureaucrat. He even resented Cammerer's particular way of chewing gum ("vigorously," as Ickes put it). But, given only twenty-four hours in the day, Ickes could not directly run both the Interior Department and the NPS at the same time. In retrospect, Ickes should have fired Cammerer. Out of step with Ickes's environmental philosophy, Cammerer slow-walked the changes Ickes wanted made. Eventually Cammerer's health failed, and Ickes was able to replace him in 1940 with Newton Drury, a man after his own heart. The head of the Save the Redwoods League, Drury's enthusiasm for wilderness rivaled Ickes's.[10]

By the time Drury took over, a new philosophy of wilderness preservation was emerging. It was given voice, in particular, by three men: Aldo Leopold, Bob Marshall, and Benton MacKaye. Marshall and MacKaye occupied positions inside the federal government; an avatar of roadless-ness, Marshall served as one of Ickes's advisors. Leopold held a professorship at the University of Wisconsin-Madison. In bedrock agreement with the views of this trio, Ickes could be expected to argue for generally leaving the wilderness alone. FDR and Ickes had long since inventoried everything they thought needed to be accomplished in the national parks. This ranged from additional development in some to leaving others primeval (apart, perhaps, from adding a few more hiking trails). Ickes wanted Kings Canyon, for instance, to become the John Muir-Kings Canyon National Wilderness Park, to be managed as wilderness with minimal roads and no hotels.[11] Still, under the emerging wilderness philosophy, did even this idea go far enough?

As early as 1934, Marshall and MacKaye were complaining of unwarranted intrusions into pristine wilderness by the National Park Service.[12] In 1935, all three participated in the founding of the Wilderness Society. Their arguments attracted national attention from conservation organizations, including the Sierra Club, and from the media. The *Saturday Evening Post* criticized the CCC for what it called a tendency "to over-manicure the wilderness."[13] From the mid-1930s on, concerns like these about the Corps only grew.

***

By the spring of 1934, the CCC had resurrected its five-camp arrangement of the prior year, with some variations. Wawona continued to host Camps 1 and 2, Crane Flat had Number 3, Merced Grove Number 5, and Cascades Number 6. The Wawona camps welcomed two newly arrived, under-strength companies from Death Valley, lucky to be in Yosemite ahead of the summer blast furnace there. These two seasonal camps were struck and dismantled at the end of 1934. What replaced them was the year-round YNP 7, known as Camp Wawona. It was situated close to the South Fork of the Merced and east of the Wawona Road – in today's maintenance area, where original CCC buildings remain in service today.

Half Dome cable replacement

Right off the bat, Camp Cascades drew a heady assignment: redoing a less-than-practical cable system on Half Dome that the Sierra Club had installed around 1919 or 1920 to assist climbers. Operating from a stub camp at the base of the dome, a CCC team replaced over four hundred feet of 3/8-inch cable with

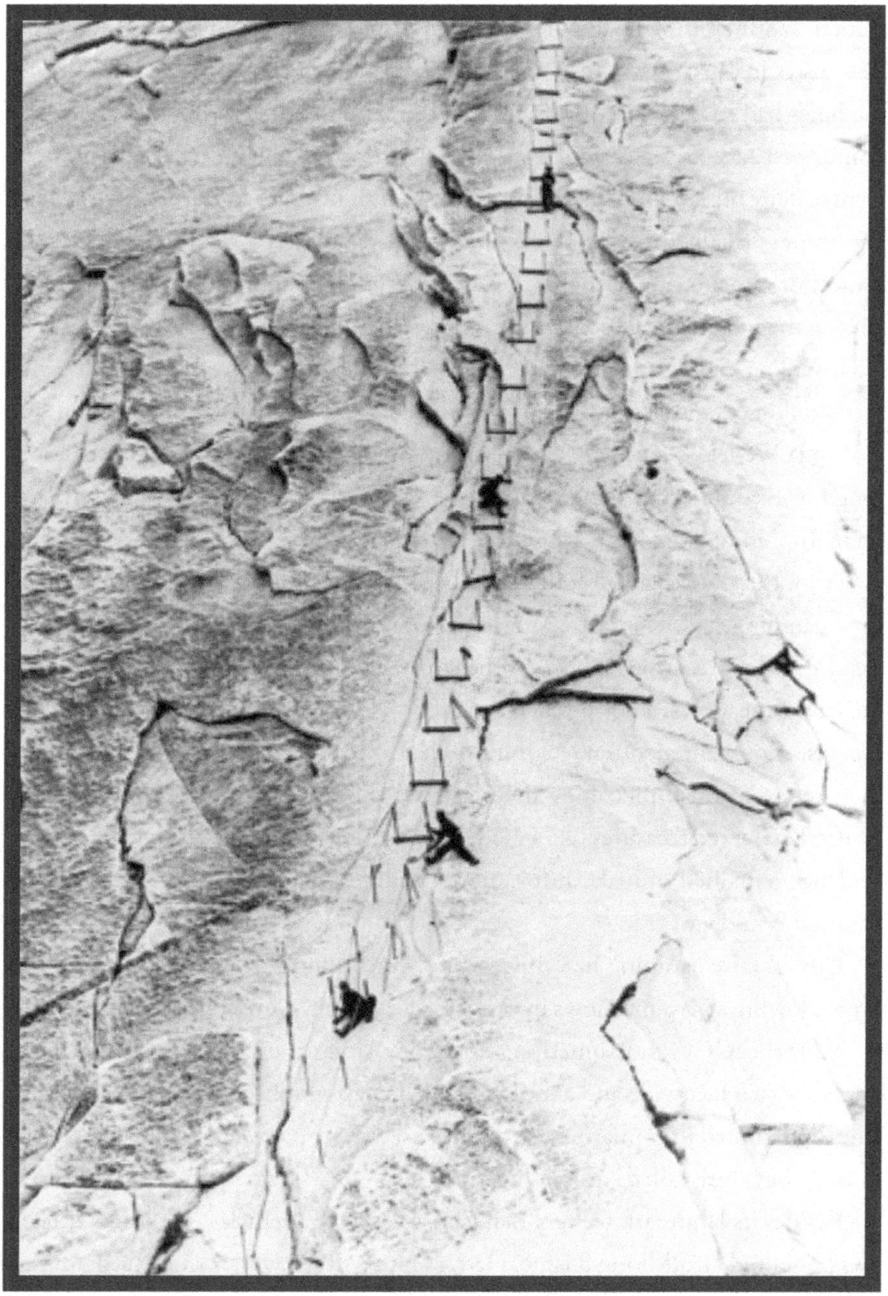

Four CCC men replacing Half Dome cables

stouter 7/8-inch cable made of galvanized iron. Some forty new one-inch posts were also sunk in the granite to an average depth of seven inches. The men boring the holes had to be secured by rope. The team reconstructed the staircase up the dome's east face and positioned wooden steps for resting at each set of posts. A terrible daily onslaught of afternoon storms – not just rain but driving wind, hail, and snow – finally drove the crew away, but later they returned to complete the project. It remains one of the CCC's most vividly remembered jobs in Yosemite, stirring the imagination today as it undoubtedly did then.

Installing cables on solid granite was about as far removed from forestry as men could get, and it showed how much the CCC was branching out by 1934. As Linda Wedel Greene has written, "the CCC initiated the largest construction program ever undertaken in Yosemite."[14] Extraordinary examples originated early on in Tuolumne Meadows, Yosemite's lofty outback.

From the time that Tuolumne had become accessible by car early in the century, camping had been a free-for-all. Despite the trouble it took to get there thanks to the precarious roads, campers managed to succeed. They drove across the iconic meadows. They pitched their tents along the Tuolumne River or wherever else they wanted, often returning each year to the same spot.[15] They dumped their refuse in trash pits along the meadows' edge, from which, as a boy in the 1940s, I extracted treasures like a Nehi soda bottle in mint condition. By then, no evidence remained of makeshift sanitary facilities, if any had existed besides the handiest boulder or tree.

Laissez-faire camping like this was not uncommon in national parks at the time. Plowing across meadows in cars was a tradition in Yosemite Valley, too. But in 1934, the CCC did something about it. Along the main roads, crews dug ditches – two feet wide and a foot and a half deep – to keep drivers off the grass. These resembled in miniature the ditches used to stop advancing tanks in World War I. They were called "moral ditches."

Besides its landmark scenery being crisscrossed by vehicles, Tuolumne Meadows presented an additional issue. Hetch Hetchy Reservoir, formed by damming the Tuolumne River downstream, was about to begin delivering water to San Francisco. Plainly, scattershot camping right along the river, with the resulting pollution, had to end. That kind of camping had been a gloriously carefree tradition, though. As Charles Thomson put it, the situation presented "a delicate job to handle since many old-timers have returned to this area year after year and now resent the fact they will not in the future be permitted to camp unrestrictedly."[16]

In July 1933, Thomson went up to Tuolumne to meet with anyone who wanted to talk with him about the coming end of wide-open camping. At evening campfires, he explained that, starting in 1934, the river would become a major urban water supply. In his report to Washington, Thomson claimed success in resolving tensions, though he did not go into detail. However understanding the campers may have been, Thomson's words had to come as a blow.[17]

The new era of public camping in Tuolumne as we recognize it today was about to debut, with the planning already in the works. During the 'twenties, Stephen Mather had wisely required that every park produce a master plan for future development.[18] The bedrock aim for Tuolumne was to cut the human toll on the natural environment. This dictated the concentration of camping within a defined campground along the new Tioga Road, which would maximize Tuolumne's open space overall (no more tents pitched hither and yon) and minimize environmental degradation in general. In 1930, Thomson had visited Tuolumne in the company of Don Tresidder and the park engineer. They agreed that in order to implement the plan, they had to begin with utilities, especially water supply. The work started that summer. Crews installed rudiments of a water system to serve the new campground, drawing water from the Dana Fork of the Tuolumne River.

Surveying and minor construction began on the campground itself in 1931. Some road construction occurred there during 1932. Now Thomson came to the realization that the original campground footprint would not be big enough, and directed that it be roughly doubled in size to over thirty-five acres. A needle-miner infestation had previously reduced to snags three-quarters of the trees that would need removing, so relatively few live trees had to come down. Getting out the dead ones would reduce hazards and fuel loads both. By hewing off one face of a log, men converted segments of the felled trees into campfire circle benches. Workers dynamited the stumps, along with obstructing boulders. (As a child I would find lengths of coiled fabric-covered wire stashed in small caves in the campground, surmised to be unused dynamite wire.)

When the CCC arrived in 1933, it arrived on a limited scale. Tuolumne never rated a full company, but instead relied for its men on the seasonal camp at Crane Flat. Located just east of the Tuolumne administrative area – referred to as Ranger Camp – the CCC stub camp consisted of tents and a mess hall. As of the summer of 1935, it housed fifty men.

In 1933, Thomson secured an allocation from the Public Works Administration to finish the Tuolumne campground project. PWA money would pay for the CCC labor involved, including on three new comfort stations, as restrooms that also contained washing facilities were called. (We will use the terms "comfort station" and "restroom" interchangeably.) Designs were drawn up for the comfort stations, and work began on the foundations and piping. The buildings themselves would not go up until the following year. I recall from early on recognizing that these Tuolumne facilities were architecturally distinguished, even though they were . . . well, comfort stations. A juvenile could see that. Today, they are all on the National Register of Historic Places.

From the founding of the park service in 1916 on into the 1940s, the prevailing architectural style for development in the national parks was "rustic." The style represented a hybrid of old pioneer architecture and elements from the Arts and Crafts movement. Overridingly, structures were intended to blend into the surrounding landscape. One way to make sure that occurred was by using building materials actually taken from the landscape. Stephen Mather wanted to make Yosemite *the* showplace national park, which must include the display of a great deal of rustic architecture. He himself largely paid for a landmark example of the style, the Rangers' Club, a residential facility for unmarried rangers in Yosemite Valley.[19]

It was not until 1935 that the NPS published *Park Structures and Facilities,* a book that explored the "rustic style" in detail.[20] The author was Albert Good, a NPS architectural consultant. Good laid out a whole philosophy of architecture, illustrated with drawings and photographs of infrastructure from around the country. These visuals, striking for the way they highlighted native materials, included the Tioga Pass entrance station and cabin, a Yosemite restroom, a park bridge, a store-gas station at Chinquapin, the fire lookout tower at Crane Flat, Big Trees Lodge in the Mariposa Grove, and the ski lodge at Badger Pass. All this suggests just how encompassing the rustic style was, and the ways in which both government and concession architecture drew on it. The CCC underwrote the book's publication, which was appropriate because by now the Corps itself had gotten well into construction. At Tuolumne Meadows, it built some of the finest examples of rustic architecture anywhere in the country.[21]

The rustic style in Yosemite called for big hewn logs and for masonry constructed with rounded boulders and cobble. Heavy shakes were used for roofing and often for exterior siding. Together with their architecture, Corps projects were distinguished for their craftsmanship. Though they learned on the job, young CCC enrollees did not possess the skills needed for this kind of work. Instead, they assisted seasoned carpenters and masons and others from the trades. Yosemite rustic inspired imitation in other national parks around the country. The CCC sometimes carried its dedication to the style to amazing lengths. In 1940, for instance, the Wawona camp paper reported that the camp now had a new grease rack for servicing vehicles. Complete with a shake roof, it was "built of heavy peeled timbers in the rustic motif so popular here in the park."[22] In any case, because of the CCC, construction in Yosemite simply boomed.

In 1934, the CCC picked up where last season's work in the Tuolumne Meadows campground had left off. Some twenty men felled trees, cleared brush, uprooted stumps, and removed boulders. They created one hundred fifty-five campsites with tables, served by newly graded winding roads. CCC crews finished building the three new campground comfort stations (plus another, smaller one on Tioga Pass) A crew of utility workers put in water and septic systems – cesspools for now, pending construction of more sophisticated means of treatment. (Eventually, the PWA funded a new sewer system that served not just the campground but the whole area.)

That same season, another new CCC project went up some distance west of the campground. Designed for federal workers, it took the name Road Crew Camp. Under the existing Tuolumne development plan, all government administrative and residential facilities at Ranger Camp were to be moved to the Road Crew area, and the old buildings then demolished.[23] Road Crew Camp, in other words, was simply phase one of an ambitious regional transformation. It consisted of a mess hall, four wood-frame four-person bunkhouses, and a restroom-shower house. From the contoured layout of the buildings to the rustic architecture, and even down to the finish (boiled linseed oil instead of paint), everything blended into the surroundings. Built like the other structures on a foundation of elevated rubble masonry, the wood frame mess hall contained a dining room, kitchen, and cook's apartment. Its roof had a strikingly sharp pitch – not just rustic in appearance, but alpine.

Tuolumne Meadows Visitor Center, today

Years later, the Road Crew Camp mess hall became the Tuolumne Meadows Visitor Center. A smattering of architectural clutter went up behind the old bunkhouses sometime after World War II, seemingly with little if any heed to the aesthetic integrity of the 1930s era design. The original buildings, though, are on the National Register of Historic Places. Ranger Camp was never relocated. It remains today exactly where it existed then.

In other parts of Yosemite during the 1934 season, the CCC took on projects that, if mostly less ambitious than the ones in Tuolumne, showed a similarly expanded role beyond straight forest work. One was erosion control, a top national priority of the New Deal. During the 1930s, the U.S. saw immense amounts of soil either wash away or else blow away in the Dust Bowl. The Shelterbelt Project, begun in 1935, planted windbreaks of trees across the prairie states so as to keep soil in place. With the CCC taking part, well over two hundred million trees went into the ground. During its nine years of life the CCC planted more than three billion trees nationwide. It is believed that this amounted to over half the reforestation undertaken throughout all American history up to the twenty-first century.[24]

In the case of water erosion, creek restoration involved hauling accumulated debris, notably logs, out of streams. While one of the declared purposes of log removal along the Merced River in the winter of 1933-1934 was cosmetic, the other was to help keep the river in its channel.[25] The salvaged logs were cut up for campers to burn.

Erosion work was extended to Yosemite and Tenaya Creeks in late 1933-early 1934. The channel of each was partially bulldozed. Men re-sloped the banks of Yosemite Creek, lined them with large rocks, and planted them with cuttings of poplar and willow. A dam was even constructed with the goal of keeping the stream in its main channel so as to prevent erosion below Yosemite Falls.[26]

Near the junction of the Wawona and Glacier Point roads, in 1934 the CCC completed a construction project that rivalled its work in Tuolumne Meadows – the Henness Ridge fire lookout. Like the pre-New Deal Crane Flat tower, the three-story Henness Ridge lookout was built in the rustic style. By contrast with the skeletal steel towers in the national forests, Crane Flat and Henness Ridge merged into their surroundings – a synthesis of functionality and art.

***

Nineteen thirty-four would prove to be a big year for road construction throughout Yosemite; yet, at the same time, second thoughts were starting to emerge about roads in general. It was becoming a truism that every improvement led to increased traffic, producing a demand for additional improvements which, if met, led to yet more traffic. Earlier, the All Year Highway, finished in 1926, had spurred an extraordinary increase of park visitors. In 1924, prior to completion, 146,070 incoming travelers were recorded. In 1927, with the new highway now open, park visitation soared to 490,430. Over 90 percent arrived in private vehicles. Harold Ickes had warned about too many roads. What about the possibility of too many visitors? What if those who thought there already were too many were right?[27] Charles Thomson wanted to reduce vehicular traffic on the roads in the park, and appointed a special committee to study the issue. Some sort of revised transportation plan was tried out experimentally.[28] Regardless, road-building proceeded apace to meet the incoming tide. So much took place in 1934 that it soaked up all the unemployment in Mariposa County.[29]

In 1933, planning had begun on a route for the new Big Oak Flat Road. This would become one of the most demanding highway projects undertaken anywhere in the United States during the 1930s. The overriding goal was to protect the magnificent beauty of the Merced Canyon. Departing from the All Year Highway as it left Yosemite Valley, the route as proposed by the Bureau of Public Roads would cross three creeks on open arch bridges. Every effort would be bent, as the park service put it, to "safeguard the natural appearance." Three tunnels would be bored "to avoid defacing outstanding cliffs of granite." Granite-block retaining walls would mask roadcuts. The park service landscape architecture division signed off on the BPR's proposal, as did Horace Albright personally before his resignation. Landscape engineers were to maintain a sharp eye on the project as it proceeded.[30]

Along the Tioga Road, Willis and Sons crews continued work on the new bridge over the Tuolumne River, under supervision of the BPR. At its core, the bridge was a modern skyscraper-era structure built of reinforced concrete. It rested on two granite piers and leaned into granite abutments. The look – granite and concrete together – appeared both rustic and modern at the same time. Construction of the wide deck called for huge amounts of sand and gravel, which lay conveniently at hand at the confluence of Dana and Lyell forks just above the bridge to form the river. The contractor transformed the area, then a sandbar, into a "borrow pit" – in other words, a quarry. After yet more borrowing for additional road stretches, the quarry became a lake up to twenty feet deep.[31] Campers called it the Poho. I used to swim in it. Over the decades since, it has been transforming itself into a meadow.

By October 1934, the first phase of the Tioga Road project, close to twelve miles long and including the bridge, was complete except for paving. That same month, the Idaho construction firm Morrison-Knudsen began work on the second phase, running eleven miles eastward from Crane Flat to McSwain Meadows (just beyond White Wolf). In 1935, the third, final leg of the road, from McSwain Meadows to Tuolumne, was surveyed. But while the entire Tioga Road had been planned for completion by the end of the 1930s, progress stalled. Along this last leg, the old track remained the only route.

Campers darkly referred to this stretch as The Twenty-One Miles. Driving it has been compared to riding a roller coaster. The driver had to navigate a track hurriedly laid out in the 1880s for wagons and teams. If there was any rock outcrop or tree stump the road did not snake around, a person cramping a steering wheel back and forth would have been unaware of it. The American Automobile Association warned: "It is not unusual to find people . . . unused to mountain roads, who just go to pieces, freeze at the wheel and park their cars in the middle of the road" awaiting rescue by some ranger or, really, anybody.[32] The same fear-induced freeze-ups occurred on Lee Vining Grade farther east. Thus, the flatland motorist had two distinct and separate opportunities to go to pieces. As a boy I watched it happen as my family navigated Lee Vining Grade, my parents commenting that some stopped driver had suffered a sudden panic attack.

***

By no surprise, given Harold Ickes's painstaking ways, it was not until 1934 that the Public Works Administration began to make a big impact on Yosemite. Early that year, a new sewer system in Wawona, begun with PWA funding, was completed using Civil Works Administration labor. That winter, workers directly employed by the PWA battled infestations of hemlock bark borer (a threat to Douglas fir) in Yosemite Valley. The PWA paid generously compared to the compensation park insect crews had previously received – over 50 percent more, in fact.[33] But tree-by-tree forestry was the purpose of the CCC, not the PWA.

By the end of the year, the Public Works Administration was finally focused on its core mission – large projects demanding skilled labor. The PWA hired carpenters to build an amphitheater in Camp 14 (today's Lower Pines), Yosemite Valley's largest campground. This consisted of a platform facing one hundred-twenty benches to accommodate audiences for the evening programs. The PWA constructed ranger residences and a ranger dormitory, ranger stations at Wawona and Merced Grove, and a restroom at the south entrance. Needed immediately to accommodate visitors to Hetch Hetchy, a new six-room park entrance station at nearby Mather went up with remarkable speed. By the spring of 1935, the PWA was at work constructing a big utility building in the valley.

Harold Ickes belonged to a parade of prominent Yosemite visitors in 1934. Robert Fechner made an inspection on behalf of the Civilian Conservation Corps that he directed. Movie stars William Powell and Jean Harlow drove into Camp Cascades to greet a friend, a former Hollywood stuntman now serving with the CCC. Their appearance caused a sensation.

The outstanding celebrity of the year, though, was Eleanor Roosevelt. In late July, Ickes and the First Lady met at Hetch Hetchy. "It was interesting to meet her in that remote nook," Ickes recorded in his diary. "She was very tanned and was enthusiastic about the park." They had dinner that night at the Rangers' Club. Afterward, Ickes went to bed early, while Charles Thomson took ER for a moonlight ride around the valley. "Anything more beautiful than that valley by moonlight," she declared, "I have never seen."[34]

ER had arrived in the park days earlier with a single traveling companion, Lorena Hickok, known to everyone as Hick. The First Lady had refused Secret Service protection, even though her husband had narrowly avoided assassination just the year before.[35] Driven down from Reno by park rangers who were accustomed to negotiating Lee Vining Grade, ER was fascinated by Mono Lake. She wrote presciently, though, that the region's incorporation into the Los Angeles water supply system might alter it.[36]

An ardent small-d democrat, ER had become a strong advocate for the construction of campgrounds as an egalitarian way in which families of limited means could enjoy the national parks alongside hotel guests staying at places like The Ahwahnee.[37] Indeed, The Ahwahnee in that era had a reputation for snootiness. It catered to the upper crust. The hoi polloi – campers, lodgers at Camp Curry – found themselves discouraged from entering the grand building at all. A doorman in livery once halted Herbert Hoover for daring to walk in wearing dirty fishing clothes.[38] Eleanor Roosevelt disdained this sort of thing, even when the victim was Herbert Hoover.

In Tuolumne Meadows on July 24, she and Hick met up with more rangers led by Yosemite's Chief Ranger, Forest Townsley, ready to escort the visitors into the backcountry on a four-day camping trip to Young Lakes. The rangers had made elaborate preparations, including for the logistics of ferrying mail and messages back and forth. Saddle horses and pack animals awaited. It looked, Hick later wrote, "as though we were starting out on a safari somewhere in Africa."[39]

The trip up covered six miles.[40] ER was a natural, graceful rider. Arriving at the lower lake, she found the setting enchanting, with a rising moon lighting up the jagged peaks. The rangers had packed in a tent on muleback, but instead the two women laid their sleeping bags out under the stars. Trying to maintain a low profile, the rangers quickly found themselves having to keep up with ER.

Eleanor Roosevelt on her trip to the high country, 1934

She took a natural interest in everything, and was having a wonderful time hiking and riding. She wanted to help cook, an offer the ranger in charge of the food fortunately declined (her culinary gifts would not have met his standards). Each morning just past dawn, she would plunge into the freezing lake for a short swim.

Ranger Billy Nelson, who had charge of the equipment, was an all-around folksy, pipe-smoking character. Probably the park's best-known campground ranger, he was also a renowned guide for visiting celebrities. He had told King Albert of Belgium, "You call me Billy and I'll call you King." Nelson gave ER a hot-water bottle to stuff inside her sleeping bag.

One morning, ER and Forest Townsley, then in his early fifties, climbed a peak described as around thirteen thousand feet in elevation (probably Mount Conness, 12,590 feet). When they returned, ER, who at forty-nine was only slightly younger than Townsley, was described by Hick as looking as though she had just taken "a stroll in Central Park." On the other hand, "I thought that Ranger was going to have a stroke. His face was purple." ER tried her hand at fishing, but in the end "I finally agreed that I would clean the fish, since I was quite incapable of catching them." She helped the rangers stock rainbow trout in a lake at the base of Conness. The unnamed lake was assigned the name Roosevelt Lake.[41] (Tuolumne also has a Nelson and a Townsley Lake.)

One gets the sense that some people ER met in Yosemite had trouble figuring out what to make of Lorena Hickok. ER had a special place for accomplished and offbeat women, and Hickok decidedly fit both descriptions. Working for the Associated Press prior to the New Deal, she became the most famous woman reporter in the United States.[42] She took a job inside the administration working for Harry Hopkins. By then, she and ER had become intimate friends – just how intimate, historians have debated.[43] A lesbian, Hick was unquestionably (to quote Doris Kearns Goodwin) "madly in love with Eleanor."[44] In advising her early on, Hick played an unmistakable role in Eleanor Roosevelt's extraordinary emergence as – easily – the greatest First Lady in American history.

The relationship had had its high and low points, but in Yosemite it hit bottom. There are hints (or more) of this in each woman's published accounts of the Young Lakes trip. Immensely possessive, Hick was jealous of all the attention the rangers were devoting to ER. A heavy smoker, badly overweight, and now packed into the high country at ten thousand feet, Hick "more or less panted" the whole time they were there, ER later wrote. On the trip back down to Tuolumne Meadows, while the mounted party forded a stream, ER glanced back and was horrified. Hick had slid off her horse, landing in water up to her chin. The rangers had neglected to tell Hick that the mare that had unloaded her loved to roll in the water.[45]

Hickok recorded another incident that, "after our camping trip, stands out in my memory above all others." At dinner, ER left Hick and Ickes alone together. Hick had become an outspoken advocate of Harry Hopkins's approach to work relief (favoring hiring as many as possible to do projects, as against using labor-saving machinery); this ran directly counter to Ickes's strategy (lots of heavy equipment, fewer jobs). "Secretary Ickes," Hick wrote, "was the last man in the world I wanted to meet at that time." She had been writing reports that went up to FDR, sharply criticizing the Ickes method. Now, sitting on the terrace with him, Hickok felt desperate to escape. There was silence. Then Ickes broke it by saying: "I've been reading your reports. Interestin'." ER mercifully returned just then, and the conversation turned to other topics.[46]

The Mariposa Grove gave ER and her party, in her own words, "a sense of time and of our own insignificance which is good for the soul." She reacted in the way that Ickes had, with reverence and awe. While the trees left her awestruck, the First Lady herself had a similar effect on other people, including the rangers who had escorted her to the Young Lakes.[47] ER and her entourage visited the CCC camp at Crane Flat. John Burgess, a seventeen year-old enrollee, watched the parade of Studebakers roll in, with ER in the second car. Burgess recalled decades later that he had "visited some with her, but was very hard-placed for words, as it was my first contact with a person of her high station."[48]

The ranger naturalist Carl Sharsmith had a similar problem. ER visited Glacier Point on one of her two trips to Yosemite during the New Deal years. Sharsmith was stationed there. She fed some ground squirrels. Sharsmith could not bring himself to tell the First Lady that she was violating park regulations.[49]

[6]
LIFE IN THE CCC

In February 1937,[1] an iconic image appeared in *Life* magazine. Taken by the famous photographer Margaret Bourke-White, it depicted downcast African American flood victims lined up in Louisville to receive emergency food and clothing. They stood in front of a large billboard picturing a family of joyful white, middle-class Americans driving in their car. The caption on the sign read, "WORLD'S HIGHEST STANDARD OF LIVING." One of the most famous pictures of the 1930s, the image has always been taken as a commentary on that time.

The picture certainly evoked Yosemite during the Depression era. The wealthy had long since found their way into the park. Subsequently, thanks to the automobile and better roads, Yosemite had become democratized. Public campgrounds for the middle class were free. Badger Pass was constantly setting new visitor records. And all the time, working constantly to make the park an even more welcoming place were thousands of CCC men, PWA employees, road crew gangs, and day laborers. As the visitors drove past, the workers remained, so to speak, in profile.

It would be easy to stereotype these workers as similar, ordinary people doing dull jobs somewhere on the periphery of things. While the hotel-denizens sipped their martinis, the golfers golfed, and the skiers sped downslope, the proletarians, it might seem, silently labored in anonymity, lucky to be off of relief rolls. Personal records of those who worked in the park for the Public Works Administration and the Bureau of Public Roads are scarce. There are richer sources for the Civilian Conservation Corps. They show how wrong any stereotype about those mostly young men would be. CCC camps were unquestionably some of the most interesting places in Yosemite's history.

Over the years, Yosemite hosted seven to eight thousand CCC men in ten permanent or seasonal camps.[2] Men belonged to one or another of twenty-four different companies (plus one briefly tucked into Wawona at the very end) representing nineteen states. A dozen of these companies came from California.

Far removed from one another, the year-round, winterized Wawona and Cascades camps served as the CCC's two hubs in the park. Cascades was occupied by Company 942 for all but the final month of the camp's lifespan, 1933-1942. Nine forty-two was designated the valley's "service company," meaning that it was the principal company in that area. Wawona was called the South Entrance service company. Originally recruited from the Bay Area, Cascades later received enrollees from all over the state. Camp Wawona hosted four successive companies; the longest-serving was Company 487 (1937-1941). Even with a single company in place, men continually came and went. During its first year in the park – October 1937-October 1938 – a total of 389 men served at one point or another in Company 487. Of the 161 original arrivals from Alabama, only 28 still remained on the rolls on the company's first anniversary in the park. One hundred ninety-eight had come and gone.[3]

The other, seasonal camps were typically occupied from May or June until October. The number of seasonal camps varied from year to year. During two years, 1939 and 1940, the park reached its combined maximum – a total of six camps, four of them seasonal. A major slump occurred from 1936 to 1938; and ultimately a tapering off set in toward the end of the program, starting in 1941.

Following is a year-by-year summary. During 1933, all the camps except Cascades were seasonal: the two Wawona camps (YNP 1 & 2), Crane Flat, Eleven Mile Meadow, and Merced Grove. In 1934, the two seasonal camps reopened in Wawona, together with ones at Crane Flat and Merced Grove; the year-round Camp Wawona finally debuted that October. Nineteen thirty-five saw seasonal camps at Crane Flat and Merced Grove. Crane Flat was the only seasonal addition in 1936. The following year, no seasonal camps opened. Nineteen thirty-eight had seasonal camps at Crane Flat and Middle Fork of the Tuolumne; 1939, seasonal camps at Crane Flat, Middle Fork, Tamarack Flat, and Empire Meadows; 1940, the same; 1941, Crane Flat and Middle Fork; and 1942, no seasonal camps at all.

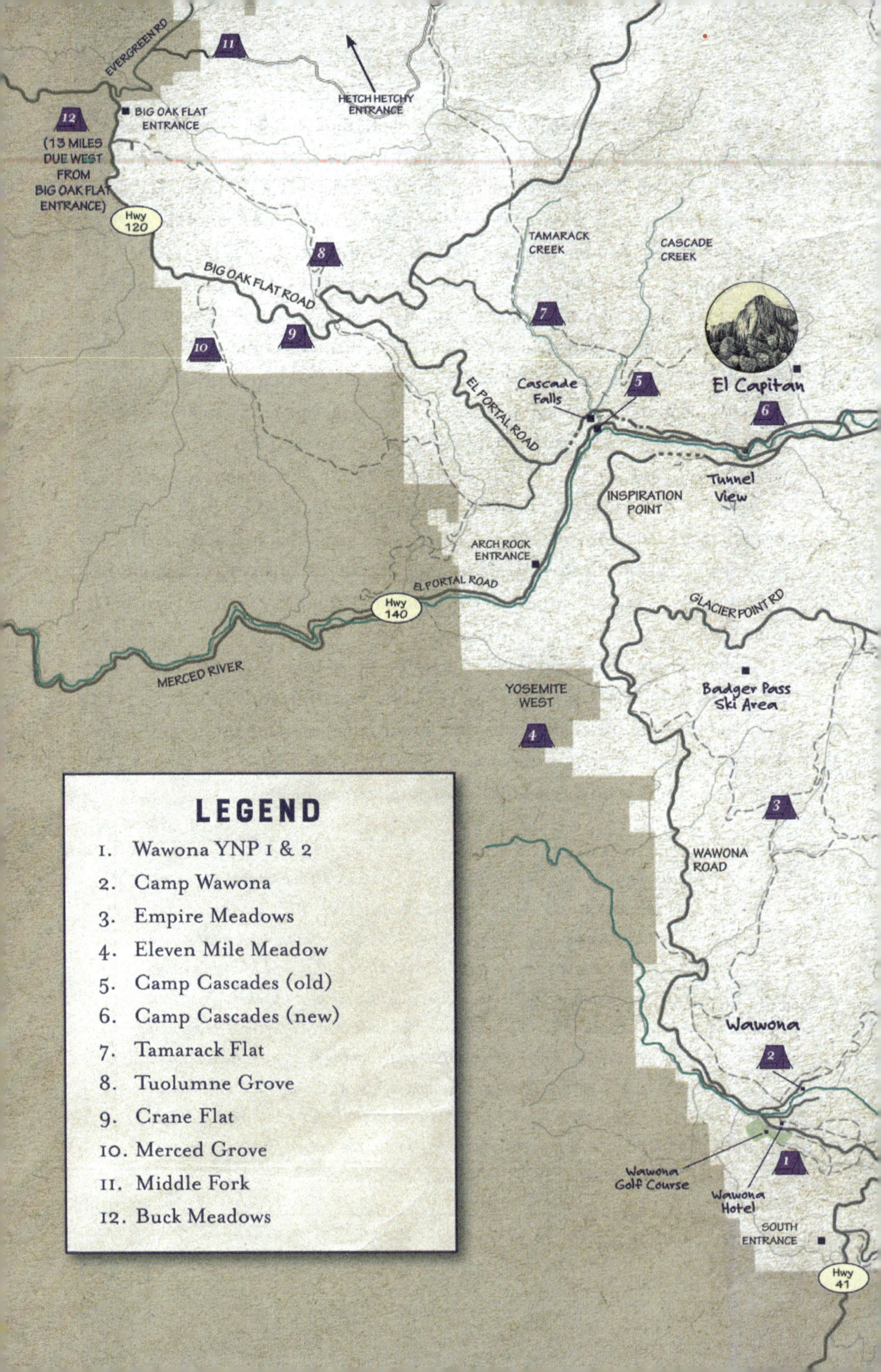
EVERGREEN RD
11
HETCH HETCHY ENTRANCE
12
(13 MILES DUE WEST FROM BIG OAK FLAT ENTRANCE)
BIG OAK FLAT ENTRANCE
Hwy 120
8
BIG OAK FLAT ROAD
9
10
TAMARACK CREEK
CASCADE CREEK
7
El Capitan
6
5
Cascade Falls
EL PORTAL ROAD
INSPIRATION POINT
Tunnel View
ARCH ROCK ENTRANCE
EL PORTAL ROAD
Hwy 140
MERCED RIVER
GLACIER POINT RD
Badger Pass Ski Area
YOSEMITE WEST
4
3
WAWONA ROAD
Wawona
2
1
Wawona Golf Course
Wawona Hotel
SOUTH ENTRANCE
Hwy 41
LEGEND
1. Wawona YNP 1 & 2
2. Camp Wawona
3. Empire Meadows
4. Eleven Mile Meadow
5. Camp Cascades (old)
6. Camp Cascades (new)
7. Tamarack Flat
8. Tuolumne Grove
9. Crane Flat
10. Merced Grove
11. Middle Fork
12. Buck Meadows

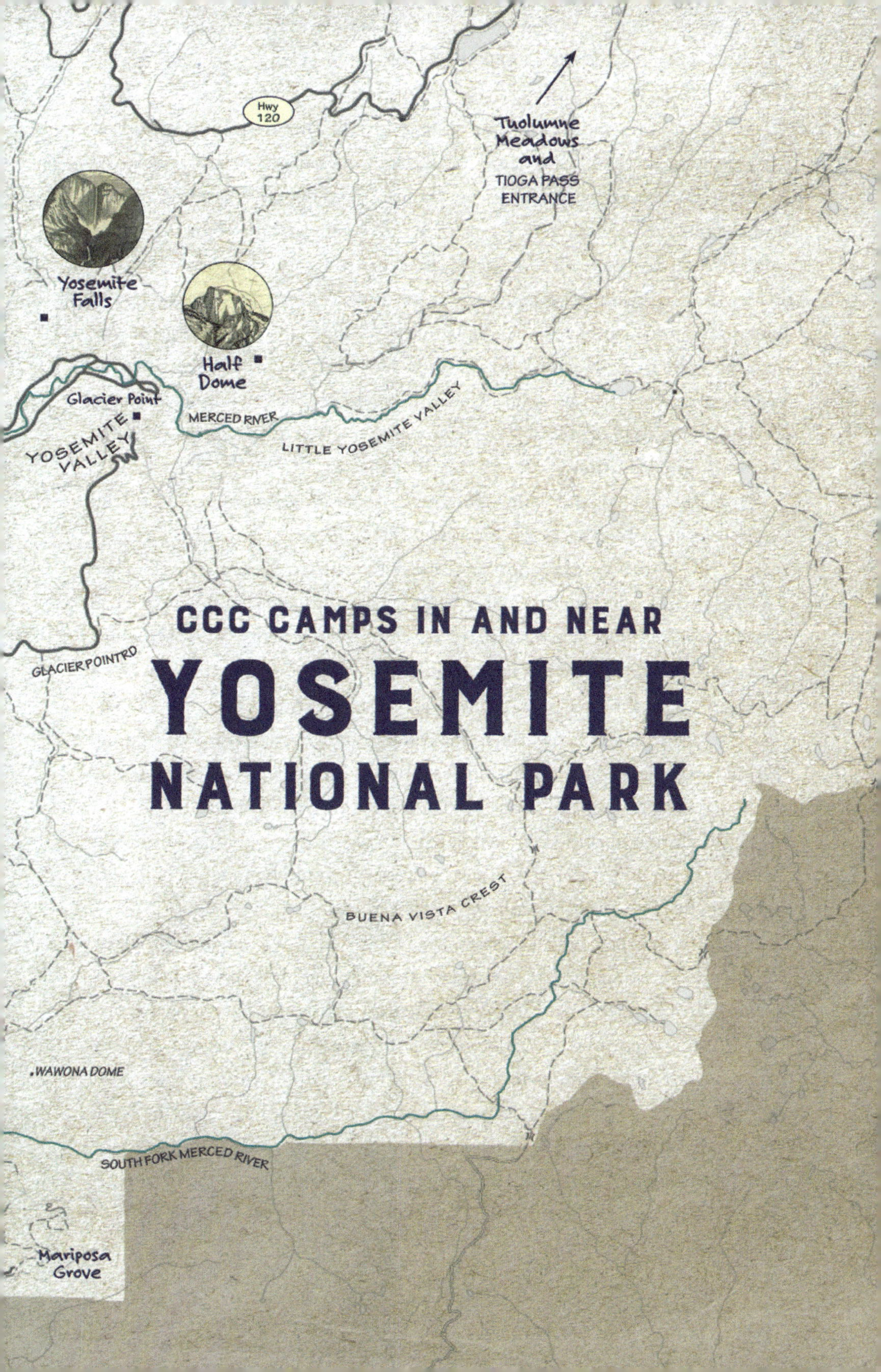
Hwy 120
Tuolumne Meadows and
TIOGA PASS ENTRANCE
Yosemite Falls
Half Dome
Glacier Point
MERCED RIVER
YOSEMITE VALLEY
LITTLE YOSEMITE VALLEY
CCC CAMPS IN AND NEAR
YOSEMITE
NATIONAL PARK
GLACIER POINT RD
BUENA VISTA CREST
WAWONA DOME
SOUTH FORK MERCED RIVER
Mariposa Grove

At the end of a season, the men assigned to the summer camps would return to their original wintertime locale or be reassigned to a new one. Al Monteverde's experience provides an example. Initially, he was stationed at a spot outside the park, then at Crane Flat, and finally at a different place outside again. In 1939, enrollee Herbert Lake came to Crane Flat with Company 1952, based at Big Sur. The men arrived in a convoy of trucks, battered by the long ride bouncing on hard wooden benches. Crane Flat was a bit more developed by now than when Al Monteverde had been there five years before. Promised a return trip by train instead of truck, Herbert's company reoccupied Big Sur in the fall. The following year, he was back in Yosemite again, this time at Empire Meadow.[4]

Over the summer, the permanent and seasonal camps would spin off stub camps of men detailed to do specific kinds of work in designated areas. The 1935 season provides the best example of how the system operated. Camp Cascades had a stub camp in Little Yosemite Valley fighting needle-miner. Camp Wawona had a stub operation at Deer Camp north of Wawona, clearing debris from old logging operations. (By 1941, Wawona men would have cleaned up some thousand acres of logged-off land in their area of the park.)[5] Fifty men from Crane Flat were assigned to a stub camp in the Tuolumne campground, doing hazardous tree and flammable debris removal and battling bark beetle. Merced Grove's seasonal camp maintained a stub camp at Porcupine Flat, combating needle-miner.

All in all, the operation looked kaleidoscopic, with everything continually changing shape and size. But a better comparison would be to a machine with moving parts. The 1930s, after all, belonged to the Machine Age.

The motto of the Civilian Conservation Corps was, "We Can Take It." There was a lot to take, ranging from the work to the spare and often spartan living conditions. The Corps constantly transported enrollees from the East or Midwest to the Far West, where most of America's remaining forests were. One had to transition from a familiar family setting to a barracks or tent encampment; from frenetic, noisy big cities to the isolated silence of the woods; from regions of the country that were as flat as a plank to rugged mountains; and, most important, from jobless idleness to highly demanding physical labor. One of the beauties of youth is adaptability. The hard labor tended to give a new meaning to life. "We sure put out the work and I don't mean perhaps!!," Al Monteverde wrote at the time.[6] Many CCC veterans looked back on the whole experience as a high point of their lives. As one man put it: "We were educated and given job opportunities, honor, respect, and a purpose in life."[7]

One thing that struck the men at the time, and always would, was the food – mainly the sheer amount of it. You could literally eat all you wanted. That was such a novelty to young men from families on relief that at first it tended to startle them. In his second inaugural address, delivered in January 1937, Franklin D. Roosevelt famously declared: "I see one-third of a nation ill-housed, ill-clad, ill-nourished." Coming from a Florida farm that raised tobacco but not enough food, Joe Bryan couldn't recall a time when he had not gone to bed hungry.[8] When North Dakotan Alf Bergly became a camp cook, it must have made him awfully popular. The Wawona camp paper ran this headline in 1940: "JIMMY ERNEST RETURNS FROM BAKING SCHOOL."[9] "I never heard any complaints about the food," foreman Howard Cox's wife, Rose, later remarked.[10] Depending on the locale, feeding a man would cost from thirty-two to forty cents a day – averaging about seven dollars in today's value.[11]

The food was basically army rations: one-size-fits-all mainstream American fare of the 1930s, plain food and plenty of it. A typical breakfast at Camp Wawona might consist of fruit, hot cereal, fried eggs, toast, butter, and coffee or milk. A typical dinner would include soup, salad, braised beef, rice, hot bread, string beans, tapioca pudding for dessert, and hot chocolate.[12]

Southerners like Joe Bryan who passed through Yosemite doubtless missed their regional dishes, the way Southerners wedded to grits or jambalaya did elsewhere around the country. Joe may have seen Southern cornbread from time to time. Possibly there was Brunswick stew, a southern dish served in Wawona and traditionally made with local small game like squirrel, possum, or rabbit. This being a national park, no doubt it was made from something else.[13]

Italian Americans like John Ricci had to make a huge adjustment. John, his son recounts, was shocked like so many others by the quantity of food. At home he had eaten nothing but Italian cuisine; now he had to get accustomed to mainstream American fare like pancakes, meatloaf, and chicken and dumplings.[14] In getting used to the unfamiliar, Joe and John had plenty of company. One CCC veteran, Mel Melvin, has recalled watching a farm boy eat a peculiar item – a banana – peel and all.[15]

Now and again, though, camp cooks would serve up spaghetti, which by then (like cornbread or chili con carne) had found its way into the mainstream American diet. In 1940, enrollee Fred Rogers (not the Fred Rogers of later television fame) immortalized in verse the spaghetti at Camp Wawona. It plainly differed from the Ricci household's.

Pallid serpents sprawled at ease
Sporting chunks of stringy cheese
Crawling from my fork to nest
Upon my shirt front, tie or vest.[16]

Rather than knowing how to twirl their pasta, most CCC men like those in Wawona would probably have cut it up with a fork.

If their job assignment was close to camp, men would return to the mess hall for lunch. For worksites farther afield, food would be prepared in the camp kitchens. Sometimes it would be packed in heat-retaining boilers and driven out. At other times, the men would eat sack lunches. A typical lunch included sandwiches, pie, and coffee. The men ate the way they worked, shirtless and grimy.

Thanksgiving dinner was special in CCC camps. Because the adjoining days were not days off, most men remained in camp rather than going home, even when home might be as nearby as Fresno. They were rewarded with a turkey dinner so sumptuous that looking at the menus makes one want to go back in time and find a place at the table, including the one, at right, for the 1935 Camp Cascades feast.[17]

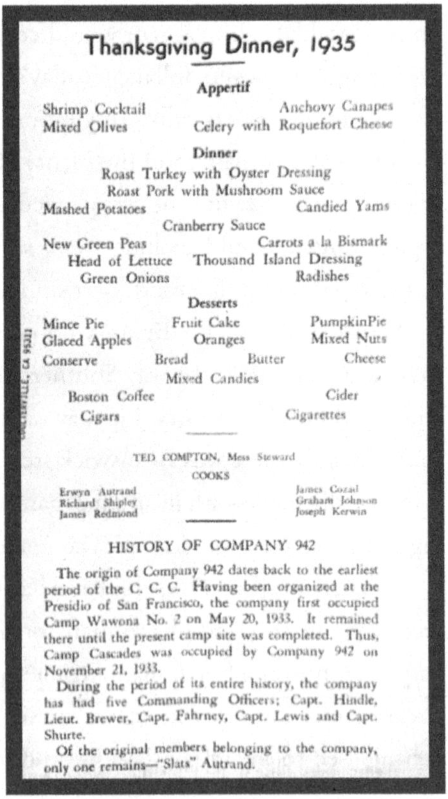

Thanksgiving Dinner, 1935

Appertif

Shrimp Cocktail — Anchovy Canapes
Mixed Olives — Celery with Roquefort Cheese

Dinner

Roast Turkey with Oyster Dressing
Roast Pork with Mushroom Sauce
Mashed Potatoes — Candied Yams
Cranberry Sauce
New Green Peas — Carrots a la Bismark
Head of Lettuce — Thousand Island Dressing
Green Onions — Radishes

Desserts

Mince Pie — Fruit Cake — PumpkinPie
Glaced Apples — Oranges — Mixed Nuts
Conserve — Bread — Butter — Cheese
Mixed Candies
Boston Coffee — Cider
Cigars — Cigarettes

TED COMPTON, Mess Steward

COOKS

Erwyn Autrand — James Cozad
Richard Shipley — Graham Johnson
James Redmond — Joseph Kerwin

HISTORY OF COMPANY 942

The origin of Company 942 dates back to the earliest period of the C. C. C. Having been organized at the Presidio of San Francisco, the company first occupied Camp Wawona No. 2 on May 20, 1933. It remained there until the present camp site was completed. Thus, Camp Cascades was occupied by Company 942 on November 21, 1933.

During the period of its entire history, the company has had five Commanding Officers; Capt. Hindle, Lieut. Brewer, Capt. Fahrney, Capt. Lewis and Capt. Shurte.

Of the original members belonging to the company, only one remains—"Slats" Autrand.

At Christmas or else New Year's, CCC men got five days of leave. For many who remained in camp, this was the first Christmas they had ever spent away from home. Christmas dinner rivaled the Thanksgiving feast. It likely far exceeded what a family dependent on the twenty-five dollars their son sent home each month could afford to put on the table. With gift exchanges, entertainment, festivities, and the meal, CCC Christmases were memorable.

The average CCC recruit could be virtually counted on to gain weight.[18] During the first two or three months in camp, a jump of ten or more pounds was common. Over time, men added an average of eight to fourteen pounds.[19] Jack Rettinhouse, who served at several camps in Yosemite, went into the CCC at age sixteen; he had gotten into trouble in high school in Fresno, and lied about his age to enroll. During two years in the Corps, his weight went from ninety-six pounds to one hundred forty-five.[20] Al Monteverde sent a joshing letter to his brother Paul, then serving in a CCC camp in Santa Barbara: "So you've gained fifteen pounds, eh? and you say it isn't all fat? well – that's fine!"[21]

If the day-to-day chow was army-issue more or less, a lot of the camp routine had a military aspect too. Before climbing aboard trucks to head out for the day's work, men would stand at attention for barracks inspection, which included bunks. These were typically double-deck. (One of a newly arrived man's first jobs involved packing straw as tightly as possible into a large sack to make a mattress.) At Camp Cascades, a single wrinkle in a blanket at inspection time meant KP duty – "kitchen police" or "kitchen patrol," i.e., peeling potatoes or other mundane jobs that doubtless included latrine duty.[22] A lot of the lingo was military – "company," "mess hall," "goldbrick" (loaf), and "KP" itself. Even so, as the word *Civilian* specified, the Corps was fundamentally a civilian organization. There was no saluting, nor any arms training. The army actually turned down an offer from the National Rifle Association to provide the men with weapons instruction.[23] Out of anxiety over the CCC looking militarized, shooting was banned as a camp sport.[24]

Like CCC companies, the army officers in charge of the camps came and went continually. Some earned considerable respect from their men, who were sorry to see them go.[25] Details about these officers are scarce. In the spring of 1935, though, the Wawona camp paper profiled one of them, the commanding officer of Company 529. Captain Otto Lewis had served in World War I. After the war, he studied at France's illustrious Sorbonne. He then embarked on an engineering career that took him to places ranging from the Arctic Circle to Mexico. A dedicated hunter, Lewis must have been amazed at all the off-limits bears and deer roaming freely around Yosemite.[26]

One of the big adjustments men had to make involved learning to live among a couple hundred other men. The Corps manual, *Your CCC,* offered an outsized amount of advice on the subject. "It's not an easy job, getting along with people," the manual acknowledged.[27]

The youth culture of the 1930s differed from the highly defined styles of youth culture that have emerged since World War II. It was less distinct from the adult world; and in any case, the Depression made kids grow up fast. Still, boys will always be boys and young men young men. They will, for instance, haze and pull pranks. Beds got short-sheeted. A greenhorn might be sent to the supply shed to fetch a skyhook. And the snipe hunt, a timeless practical joke, was a rite of passage in CCC camps. The new man would be furnished with a bag and a flashlight, and told to track down a snipe in the woods in the dark. (The snipe is literally a type of bird, but in a snipe hunt the bird being chased is a wild goose.)

Sometimes a practical joke would have a practical purpose. Darrel Stover (Camp Cascades, 1934-1936), recounted a story about a man assigned to a top bunk who, in the process of undressing after nightly taps, would constantly drop his boots to the floor with a crash. The man's annoyed dorm-mates nailed them to the floor. Another enrollee refused to shower. His mates put him into a wash tub and did the job for him, using laundry soap and a scrub brush.[28] (It is unrecorded whether the man's reluctance had to do with having to parade naked along with all the other Cascades men through cold and snow to the shower house.)

In 1934, Wawona Company 529 decided to divide its four barracks into squads of eight men to improve the organizational setup. This also applied to the mess. The camp paper declared that "our louder and less mannered messmates will be given the imperative opportunity of waiting on their table until another tablemate commits a greater breach of etiquette."[29] As Clair Nelsen, who was stationed at the Buck Meadows camp outside the park (and who apparently crossed paths with Al Monteverde), later wrote: "Peer pressure kept the more slovenly in line while the worst offenders found themselves isolated or sent home – the last thing that most of them wanted."[30] Lawrence DiCandio said that very thing in an editorial in the Wawona camp paper at the time: "The rookie enrollee soon learns the telling effectiveness of social criticism and finds that he must cooperate or be outside the pale."[31]

Little record remains of bullying, although some teasing – "razzing," in the idiom of the era – surely would have morphed into bullying. By the mid-'thirties, officers began to put a damper on outright hazing. In 1941, Lieutenant Leslie Wood, the Company 487 commanding officer, wrote an editorial about hazing in the Wawona camp paper. He pointed out that there were regulations against hazing because, in the past, some CCC men around the country had gotten seriously hurt or even killed during these rituals. Certain kinds of hazing were expected and acceptable, Wood allowed, and he specified examples: sending a rookie to fetch a can of striped paint, a left-handed monkey wrench, or two yards of red tape, or directing a newcomer to water the flagpole. Beyond these pranks lay forbidden territory.[32] As for bullying per se, less sensitivity existed to it then, and the victim was expected to settle his own accounts or endure it. John A. Salmond records that while bullying did happen, it plagued only a few camps nationwide.[33] One would hope so.

Many of the Local Experienced Men assigned to Yosemite camps were middle-aged or older. Those at Camp Cascades came from the Fresno-Merced area. They served as foremen or supervisors. Enrollee Darrel Stover recalled that these men "added stability to camp life among all those in their teens and twenties."[34] When interacting with the younger men, World War I veterans likely had the same effect.

A priority wherever young men congregate, recreation provided a way to blow off steam and have fun. The Wawona camp paper admonished: "On days when there is no work do not succumb to the temptation of sitting on yor bunk all day."[35] Some recreation was programmed, some informal and spontaneous. Men went hiking, or swam and fished in rivers and lakes. They played basketball, baseball, and softball. Camp Wawona had a football field. YP&CCo allowed men stationed there to use the company's tennis courts; in 1940, the camp built its own. Teams from camps in one part of the park would be trucked to play against other camps' teams. Or a team would take on an opponent, say, from the Bureau of Public Roads or the Wawona Hotel. Barracks played against other barracks.

Sports simply flourished. There were boxing matches, volleyball games, pool and horseshoe competitions, bridge tournaments. Men played chess, cards, checkers, bingo, and ping-pong, During the winter, they entertained themselves with skiing, ice skating, tobogganing competitions, and other diversions.

CCC men dive in

From time to time, Carl Sharsmith would lead organized hikes up one mountain or another for CCC crews stationed in Tuolumne Meadows. A number of these men were tough second-generation Polish-Americans who came from the industrial cities bordering Lake Erie. A sergeant who spoke Polish would come along to keep the men in line.[36]

Because so many newly arriving men thought Wawona was like the far side of the moon, efforts were made to break down the sense of isolation. Camps across the country held dances, with music provided by their own swing bands. These were a regular feature of life at Camp Wawona in the late 'thirties and early 'forties, phonograph records playing if a band wasn't on hand. In 1938, the men tapped their camp fund to buy some Carter Family records. The initial generation of the legendary Carter-Cash musical dynasty, the Carter trio was the first country vocal group to achieve stardom. Almost any night, if you happened to be in listening range of Camp Wawona, you would hear Sara Carter on rhythm guitar or autoharp, Maybelle on lead guitar, and A.P. adding a male voice, singing songs like "Keep on the Sunny Side" and "Coal Miner's Blues."[37]

Movies helped reduce Wawona's sense of isolation, too. These might be accompanied by cartoons, shorts, or newsreels – the famous *March of Time.* During the late 'thirties, the camp had movie nights on Thursdays and Saturdays; many were current-release feature films.

CCC camps staged their own plays and musical productions. Following its Thanksgiving meal in 1936, Wawona Company 2548 scheduled games, a musical, and a play performed by the Wawona Thespians – a comedic adaptation of Longfellow's "The Courtship of Miles Standish." The production was directed by a member of the WPA's Federal Theater Project.[38]

Park rangers led campfire programs for the men. In 1933, these occurred at each camp twice a week. In some ways, they echoed the programs for campers. Having charge of one of the weekly campfires, a ranger naturalist would talk about flora and fauna. A park service official would run the other weekly campfire. There was a good deal of talk about the national parks in general. Local Indigenous Americans were invited to share lore and perform dances. And there were activities and singing. CCC quartets and instrumentalists pitched in. On September 16, 1933, six hundred CCC men were brought together from the far-flung camps for a day of races, a tug-of-war, boxing, and other events. The day concluded with a big campfire program featuring singers and instrumentalists, with a prize awarded for the best performance.

And there was radio. Darrel Stover later recalled listening to *Your Hit Parade*, a popular show of the era, in the recreation hall at Camp Cascades.[39] In February 1935, the Wawona camp paper proudly reported: "After almost giving up all hope Company 529 was rewarded Monday with the finest radio money can buy. It is a Scott all wave, using 11 tubes, and is run entirely from batteries."[40] The men would decide collectively on programs by writing down their preferences and depositing them in a box. They had quite a choice, not just CBS and NBC but foreign broadcasts, airplane and ship transmissions, and police calls.

Reading provided yet another diversion. In March 1935, Wawona Company 529 took a tally of how many books had been read that month. One man had devoured ten; a couple more had read five. "Those who thoughtfully read . . .

fewer experiences need," the camp paper advised. "The library has a number of very thrilling detective and mystery novels in stock now. Any one feeling the need of a nice harmless, blood curdling hour or two, just drop around between 5 and 7:30 PM."[41]

As a routine at CCC camps around the country, on Friday and Saturday nights trucks would transport the men to town. In Yosemite, that might be a short trip. On Saturday evenings, men would ride trucks from Cascades to a motion picture at Camp Curry or a dance at the Old Village. Riding back to Crane Flat one night after seeing a movie, Al Monteverde recalled freezing inside his heavy army coat.[42]

Excursions by truck to points of interest in the park made another welcome routine. Had these not been offered, it is easy to imagine men working for six months or a year in one part of Yosemite but never getting to see the others. These excursions extended to CCC men stationed outside the park, who would tour Yosemite and sometimes camp in the park. On weekends, trucks would transport men to the start of hiking trails.

In March 1935, as a gesture of appreciation for their work, a Mr. Poetker hosted half a dozen Wawona men for a trip to Fresno. Normally enrollees paid for food, movies, and rooms out of their own pockets, but not this time. An army truck took them down. Dinner at Tiny's Broadway Café was topped by "pie that even mother would have had a hard time making," the camp paper reported. After dinner, cigars were passed out, "the result of which gave the appearance of a bankers convention." Men then dispersed to take in a movie or visit Chinatown. They rolled back into Camp Wawona at 4:30 in the morning, with snow falling. "The sensation of Civilization," recorded the paper, had been experienced "in a big way."[43]

Stationed at an isolated mountaintop CCC encampment a short distance west of the park boundary (where the job was to build a forty-five-foot fire lookout tower on Trumbull Peak), Al Monteverde recounted that "there was no recreation of any kind – except what we dreamed up." For example, "two of the men got the bright idea to take up a collection," head off for Indian Flat (which featured a store and café and not much else), and buy a gallon jug of wine. To accomplish this, the two had to descend along nine thousand feet – almost two miles – of steep logging incline railroad track. Then they crossed the Merced

The Trumbull fire tower goes up

River using a hand-powered cable car that, in a stroke of luck, happened to be unlocked. Once across the river again with their prize, they hauled themselves back up the incline railroad track. Darkness having fallen, they received a warm greeting for "something novel as a form of recreation."[44]

Al considered stub camps like this one "a lot better" than the bigger, more established camps because, in his experience, a stub camp would disregard formalities like roll call and retreat.[45] The boss of Al's twenty-man stub camp, Bill Fiske, had been the Sheriff of Mariposa County, making him the ultimate Local ienced Man. Al idolized him. Fiske had an easygoing perspective on the . He let the men keep guns. This meant a lot to Al, who had just bought a age rifle. Al took it hunting, and from time to time the crew got to dine on nison.[46]

Once, Al's crew convinced Fiske to let them make an overnight trip to Merced. Fiske released a truck to get them there. In town they went sightseeing, but Merced in the 1930s offered only so many sights to see. As Al later wrote: "Come nightfall, and the guys got a brilliant idea – let's go across the tracks! They had heard of some ladies on the other side of the tracks." Egged on by Slim, a Local Experienced Man in his forties, six or seven young enrollees "got our nerve up and we started walking." They arrived at a line of small houses, with women lounging on the porches and "probably laughing inside upon seeing this unlikely little group standing on the sidewalk with very sheepish looks on their faces. . . . Well anyway, we saw them, and we knew all the time we were starting something we couldn't or wouldn't finish. Slim was the winner – he had his joke!"[47]

In later years, John Ricci – who was posted to Yosemite as a fire warden – loved to tell the story of how CCC men invented a new kind of firefall. Near the top edge of Bridalveil Fall, they would line up big metal barrels filled with dry pinecones, douse them with kerosene, light them, and tip the blazing cones over the side. John said the sight was gorgeous against the black of the night, and that all the hooting and hollering could probably be heard for miles.[48]

***

Strictly speaking, of course, extracurricular activities like these did not fall within the federally authorized mission of the Civilian Conservation Corps. The mission did expand, though, beyond the two original goals of employment and conservation, and beyond the superimposed priority of construction projects, to take in yet another objective – education. In and of itself, the CCC constituted a profound learning experience for the men. It taught them how to live together in groups, work in teams, use tools, cope with the woods, appreciate the mountains – and how to grow up. It framed all this in the context of the 1930s – a time when hard physical labor was more prevalent, and formal education far less prevalent, than today.

CCC men in Yosemite, and all over the country, were learning about conservation at ground level and on a daily basis. "Conservation" was, after all, the word at the center of "Civilian Conservation Corps." Conservation had previously been a concern of the privileged. By bringing unemployed, largely working-class young men into this kind of endeavor, the Corps democratized the cause. As Neil M. Maher has put it, the CCC became "synonymous with conservation." Following World War II, the newly named environmental movement would take on a grassroots nature that conservation had never had before, in part, Maher argues, because of the CCC experience in itself, and in part because of all the media coverage it attracted.[49]

Today, 90 percent of Americans finish high school, and more than a third have a college degree. In 1940, fewer than a quarter of the population possessed a high school diploma, and well under 5 percent a college degree.[50] Most CCC enrollees were both unemployed *and* unskilled.[51] The average enrollee had not graduated from high school; some could not read or write. Any kind of learning program had to base itself on these facts, together with a sense of the direction in which trends were going. As Al Monteverde's motherly older sister, Catalina, wrote to their brother Paul, "like they say, it is the age of 'intellectuals' and the others haven't much chance to get anything. So do everything in your power to learn something if possible."[52]

Improvised CCC educational programs started right away, as early as 1933. Meanwhile, Washington – realizing that the camps offered a rare chance to benefit young men with opportunities to learn – worked out a more organized, professional approach. As camps were set up, books actually preceded barracks. Taking advantage of men's desire to read, the camps received their own libraries of books and magazines. Traveling libraries of a hundred to two hundred titles circulated additional fiction and nonfiction from company to company. The Yosemite Museum opened its reading room to CCC men on the weekends.

Starting in 1934, every army corps area, and every CCC administrative district within a corps area, was assigned an Educational Advisor (EA). Each camp, in turn, received its own EA, appointed by the United States Office of Education and working subject to the army chain of command. The advisor could count on the help of one CCC member, who was ranked as "Assistant" and earned thirty-six dollars per month (the pay grade of an Assistant Leader). Unemployed teachers on work relief were also assigned to the camps by the WPA and other federal relief agencies. The average camp had fourteen teachers, some of them serving purely as volunteers alongside those on relief.[53] By 1937, every CCC camp also had its own education building.

The administrative set-up for Camp Wawona during the summer of 1937 clarifies how the education program fit into the camp's table of organization. The commanding officer was a first lieutenant, the adjutant a second lieutenant. The medical officer was a first lieutenant. The camp had an education advisor, a drama instructor, and, for men just getting a start on their education, an elementary school teacher (a woman). To these staff, the park service added a project superintendent, a senior foreman, four foremen who supervised work in the field, and a head mechanic.[54]

As Ray Hoyt observed in a 1935 book about the Corps, the CCC education program amounted to a great experiment. "There are no entrance requirements, no definite curriculum is adhered to, and students attend, or not, as they wish."[55] The teachers faced opportunities and challenges aplenty. The CCC ran the gamut, from college graduates (a few) to men who resisted traditional education altogether. Undoubtedly, to some enrollees the Corps meant little more than three square meals and a bed with a roof over it.[56] Classes had to prioritize the interests of the students, including skills they might want to acquire that could translate into private sector jobs. Many would need assistance in earning a high school diploma. The CCC's education strategy was an informal one that shunned rigidity while stressing personal incentives, spontaneity, and give-and-take. Going beyond the conventional blackboard and chalk, educators also made use of vocational films.

It worked. The CCC always and continually emphasized self-improvement, which provided a backdrop to its education campaign. And the men took learning seriously. Drawing heavily on national data, a 1937 report suggested that 90 percent of CCC men were involved in one or another educational program, and that half of all the younger ones were taking vocational instruction. Nearly all of the ten thousand illiterates, the report indicated, had enrolled in the literacy program. During its lifetime, the Corps taught an estimated one hundred thousand men to read and write.[57] In March 1941, six members of Camp Wawona received literacy diplomas. Men were finishing grade school or completing high school.[58] Some, undoubtedly, were enrolled in college-level courses.

By January 1934, evening and Saturday vocational classes were being offered in Yosemite on forestry and the repair of cars, trucks, and tractors. These courses related to everyday work activities, of course, and to learning a trade; but students could also study electrical engineering, geology, business, English, arithmetic, photography, and other subjects.[59]

In 1936, the Educational Advisor for Wawona Company 2548 was Curtis Stricklin. The holder of bachelor's and master's degrees, Stricklin, the camp paper indicated, was working on a Ph.D. in an unidentified field at a campus of the University of California. This was not his first EA position; he had been serving elsewhere for the prior two years.[60]

Stricklin had a ready-made teaching facility to work with. In February 1935, the paper had proclaimed with tongue-in-cheek pride: "With a ruffle of drums and a blare of trumpets, figuratively speaking of course, the Wawona Institute was thrown open to the public last week. . . . Camp Wawona is quite proud of her 'little red schoolhouse,' as it is one of a very few in our district."[61] The "Wawona Institute," consisted of four small rooms. It somehow accommodated a library, a darkroom, and enough space for shop classes. Critically for the men, it also housed a radio. In 1938, with education buildings now standard in camps across the country, a second building, measuring eighty by twenty feet, went up to supplement the Institute.

The Wawona Institute also made a convenient place to offer Sunday school classes. Nationally, CCC camps held religious services on Sundays, which men were free to attend or not. Army chaplains or civilian clergy (some volunteers, others hired from the local area) provided for worship in the Protestant, Roman Catholic, and Jewish faiths. A chaplain would be assigned to cover a total of eight camps. Most services were sufficiently general in nature that an enrollee could join in regardless of his religious affiliation.[62] Many men were quite observant. During the summer of 1933, for instance, a priest visited Wawona. Enrollee Arnold Seibel went to confession Sunday night, then, the following morning, volunteered as an altar server, attended Mass, and received Communion.[63]

Working with an EA like Curtis Stricklin, a CCC man could obtain education in either of two ways. He could take evening classes at the Institute, or else complete correspondence courses in his spare time. Through the Institute, the California State Department of Education offered correspondence courses at no charge to the student, and covered postage. These courses included "practical photography," auto mechanics, business English, business law, chemistry, journalism, geography, psychology, forestry, radio, mechanical drawing, aeronautics, blueprint reading, placer mining, and other subjects – a total of more than three dozen correspondence courses as of 1940. Most fundamental of all was a class called How to Study.[64] A man would turn in a finished lesson to the EA; the advisor would send it back to the Department of Education where it originated; and, having marked and graded it, the department would return it to the camp. Once the full course had been completed, the department would issue a certificate.

It wasn't just professional teachers who did the teaching. In 1936, the Camp Cascades commanding officer, Captain Clarence Collins, taught an archery class. During 1938, the popular and long-serving[65] Camp Wawona CO, Captain William Spencer Rockwell, taught courses in business English as well as shorthand. A man in his thirties, Rockwell had earned a law degree before taking over Company 487. During his time as CO, Camp Wawona mounted an education contest, with prizes awarded, for example, for the number of correspondence course lessons completed in a month, or for the grades received. It was not all correspondence courses or shorthand, though. In 1940, the camp's second-in-command, Lieutenant James Stone, directed a forum for the men on the relationship between psychology and social issues. The following year, a park service surveyor taught a course on surveying.[66]

Al Monteverde earned a special assignment: "I talked myself into the job of official photographer for the records." A ranger who ran the graphics shop at park headquarters supplied him with a camera, film, and access to a darkroom. (Al later recalled sharing a darkroom with a rather aloof Ansel Adams.) Al wound up traveling around much of the park taking pictures, which were transmitted to Washington. At the time, a young ranger naturalist was teaching men about the different types of trees and how to identify them. This ranger recruited Al to accompany him to the Merced Grove, where the naturalist laid out grids using lengths of string. He took notes on the living things that grew within each square, and had Al photograph them. Later, the ranger would return to the site from time to time to study what had changed.[67]

In Yosemite Valley, the integration of the park naturalist program and the CCC went beyond a single ranger and a single enrollee. Carefully selected men from Company 942 were trained to carry out responsibilities as interpreters and guides for the general public, under the supervision of park naturalists, The men considered this "honor duty" an extremely desirable assignment. Those few good enough to be chosen carried out their role in full dress uniform. As interpreters, they were also active teachers.

Wawona offered one very special form of instruction – in art as taught by the unique Cornelius C. Sampson. Born in Billings, Montana, Sampson grew up on a ranch. Initially a self-taught artist, he loved portraying the Indigenous Americans of the region, particularly the Crow. From 1929 to 1934, Sampson studied at the Chicago Art Institute. He earned tuition by driving cattle all the way from Montana to the Windy City. Leaving the Art Institute just four units short of a degree, Sampson then moved to Yosemite and became an official (or perhaps quasi-official) park artist in residence.[68]

The New Deal employed a great many needy artists, including some of the country's most famous, on federal work projects. The 1930s was a landmark era for art and design, and much of the artistic legacy of the time came out of programs like the Federal Art Project. This raised predictable complaints that the government had absolutely no business hiring artists. Art wasn't "real" work, and anyway a lot of artists were peculiar or radical. "Hell," Harry Hopkins responded, "they've got to eat just like other people!"[69]

Given Cornelius Sampson's background, it was likely no accident that Camp Wawona put a big emphasis on Indigenous American lore – a theme captured in the name of the camp newspaper, the *Pow-Wawonian.* Toward the end of 1934, a stone mason and a bricklayer from Merced spent a week in camp erecting fireplaces. Enrollees collected and hauled in an estimated twenty-five tons of river rock.[70] One fireplace went up for the recreation hall. Above the fireplace, Sampson painted a scene of his favorite plains Indians on horseback.

Cornelius Sampson mural, Camp Wawona

Sampson was a fixture at Camp Wawona. He painted the scenery for "The Courtship of Miles Standish." He offered courses on elementary drawing, composition, figure sketching from life, and color theory. And he served as art editor for the camp paper.[71] In 1939, Sampson moved to San Francisco as art director of the Golden Gate International Exposition, on Treasure Island. After that ended, he established a free-lance industrial design business in San Francisco. He became renowned for designing everything from a famous style of fire hydrant, to color schemes for transit buses, to company logos like the distinctive "S" in Safeway. Various of his designs went on display in the Smithsonian.[72]

***

The Happy Days Publishing Company, based in Washington, produced a national independent weekly newspaper, *Happy Days,* that circulated to camps around the country. The paper's motto was, "A Newspaper by the CCC, for the CCC." Upbeat in tone, *Happy Days* provided its readers a national perspective by reporting on CCC activities and individual camps around the country. Yosemite was often featured. The paper sold for a nickel. It carried ads for things like candy bars, cigarettes, and such CCC merchandise as buttons, decals, and pennants. ("Happy Days Are Here Again," incidentally, was the theme song of the Democratic Party and of FDR's 1932 campaign.)

Nearly every CCC camp also produced its own individual newspaper, which provided information, entertainment, and, for its staff, journalism-class training. Some camp journalists later landed careers in the profession. Papers ranged from tabloid format to magazine style. Archival remnants survive from the various companies stationed in Yosemite, including issues of five Wawona papers. Chronologically, they are the *Wawona Bear Claws,* the *Pow-Wawonian,* the *Wabama News,* the *Valley Scavenger,* and the *Wawona Wolverine.* Together with the memoirs and correspondence of individual enrollees, papers like these provide our best window into what life was like in the Yosemite CCC.

Camp newspapers were typically produced as a kind of lab project. The content of the Wawona papers, like others around the country, would be typed or hand-drawn directly onto a stencil. Copies would then be run off on a mimeograph machine – a hand-cranked duplicator that forced ink inside a drum through the stencil and onto the paper. Typically, newspapers ran just a few pages. Looking at them today,[73] most seem a bit free-form. Good enough was good enough. That looseness gives them a great deal of charm.

The papers contained a lot of what one would find in a small-town newspaper – headline stories, gossip, editorials, cartoons (some of them well-drawn and clever). Page-one news for January 1935, as reported by the *Bear Claws,* was that Camp Wawona now had a gasoline-powered washing machine.[74] Relegated to page six of a 1939 *Valley Scavenger* was news about the company's new latrine, a "14-holer."[75] There were philosophical musings, columns offering personal advice, and articles on new developments in science and technology. The papers covered sports, of course. They often contained a lot of amusing doggerel, and once in a while an example of real poetry.

But very seldom through most of the years did a paper refer to the men's ordinary daily work routines. What counted was what happened when not out in the field. The *Bear Claws* ran a regular "Scratchings" feature that captured the men's doings (and antics) in snippets. For example:

> Harris wants his barracks to call him Sergeant. Me thinks he is putting on the dog. . . . Someone put snow in Frank Cabanski's bunk the other night, and him a 36 dollar man. . . . It was reported that Baldwin was trying to play music on the icicles hanging from the roofs.[76]

The papers were upbeat, lighthearted, and often humorous in a way that still brings chuckles today. They had a range, though, and could occasionally be quite poignant. In March 1935, eighty-six men, nearly half of Company 529's members, were about to return to their homes in the East. Their enrollment period had expired. A lot of them, judging from their names, came from immigrant families of southern or central European origin. Most of the men had no clear job prospects. On page one, the *Bear Claws* reflected on their experience:

> We don't regret the help our stay here has been to those we love. We have no regrets about returning to them. That is a joy. We don't regret the weight we have gained; the height we have added to our stature; the bulging muscles we have built – physically, mentally and spiritually. . . . Living together is an art . . . an accomplishment.[77]

This issue of the paper also contained an article on how to get a job. Four years later, in 1939, one man wrote this poetic lament for the *Valley Scavenger*:

> Now that I'll be heading home
> To sit and listen for the phone
> To wait for work that never comes,
> To sit and twiddle both my thumbs,
> Ah me! No wonder that I groan.[78]

Sometimes a newspaper would actually come out in printed form. In 1940, the fairly amateurish mimeographed Wawona papers were succeeded by the *Wawona Wolverine,* named for a rare high-elevation mammal found in the park (its presence at all today is uncertain). By contrast with its predecessors, the *Wolverine* had a very professional feel. Gone were the freehand drawings, silly cartoons, and irregular publication dates; this was a monthly. The paper contained a lot fewer illustrations, and more educational articles on everything from nature to history to sociology. Many of these were written by the Educational Advisor. The *Wolverine* also summarized the current state of work projects. Journalism in Wawona had decidedly turned more serious.

***

Any time you concentrate hundreds of men together, a number of them will misbehave. Working around California and in Yellowstone, foreman Howard

Cox found that the most unruly CCC camp he dealt with consisted of World War I veterans. In pleasant contrast was a company of young men from New York's gritty Hell's Kitchen – some of them with records – who were regularly sending money home to their families. They typified Cox's general experience. "Always, Howard spoke highly of the boys' attitude and willingness to learn," his wife Rose later recalled.[79]

Surprisingly little misbehavior was recorded in the Yosemite CCC, but a number of men did get into trouble. The War Department had imposed a national discipline code, and company commanding officers were responsible for enforcing it. Among other forms of punishment, men could face discharge, admonition, or suspension of privileges. A dishonorable discharge meant ouster from the Corps without pay. Offenses subject to dishonorable discharge included refusing to work and homosexual activity. An administrative discharge involved separation with pay. All told, a fifth of CCC men nationally were separated under an administrative or a dishonorable discharge.[80]

Some of the mischief men got into involved automobiles. Even the desperate Joad family in John Steinbeck's *The Grapes of Wrath* drove a creaking Hudson; but the CCC disallowed men from having cars on the theory that genuine neediness did not comport with owning so much as a jalopy. Across the country, some men flouted the rule by hiding their cars away from camp. That may explain how it happened that an enrollee from Cascades got arrested in 1935 for drunk driving, followed by a ninety-day jail sentence. The same year, a Crane Flat fellow drew a forty-day sentence for disorderly conduct in camp, together with a (presumably dishonorable) discharge. Another man faced sanctions for stealing curios from Camp Curry.[81] Darrel Stover remembered that "a couple of the guys had too many beers at the dance one sat. night, and spent the night in the Park hoosegow." The company CO bailed them out in the morning.[82] Carl Sharsmith was outraged when CCC men in Tuolumne Meadows rolled glacial erratic boulders off of Lembert Dome.[83] Occasionally, men would get fined for violating park (as opposed to CCC) rules. During that era, for example, gates at park entrances were closed overnight, but occasionally men would try to slip through after hours.[84]

During the winter of 1937, morale in the camps plunged when bone-chilling weather gripped the park. The fifty-two-man barracks at Camp Cascades were heated by two puny wood stoves, which in normal times had to suffice as foot-long icicles hung from the eaves outside.[85] But January 1937 was not normal. Temperatures dropped to the lowest levels that had ever been recorded in the park. Yosemite Valley hit 5.5 degrees below zero Fahrenheit while snowfall reached 78.5 inches. In Wawona, a record low of 22 below zero was registered on January 21. The Corps had not issued clothing that would protect against such temperatures. Late that month, Camp Cascades was quarantined because men were getting sick, with concern developing about a possible outbreak of influenza. In Wawona, some of the men refused to work. Under the discipline code, that spelled an automatic dishonorable discharge. They were duly ejected from the Corps and sent home.[86]

Again, to generalize, the record shows CCC men in Yosemite as surprisingly, even astonishingly, law-abiding and rule-observing, especially considering their numbers and their youthfulness. One has to hunt to locate even mention of the infractions highlighted above. It would be a fair guess that, based on the record, far more tourists and YP&CCo employees per capita got into trouble than CCC men.

There was, though, one other category of infraction that did not apply to rule-breaking tourists or employees – desertion. Also known as going "over the hill," or, in army terminology, absent without leave (AWOL), desertion from a military unit in wartime carried a potential death penalty. The CCC was not *that* punitive, but when men signed up for a six-month hitch in the Corps, it meant six months. If an emergency arose at home, or if a private sector job materialized, a man could receive an honorable discharge. (This did happen in Yosemite.) Otherwise, his next six months belonged to the CCC.

The motto of the Corps was, "we can take it." Even better, as a Wawona camp paper put it, was to be able to "take it with a smile."[87] But there were those who could not. Men who fled had their reasons – spartan camps; regimentation; demanding day-to-day labor; homesickness. Al Monteverde recorded that while most of his fellow recruits took to the tough work, one or two got homesick and went over the hill.[88] But reasons were not excuses. Unless a man who bolted reappeared within ten days, he received a dishonorable discharge. During the CCC's first several years, the national desertion rate remained low. At the same time, though, it was steadily mounting. Efforts were made to raise morale, but the rate kept on rising. In 1933, it was 8 percent. By 1937, it had reached 18.8 percent, and by 1939 very close to 20 percent. Some were deserting to grab private sector jobs without getting a discharge first; some families no longer depended so much on their lion's share of an enrollee's paycheck. Regardless of cause, the pattern worried CCC administrators. The high correlation between the desertion rate and the discharge rate explains itself.[89]

For the great majority who stuck it out, praise for good behavior vastly exceeded admonishments for bad. One thing that widely endeared the CCC to the public was its eagerness to tackle any emergency, from a fire far in the backcountry to a search and rescue. As a young ranger naturalist in 1935, Carl Sharsmith came close to getting killed. He was part of a group that climbed Mount Lyell, then later in the day took on Mount Maclure. At the top of Maclure, Sharsmith slipped and tumbled, spinning downward uncontrollably. When he finally came to a stop, his feet were swinging over the edge of a fifteen-hundred-foot cliff. He was bloody and in shock. A litter was improvised, and relay teams of fellow climbers transported him down to the base camp. A CCC crew arrived, led by a foreman, to carry him the rest of the way out to a waiting ambulance. Though the doctors could never confirm any fractures, it required two months in the hospital for Sharsmith to recover from the pounding he had absorbed. Once well again, he would lead group hikes up Mount Lyell on into the mid-1950s.[90]

CCC men themselves died tragically, or got injured; so did members of the road crews. The work was often dangerous, compounding the fact that Yosemite itself is inherently dangerous. Car crashes, drownings, and mishaps took a steady toll of park visitors in the 1930s just as they do today – an average of seventeen deaths per year between 2014 and 2019. If tourists suffer a toll like this, one can imagine the added risks young enrollees encountered felling trees, maneuvering heavy equipment, using power tools, and setting off dynamite. The wonder is that more weren't hurt or killed. A national CCC safety initiative launched in 1934, the year after the program began, cut the accident rate by two-thirds over four years.[91]

Even so, things happened, some of them freakish or unpredictable, others random or mundane. In the mundane "lesson learned" category, during the summer of 1934 a man attached to the Merced Grove camp got to playing with a bear cub. The mother bear lit out after him, and in running for his life he tumbled and sprained an ankle. In 1936, Camp Wawona enrollee Lloyd MacLaughlin broke an ankle sliding into second base in a game against Camp Cascades. One of Al Monteverde's CCC mates fractured a collarbone in a skiing accident. In 1940, enrollee Bryant Higgins cut off a finger with an axe. In May 1941, measles broke out in Camps Cascades and Wawona. While the army routinely vaccinated men coming into the Corps, no vaccine for measles existed yet. Cascades had to go under quarantine.[92]

Then too, there was the category of might-have-been-worse. Al Monteverde loved driving bulldozers, but he once came close to flipping one down the side of a hill. In 1935, Glenn Strouse of Camp Wawona had an explosives accident and wound up in the infirmary recovering from powder burns. Al Monteverde got a lot of experience working with dynamite, and his advice to his brother Paul, who was doing the same thing with the CCC in Santa Barbara, was, "don't ever trust anything or anybody with it!" In 1939, three employees working for a contractor on the Wawona Road cheated death, injured but alive, when a dynamite charge went off unexpectedly.[93] Near-misses – the axe stroke that nearly split a shin, the shovel handle that almost struck an eye – went unrecorded.

When accidents did occur, the CCC had doctors on hand. The doctors, like everyone else, were transferred from place to place. In 1938, the physician serving the CCC camps in Yosemite was Ralph Barnard. Arriving from Wyoming, he served for less than a year before moving on again.[94]

Sometimes tragedies happened. In November 1934, near Camp Wawona, Louis Miller, an eighteen year-old CCC man from Ohio, was tending a drum hoist – a motorized lifting machine that operated by wrapping a boosting cable around a rotating drum. The machine was being used to drag a log. Apparently, Miller lost his footing and got caught between the moving cable and the drum. He probably died instantly. No one saw it happen. In a similar tragedy, in 1939, near White Wolf, a young worker on the new Tioga Road died after getting entangled between a belt and pulley on a big compressor.[95]

For workers on New Deal projects in the park, roads and vehicles proved to be the worst killers. In 1935, a BPR powderman on the new Big Oak Flat Road blasted out a roadcut but died in the rockslide his charges set off. In 1937, a government engineer on the same project dropped off a roadside cliff, later dying of pneumonia in the valley's Lewis Memorial Hospital. A couple of months later, a Big Oak Flat worker, taking shelter from blasting beneath a dump truck, died when the driver, unaware he was below, rolled over him. That same year, two CCC men – Ernest Gance and Owen Meeks, both from West Virginia – died when their car plunged down a hundred-foot embankment in Wawona. The following year, a big CCC truck was carrying more than two dozen men based at Buck Meadows into Yosemite on a routine excursion. The driver was going too fast. As he turned sharply into the icy viewpoint parking lot east of the tunnel, the truck rolled over, hurling all the men onto the pavement. Nearly everyone suffered serious injuries. Earl Arthur of Oklahoma, age twenty, later died.[96]

Darrel Stover recalled a particularly poignant incident from his twenty-one-month service at Camp Cascades. During the winter, it was standard practice to drain truck radiators each night so they would not freeze. One of the men in camp developed what medical staff later termed "race-horse pneumonia." Doubtless in a hurry to get the patient to Lewis Memorial, the assigned driver forgot to refill his radiator. His overheated engine seized. By the time a replacement truck got the patient to the hospital, it was too late.[97]

In view of such losses of life, a striking fact remains from the Civilian Conservation Corps experiment. Despite all the dangers of their work, CCC men had a lower mortality rate than did men in the same age bracket who never joined the Corps. The disease rate was lower as well.[98]

[7]
BIG NEW INITIATIVES: THE MID-1930s

In a burst of energy, the New Deal launched a rush of projects during the mid-1930s that permanently changed Yosemite. As the Civilian Conservation Corps branched out, road improvement proceeded mile by mile, and the full impact of the Public Works Administration came into play, the park changed physically. Some of the changes have faded away over time. But much of the legacy remains in clear view today – taken for granted as if, like the scenery, it had existed from time immemorial.

Many of the new initiatives involved the definition and use of space. Landscaping projects were a mainstay of CCC work in the park. Men landscaped such places as the new south entrance station and Badger Pass. They installed drinking fountains along the Wawona and Glacier Point roads. (During its lifetime, the CCC placed some two thousand fountains in tourist areas nationwide.)[1] And crews planted a great many trees and shrubs in the campgrounds, adding watering systems to keep them alive.

The definition of space often meant the redefinition of space, which included a good deal of building demolition. The thought of razing old wooden structures may cause a melancholy twinge today, but in reality the nature of the typical teardown would tax all but the most devoted antiquarian's capacity for nostalgia. The trade for natural open space was worth it.

Many of the park's structures were built to last about as long as an early tarpapered CCC barracks. In fact, the lounge and dining room of the Yosemite Lodge consisted of two old army barracks pushed together end to end. David

Curry was not Yosemite's first aggressive entrepreneur; before him, there had been a whole parade of them. In the nineteenth century, the park saw a profusion of hotels, ranging from the respectable to the ramshackle. One, dubbed La Casa Nevada, even materialized between Vernal and Nevada falls. A fire incinerated this chalet, like quite a number of the other establishments, but derelict buildings, ripe for demolition, still dotted the landscape in the early twentieth century.

Ironically, the collection of expendable buildings included nearly the entire Old Village, the hub of Yosemite National Park. This explains why – except for the chapel, which was rescued – the site on which the Village once existed has returned to nature. Today it offers some of the finest open views on the valley floor. During the 1930s, the terms Old and New Village were used to designate a transition to what today is simply called Yosemite Village. At first, the New Village was also called the Government Center, since official buildings, including the administration building, the post office, and the museum, were some of the first to go up there. The complete move would take years, but it had already gotten well under way as early as the mid-1920s. By 1935, in fact, most of the New Village as planned had already been built.

The CCC cut its teeth on demolition projects by knocking down derelict buildings in Wawona and Tuolumne Meadows early on, but demolition began in earnest in 1937, when the men razed buildings that had been condemned in the Old Village. The following year, the Corps demolished the derelict Sentinel Hotel there. Originally constructed in 1877 on the bank of the Merced River, with a fine view of Yosemite Falls, the hotel's long-term prospects were dampened when the river changed course. If the hotel still existed today, guests would require waders or maybe a raft. The CCC also demolished the hotel's adjoining Cedar Cottage – a famous attraction in its day because it had a cedar growing up through the roof. Emerging from the demolition unscathed, the tree made it into the twenty-first century. Other cottages came down too. In 1940, the federal government purchased the Carl Inn, a rustic resort just inside the park on the route to Hetch Hetchy. The inn had previously been demolished twice by flood, once by fire, and once by snow.[2] The CCC performed the final, definitive act. Nineteen forty-one saw more CCC teardowns in the park, including remnants of the Sentinel Hotel complex and some disused buildings in Wawona.

The big milestone that year, though, was the demolition of the old bear-feeding attraction in the lower valley, and restoration of its parking area. In Yosemite, bear feeding shows had been terminated in 1940, part of a national trend in the parks. The superintendent reported that a "control feeding" site on the valley's north side was successfully luring bears away from the campgrounds, residential areas, and roads. Clearly, the goal now was not public entertainment, but to divert the garbage-habituated, exceedingly overpopulated bears away from the humans.[3] In Tuolumne Meadows, where the dump was well removed from places people camped or stayed, visitors continued lining up to watch the bears. Meanwhile, signs warning people not to feed them sprouted throughout the park.

Looking back, one is struck by the amount of work the CCC devoted to Wawona Meadow, which became both a demolition and a reconstruction project. It may well have received more attention – certainly per square yard – than any other meadow in Yosemite. Part of this is easy to explain, because Wawona constituted such a major CCC hub. From May 1933 through October 1934, indeed, Yosemite CCC camps 1 and 2 were situated right on the meadow.

Part of the CCC's focus, though, originated in the prior history of Wawona Meadow. For millennia, Indigenous Americans used fire to shape the ecology of Yosemite Valley, favoring open meadows so as to encourage useful plants and provide grazing for prey deer. In nineteenth and early twentieth century Euro-American thinking, too, meadows existed to be put to use. The idea of not using them (for example, not pasturing livestock on them) seemed counterintuitive – *wasteful.* During the first half of the twentieth century, as Mark Arax has written, conservation had a very inclusive meaning. "Dams were conservation. Canals were conservation. Not letting a drop of water go unused by farms and cities was conservation."[4] The same with meadows.

Walking around Wawona Meadow today on the three-and-a-half-mile Meadow Loop Trail, one spots at a glance tumbledown rail fences and rotting cattle chutes. Well-placed interpretive signs explain their story. From the mid-nineteenth century until Wawona came into the park in 1932, the meadow served as a pasture for cattle, horses, mules, and hogs. In fact, horses from the Wawona Stables grazed there into the 1970s, and an old slaughterhouse still stands today. A hayfield (which had earlier served as an army rifle range) provided winter forage. Fruits and vegetables were raised for hotel guests; ancient apple trees still bud out each year. In 1918, the lower end of the meadow was turned into the first golf course in the Sierra. Next came airplanes. The middle of the meadow was graded into a landing strip. The first aircraft, two dated World War I Jenny biplanes, landed in December 1925. Before long, an intrepid entrepreneur was offering passenger service from Merced. A canvas hangar went up; it resembled a circus tent, but perhaps warranted the new name, Wawona Airport. Don Tresidder flew his personal plane in and out.

No surprise, then, that Wawona Meadow was a magnet for the CCC. In effect, it was turned into a demonstration project for some of the ecological theories of the 1930s. Early on, today's Meadow Loop Trail – then a proper road – came in for particular attention, with a lot of timber thinning along the edges and a coat of oil.

The meadow makes up a complex ecosystem. In its natural state, like other Sierra meadows, it depends on a high water table; it also depends on a flow of water gradually shimmering downhill across its surface. The whole natural system represents a delicate balance between hydrology, flora, and fauna. Everything depends upon everything else. Change one element, and you break the equilibrium.

Beginning in 1934, the CCC further upset what equilibrium remained when men were directed to begin cutting ditches that would divert the flow of surface water out to the flanks of the meadow. In 1935, the ditches were paved. The intent was to improve grazing and agriculture – to make the meadow better by making it more useful. In 1936, CCC men built check dams in the diversion ditches to retard erosion by slowing down water velocity. That spring, the meadow became the focus of all CCC activity in Wawona. In tandem with the digging, men planted the meadow and ditch-banks with twenty-five thousand willow cuttings.[5]

Meanwhile, CCC men had been improving the surface of the landing field. Wawona's incorporation into the park had made the Wawona Airport a sore thumb because private planes were not allowed in national parks. After the NPS purchased the property in 1932, it terminated private use. The field was redesignated as an emergency landing strip. This made good sense. Helicopters were then in the development stage and would not come into general use until after World War II. By definition, emergency flights until then remained fixed-wing.

***

Throughout Yosemite, CCC crews constantly undertook landscaping projects in administrative, residential, and concession areas. They planted trees, shrubs, and ferns; laid out paths; and set down log curbing. At the museum, they developed a meadow of wildflowers augmented by both a small stream and a spring.

Perhaps the outstanding example of this genre of landscape design on the floor of Yosemite Valley was the Fern Spring project of 1936. Today's visitor passes the spring, located near the Pohono Bridge, when driving along Southside Drive between the El Portal and Wawona roads. There, CCC men built a rock garden surrounding a pool, planted with ferns, ground cover, and wildflowers to create a naturalistic setting. Seats fashioned from logs were situated around the site, with a log guardrail designating where to park. Today, the perishable soft tissue – the wooden part – has disappeared. But the bones of the project endure – a crystalline pool and, below it, stone steps down which the water flows. Fern Spring remains a magnet for passersby. For Indigenous Americans, it is a deeply spiritual place, considered a source of life.

***

In June 1935, the National Park Service declared that a boom was occurring in outdoor recreation, sweeping up Americans from every walk of life. The park service offered three explanations. First, the unemployed had time on their hands. Second, camping, hiking, and other forms of recreation were broadly affordable if not free. Finally, cars made it easy to get from cities to the parks. We have seen how these three factors interacted in Yosemite. Across the country, national park visitation was skyrocketing. During 1933, the parks attracted some 3,500,000 visitors; in 1938, 16,000,000; by 1941, 21,000,000. The park service diagnosed a "recreation problem" – a nationwide recreation resource deficit. This deficit, it recommended, should be filled by CCC projects. A good deal of push came from the White House. Conserving the public health and well-being was akin to conserving forests. Human conservation in an outdoor environment, after all, was the CCC's own core purpose.[6]

Before the summer of 1935, the Corps on the national level had been focused on forestry, with little attention to carrying out projects for tourists. Scant attention had gone into developing recreational facilities. Yosemite ranked among the exceptions – for example, in developing or improving the Tuolumne and valley floor campgrounds.

In June 1935, the same month the NPS announced the recreation boom, the Corps declared that it would commit one hundred-twenty thousand men to developing recreation facilities under the oversight of the National Park Service. This represented a big boost in CCC personnel for the parks. Parks nationwide undertook an extraordinary variety of improvements, including some that would receive particular priority in Yosemite – new or upgraded campgrounds, picnic areas, roads, bridges, trails, and parking areas. It is worth emphasizing that more CCC camps by far existed in state parks than in national ones, and that the recreation initiative spanned both types. The boom in national park visitation during the 1930s resulted, Arno Cammerer declared, from the endeavors of the CCC.[7] He was undoubtedly exaggerating, but by no means completely.

As with campground construction, the Yosemite CCC got into trail work early on, in 1933. Recreational hiking was a less popular activity then than it has become today.[8] By the early 'thirties, most of the park's trail system was already complete, limiting the need for more.[9] Even so, a good deal of trail (and trail bridge) construction did take place in the 1930s – much of it done by the CCC, but much also done by other crews. The preexisting trail layout required ongoing attention and maintenance as well. Over the years, the CCC upgraded trails that the army had built when it administered the park so as to meet modern NPS standards. By the end of its life, the Corps had constructed, rebuilt, or restored hundreds of miles of hiking trails in Yosemite.

Examples abound. To control dust, men applied oil to the top stretch of the trail that ran from Glacier Point to Yosemite Valley – then called the Eleven Mile Trail, today known as the Panorama Trail. At least half of the trail, the high-traffic route leading from the valley floor up to Nevada Fall, was paved to an average width of five feet. The asphalt was made from a combination of oil and decomposed granite, of which there was no shortage. The oil had to be hauled up by mule. The trail through Little Yosemite Valley also got paved. Trail oiling (as opposed to hard-surfacing) had caused complaints in the 1920s, when hikers tracked the goo onto the Persian rugs in The Ahwahnee.[10] Presumably, putting it as far away as Glacier Point was safe enough.

Horse trails became a priority. In 1936, for instance, Camp Wawona men renovated and oiled the bridle path between Wawona and the Mariposa Grove. Led by a foreman, a crew of fourteen used two tractors to smooth down the trail, which they oiled. The project moved along at a rate of eight hundred feet per day.[11] In 1937, a bridle path was built within the Mariposa Grove.

That same year, men from a stub camp at Porcupine Flat went to work constructing trails at May Lake and Snow Flat. Toward the end of the 'thirties and into the early 'forties, trail work continued in that vicinity. To tie the new High Sierra camp at May Lake into the High Sierra loop, a CCC crew led by a park service foreman was directed to build a trail over the shoulders of Mount Hoffmann and Tuolumne Peak for a new route to Glen Aulin. (A couple of decades later, the route was superseded by another one that was carved across slick granite faces using a good deal of dynamite, which was cheaper than labor.)[12] CCC crews worked on a long fire road near Lake Eleanor. Other crews built and paved a horse trail between the Wawona Meadow Loop and the Wawona Road. In 1941, CCC men laid out a horse trail along the Tioga Road.

One of the biggest recreational priorities for the CCC – higher in Yosemite than trail work, it is fair to say – involved winter sports. As we have seen, momentum was already running strong thanks to Don Tresidder. During the 1920s and '30s, skiing as an American sport experienced its greatest growth. Formerly considered an elite pastime, it began to become democratized and middle-class. Through articles and ads, skiing found its way into popular culture. Places like Badger Pass had a big role in making skiing, like camping, conveniently accessible by car and affordable enough to dot the slopes with skiers. There and around the United States, the CCC played a tremendously important part in creating and improving skiing venues.

By the mid-'thirties, Badger Pass was attracting more skiers than ever before, especially on weekends. It proved a bonanza at a time when YP&CCo needed one, and the company did everything imaginable to keep the skiers pouring in. YP&CCo installed an early-model ski lift – something the proprietors of ski venues had recently begun doing everywhere in order to draw more crowds. The Bureau of Public Roads allotted one of its cabins as a place for wet, cold skiers to warm up. The company rented skis out of the same tight building, compounding an already claustrophobic effect. No parking lot existed; drivers simply parallel-parked along the Glacier Point Road. Visitors had to make do with pit toilets. Despite it all, the Yosemite Winter Club sponsored invitational ski events that winter which drew some of the state's premier skiers. In both February and March 1935, five thousand people piled into Badger Pass.[13]

Clearly, the time had arrived for a whole new ski complex. YP&CCo launched accelerated construction of the Badger Pass Ski House. Designed to handle hundreds of visitors, the facility would feature a big fireplace, lounge, and ski and equipment storage, and it would sell food. A ski school would offer lessons. In anticipation of the 1935-1936 onslaught, work also began on entry road improvements plus a parking area for two hundred cars. The Ski House opened in December 1935.

During the autumn of that year, men from Camp Wawona got busy clearing routes for ski runs (which would become an annual assignment). They carved a ten-mile run from Badger pass to Yosemite Valley – a four thousand-foot elevation drop. A second run with a two thousand-foot drop ended south of Chinquapin.[14]

It was a good thing that the concessioner and the CCC had prepared for crowds. During January 1936, Badger Pass drew some ten thousand visitors – nearly as many as during the *entire* 1934-1935 season. January 26, a Sunday, saw fourteen hundred arrive, overwhelming the new Ski House and jamming the new parking lot. By the end of March 1936, in round numbers, Badger Pass had attracted thirty-two thousand winter visitors, compared to twelve thousand the prior winter. (The Mariposa Grove, open for visitors despite the snow, received only a tenth as many; people definitely wanted to ski.)[15] The following October, in preparation for the coming season, a full CCC stub camp at Badger Pass cleared the runs and built a small ski jump.

Again, though, it was scarcely possible to keep up with mounting demand. In February 1937, a cold and stormy month, heavy snowfall brought a huge spike in skiers. The parking lot at Badger Pass was so completely overrun on Sunday, February 21, that cars were parked for two miles up and down one side of the Glacier Point Road. On Sunday, February 11, 1940, a single-day record of 751 cars jammed Badger Pass. This time the overflow stretched for two and a half miles. Three thousand people were estimated to have enjoyed the fine snowpack that day.[16]

In August 1940, a CCC stub camp was set up at Ostrander Lake to house a team constructing a ski hut – a touring shelter that would become a landmark of Yosemite architecture.[17] The crew consisted of two foremen, two stonemasons, a carpenter, and twenty enrollees. They made quick progress; by the end of September, the job was mostly complete. A year later, a small stub camp team added the final touches.[18] Built of stone with wood trim and a steeply pitched metal roof, the hut is a monument of the rustic style. Today, it is on the National Register of Historic Places.

Meantime, the CCC labored – yet again – to get ahead of soaring demand at Badger Pass. In 1940, carpenters assisted by a CCC crew finished building a ranger residence there. A new thirty-meter log-and-earth ski jump was begun; a twenty thousand-gallon water tank and a comfort station went in. All were CCC projects. Men planted signs for ski trails. Parking was expanded beyond the original, totally inadequate two hundred spaces, with enrollees excavating for underground drainage lines and gentling earth cuts by hand-sloping them.

The final winter before Pearl Harbor, 1940-1941, saw visitor records at Badger Pass exceeded once more. January 1941 set a new record for the month, just shy of eighteen thousand. The Ostrander ski hut officially opened, the guests including a large group from the Sierra Club. The newly expanded four hundred-space parking lot at Badger Pass was overwhelmed in February, with the overflow spilling, in time-honored fashion, onto the Glacier Point Road.[19] October 1941 saw a tremendous windstorm topple more than seventy large trees across the ski runs and slopes. The CCC concentrated on clearing away the mess before snow fell and the ski crowds returned.[20] The upward momentum seemed inexorable. Two months later came Pearl Harbor, which brought a swift end to it all.

***

The overall boom in recreation and tourism, Badger Pass included, constantly taxed the park's ability to keep up. By stretching beyond its original mission, the CCC could carry the load of building infrastructure up to a certain scale. Above that scale, the Public Works Administration took over. Today the term "good enough for government work" has an ironic twist suggesting barely adequate, mediocre. Back then, it meant work executed to the topmost standards. That was the context in which the PWA operated, with Harold Ickes poring over every contract.

The first truly massive PWA project to go up in Yosemite was a new utility building that opened in the summer of 1935. Looking at the Group Utility Building (as it was then known) today, you recognize it as a product of the federal agency that brought forth the Lincoln Tunnel and Grand Coulee Dam. Located in the midst of a congested service, maintenance, and storage area north of the museum, the building stands out today the way a sequoia does amid fir trees – except that this is no sequoia. Though actually designed by the park service, the building challenges anyone who embraces the warmth of rustic park architecture. It is big, stark, gray, and functional. A combination of single and two-story construction, when opened the massive reinforced concrete building measured 260 feet long and totaled 18,548 square feet. Steel columns supported the steel trusses which held up the roof. The complex replaced a lot of wooden structures by consolidating their functions inside. It housed a fire station with three fire trucks, together with machine, carpentry, paint, plumbing, electrical, blacksmithing, and other shops and the central CCC garage. Fire trucks still wait there for action today, and the weathered building looks as solid as a block of granite. Nothing could suit it better than its popular nickname, Fort Yosemite.

In the late 'thirties the PWA[21] tackled the valley's water and sewer infrastructure – mundane and easily taken for granted, but obviously critical. After a good deal of trenching, a new twelve-inch water main was laid, and water purifying facilities went in. Sewage disposal was an old issue in Yosemite. Camp Curry's rapid growth early in the century notoriously outpaced its sewage capacity, making the camp an odoriferous locale at night. In addition, one wanted to take particular care where one stepped. A competitor of Camp Curry's, Camp Lost Arrow, hit on an elegant solution to the problem by diverting its effluent directly into Yosemite Creek.[22] The PWA now made sure that the valley sewage treatment system got an upgrade. In Tuolumne, the PWA integrated the CCC's comfort stations into a modern system combining pumps, a sump, water lines, and the omnipresent manhole cover.

One of the biggest PWA projects in Yosemite raised the height of the O'Shaughnessy Dam at Hetch Hetchy by 85.5 feet. Run by the City of San Francisco, this undertaking reopened old, unhealed wounds. That Hetch Hetchy would be flooded at all is unimaginable today. From his reports to Washington after the dam-raising project got underway in 1935, one gets the impression that

Charles Thomson felt the same. A great deal of CCC time and energy went into cleaning up the massive amount of construction debris and general mess left by Hetch Hetchy contractors in the 1920s. Following phase two, the CCC returned and did it all over again.

So it went, project by project. A mile-long, fifty-four-inch penstock, built of wood staves, was constructed to replace an older, flood-ravaged wood stave line that funneled water to the valley's hydroelectric plant. CCC crews pitched in. A new standby electric plant went up. And PWA money funded new employee and ranger residences, the same kind of construction the CCC was doing.

Tuolumne Meadows contact station

Not to be left behind, in 1936 the CCC built a "contact station" adjoining the entrance road into the Tuolumne campground. The contact station echoed the rustic architectural themes of the nearby comfort stations, integrating native stone with rough wood. Like them, it is listed on the National Register. And, like the other New Deal buildings in the park, having gotten plenty of use over the years, it has proved remarkably durable.

In 1936, CCC men worked on a footbridge across the Merced River near the

Old Village, rebuilt a bridle path bridge across Yosemite Creek installed guard rails along roads, and built a cabin near Lake Eleanor. In 1937, a CCC crew put up a schoolhouse in Wawona. They also installed pipes and water faucets in Yosemite Valley campgrounds as well as a water system at May Lake, where the new high Sierra camp was going in. Crews built several residences in the valley. That summer of 1937, in fact, all of the construction projects in the park, with two big exceptions, were being done by the CCC.[23]

One of the exceptions involved the City of San Francisco-PWA dam-raising project at Hetch Hetchy. Near that operation, the CCC constructed additional dams plus weirs, a fish trap, a fish ladder, and egg collecting stations at Lake Eleanor.

The other exception was roads.

***

In 1935, work began on the new Big Oak Flat Road, The next year saw the intricate projects commence that make the road a masterpiece of scenic highway design. Of its three planned tunnels, the two shorter ones (downhill from the longest) came first. Initially, a pilot tunnel would be bored through, tall enough for a person to stand in. This passage would then be expanded using drills and explosives. Each tunnel got a concrete lining. Finally, a stone arch ring was added to the portals. This stonework, done under subcontract, is among the best in Yosemite, and is complemented by the stone guard and retaining walls along the route.

Big Oak Flat Road today, showing tunnel to lower right

Never had road construction at this level of difficulty and complexity been attempted in the park before.[24] A tremendous amount of study and planning went into it. Looking at the road from the opposite side of the Merced River Canyon, one can see that a lot of it rests on what was originally thin air. The overriding goal, as a park statement put it, was "to prevent unsightly scars from deep cuts which would otherwise be necessary."[25] So engineers had to design the highway to rest on fill or to be cantilevered out from the cliffs. Drilling and blasting were even carried on in a way to least disturb plant life. One is struck by the retaining walls, built of irregular granite blocks in order to look as natural as possible. The blocks were lowered into place using hand-operated derricks. Each derrick was pulled from place to place by mule train.[26]

To meet the challenge of the long tunnel, the Bureau of Public Roads assigned a resident engineer, B. H. McCain, to the project. This tunnel would demand boring more than two thousand feet through granite. A machine was custom-built for the job. Mounted on a five-ton truck chassis, this "Jumbo" cut holes in the granite using six individual drills. The holes were then packed with explosives and blown. The apparatus moved in an upward direction, against the angle of the grade. The tunnel was holed through in April 1938.

Three bridges also needed building, each one an open-spandrel arch structure made of reinforced concrete. These designs were dramatically different from the conventional rustic-looking Yosemite bridge – far lighter and airier. To get things started, temporary bridges were thrown across Cascade, Wildcat, and Tamarack creeks.

By the end of 1939, work on the tunnels and bridges had been completed. Not for two more years, though, with the stone guard walls up and the paving down, was the formal dedication ceremony held celebrating the opening of the new Big Oak Flat Road. Staged at Crane Flat on June 23, 1940, it was Yosemite's equivalent of driving the golden spike. A crowd of eighteen hundred gathered. The keynote speaker, William E. Colby, had served as secretary of the Sierra Club for the past forty years. Colby stressed the importance of roads in opening up the Sierra to auto travel. A big log had been laid across the new highway, and two teams of CCC men held a sawing competition to rip through it – perhaps the brawniest version of a ribbon cutting on record. The Crane Flat home team beat Cascades.

Festivities included a barbecue lunch, American Indian dancing, band music, and rope spinning. No one there could ever have forgotten it.[27]

Over the five-year time span of the Big Oak Flat project, other roadwork had been proceeding steadily as well. By 1934-1935, with the surfacing project on the new seventeen-mile road to Glacier Point still in progress, a driver could count at least on an oiled or graveled surface most of the way. In the dead of winter 1936, the road was kept open beyond Badger Pass, consistent with the ongoing goal of making this a year-round route.[28] By summer 1940, one could drive all the way on paved surface. In October 1940, after twelve years of work – most of it under the New Deal – the Bureau of Public Roads at long last turned over maintenance of both the Glacier Point and Wawona roads to Yosemite National Park.

Progress had also continued on the new Tioga Road. Rough but passable, by 1934 it stretched from Cathedral Creek, in Tuolumne Meadows, up to the Tioga Pass entrance. But thanks to mismanagement by a San Francisco contractor, paving that run – a total of less than twelve miles – proceeded by what seemed like inches. Stretching into its third season as of June 1937, the exasperating job was less than half finished yet had exhausted every hour of its allotted contract time. Reading Charles Thomson's reports about the project, one almost can still hear his teeth grind.[29] The work came to an end at long last that September. This meant that the first finished stretch of modern highway on the long trans-Sierra Tioga route was, ironically, in the highest, most isolated part of the park.

Motorists headed in the other direction, from Tuolumne to Yosemite Valley, could expect the next thirty-four-plus miles to consist of rough and dusty stretches of old, narrow, dirt mountain road twisting through the woods and up and down the grades. Even though a coat of oil eventually knocked down the dust along most of the route, drivers still had to cope with maneuvering modestly powered cars that lacked power steering. House trailers were definitely not recommended. Dissatisfied with the high bids it received, in 1936 the Bureau of Public Roads took on direct construction of one stretch around White Wolf. Along the 14.5-mile Crane Flat-McSwain Meadows run, Morrison-Knudsen built a fairly rustic-looking reinforced concrete-and-steel bridge across the South Fork of the Tuolumne River.

With work progressing or finished on the Tioga and Big Oak Flat routes, and the All Year Highway well established as the main artery in and out of the park, there remained the sore, longstanding issue of access to Yosemite from Los Angeles. As of 1937, two-thirds of visitors to Yosemite entered via Arch Rock. Just 16 percent came through the south entrance. This is a striking fact because San Francisco, which was served by the Arch Rock (together with the Big Oak Flat) entrance, had well under half the population of Los Angeles. That year, though, all the runner-up routes into the park showed big gains in traffic. The superintendent attributed this largely to road improvements, noting that the biggest percentage gain was on the Wawona Road.[30]

By 1938, one could travel on paved highway out of Fresno for some twenty miles, with decent oiled road continuing from there. Incoming travel via the south entrance skyrocketed that year, while traffic fell on the storm-damaged All Year Highway. It wasn't until spring 1939 that the project of actually paving the Wawona Road began. Mercifully, it went a lot better than in Tuolumne; by fall, the paving project inside the park was complete. From Los Angeles, driving time to Yosemite by way of Fresno, or via Merced on the All Year Highway, practically equalized.[31]

[8]
THE END

On March 23, 1937, Charles Goff Thomson died of a heart attack in Lewis Memorial hospital. He was only fifty-four. His memorial service was held at the new Wawona Tunnel viewpoint, with Bridalveil Fall and Half Dome as the backdrop. Frank Kittredge – an expert on national park roads who had worked with Thomson[1] – delivered the eulogy. Kittredge emphasized all that Thomson had done to keep development of the park in balance with the natural environment. Kittredge described Thomson's "keen sense of the fitness and desire for the harmony of things. . . . He recognized the importance and practicability of restricting and harmonizing necessary roads and structures into a natural blending of the surroundings."[2] In the ways that Kittredge described, Thomson had left an indelible mark on the park. No one connected to Yosemite had wrestled harder with the big issues, or shown more adaptability as the shape of the issues changed, than this complex and contradictory man. The sad blot on Thomson's legacy was his isolation and removal of the Indigenous Yosemite.

That summer, Lawrence Merriam was appointed to succeed Thomson as superintendent. Harold Ickes had previously tapped Merriam, a trained forester who had served as a CCC district director, as the NPS senior conservationist. Kittredge, in turn, succeeded Merriam in 1941, when Merriam moved up the park service chain of command.

Thomson's unexpected death was an omen of the kind of year 1937 would turn out to be in Yosemite. Apart from the blow of losing the park's transformational superintendent, though, it did not seem that way at first. Everything proceeded more or less as normal. The spring and summer saw a great deal of activity on all fronts, from forestry to roadbuilding. Unlike plenty of other years, no massive fires brewed up. On the whole, nature seemed benign.

The CCC went about its ambitious but routine business, which included carrying out flood control work along the Merced River. Undercut banks were re-sloped and re-vegetated. A CCC team built a rock wall at Happy Isles to prevent road flooding there. Although Yosemite Valley had not seen a major flood in thirty years, it was as though the work was driven by some sort of premonition.

Looking back, one is struck by how hard the CCC and other New Deal agencies struggled to improve and manage Yosemite Valley as a setting for peaceful encounters with nature – a place to refresh the spirit. In trying to accomplish this, they came up against the forces of geology, hydrology, and gravity. The valley is a highly dynamic, unstable place. I recall casting flies for trout in Mirror Lake during the 1960s. Thirty years before, the CCC had taken pains to restore and reinforce the rockfall dam that originally formed the lake. Though rebuilt time and again over the decades after high water events, using granite and even sandbags, the dam could not stop sediment from continuing to flow down Tenaya Creek and fill in the lake. So the lake was dredged, until that eventually came to a halt in the early 1970s.[3] Today, the place where I waded hip-deep in water is dry land.

Old Big Oak Flat Road, as seen from Dewey Point

Anyone who questions the dynamic nature of the valley might wish to hike a distance along the old Big Oak Flat Road as it departs the valley floor heading west, or follow the old Wawona Road up to Inspiration Point (a route the Wawona Tunnel, with its Tunnel View, superseded). Rockfalls and washouts, not to mention fallen timber, render these slow and precarious trips. The terrain is making fast work of returning to nature – not just in geologic time but in human time. More than one park trail I used to follow has reverted so completely that I have to bushwhack my way now from memory, keeping an eye peeled for an old tree blaze or maybe a remaining cairn (duck). John Muir famously and ecstatically described the mammoth earthquake that shook the Sierra Nevada in 1872, when he was living in Yosemite Valley.[4] In a sudden explosion of falling granite, the valley violently altered its topography. In 1996, a mass of granite estimated at eighty thousand tons peeled off Glacier Point, causing a fatality and numerous injuries.[5] Like Mirror Lake and Glacier Point in living memory, the valley, in geologic time, is filling itself in. During the mid-1930s, a team from the California Institute of Technology undertook the first scientific study of how much it already had, gauging sedimentary deposits by the resonance from blasts they set off.[6]

During the 1930s, Yosemite experienced a series of exceptionally heavy winters. In January 1935, one of the biggest snowstorms on record presented CCC men with the challenge of getting snow off the roads and sanding them. That spring, the principal trails had to be shoveled open. As it turned out, 1935 was merely a foretaste.

On December 9, 1937, a span of rain warm enough to melt the accumulated early snowpack let loose one of the biggest floods in the history of the park. Yosemite Valley turned into a biblical scene. Never before in recorded time had the park faced devastation on this scale. The center of the valley became a lake. Inundated by four to five feet of water, cabins at the Yosemite Lodge were swept off their foundations. Several feet of water coursed through the Old Village, where store merchandise quickly dissolved into waterlogged trash. The unfinished long tunnel along the new Big Oak Flat Road resembled a well, with ten feet of water backed up in the downhill end. B. H. McCain, the supervising engineer, had his mouth ripped away when a pine crashed down on his car.[7]

The All Year Highway took staggering damage. Several long stretches were simply washed away. Cascade Creek lost its metal bridge. Sliding down from the new Big Oak Flat Road onto the All Year Highway, fill material buried the park's arterial route in four or five feet of granite and mud. A major building at the Arch Rock entrance station rolled off its foundation. Miles of railroad track along the Merced Canyon washed out.[8]

Camp Cascades flood damage

Nothing suffered greater destruction than Camp Cascades, which all but ceased to exist. It had been built on a flat floodplain just a few feet higher than the level of the Merced. At an angle of ninety degrees immediately upriver, Cascade Creek emptied into the river. The camp was vulnerable to torrents of water coming at it from two different directions. The surge washed most of its buildings, including four barracks and the officers' quarters, down the Merced. The structures would slowly lift off, slip into the current, and be pounded apart. Some men snatched what they could carry and clambered out of windows. A number took refuge in the recreation building, but the onrushing tide forced them to chop their way out the back. Struggling through water and mud, sometimes forming human chains to get through, the men worked their way on foot out of the park and down to the hamlet of El Portal. But El Portal was cut off. Food had to be airdropped to the town. By great good fortune, no one drowned.[9]

CCC men in Wawona had almost completed a footbridge across the South Fork of the Merced that would connect to the new schoolhouse, making the daily trip shorter for children who lived on the opposite side of the river. The surging floodwater left nothing of the bridge behind but the abutments and piers. (In Yosemite Valley, too, bridges took a terrible beating.) For a time, Camp Wawona was cut off except for shortwave radio. The camp's water supply system was destroyed. CCC construction work across the park came to an abrupt halt.[10]

Building foundation remnant at new Camp Cascades

Now the priority immediately turned to reconstruction. In January 1938, clearing and grading began for a new Camp Cascades farther up the valley, near the southwest base of El Capitan and well away from the river. In April, the men were able to move in. Meanwhile, crews had returned as quickly as possible to the valley to help clean up the flood mess and put things back together. The 1937 flood required reconstruction of over six hundred miles of trails in the park; the CCC played a critical role. Some trails and trail bridges had been washed into oblivion. Complicating things even more, deep snowpack stubbornly persisted. Much of the high country did not open up until the following autumn.

The All Year route was shut down until the first of January. Repair crews worked in day and night shifts around the clock. One-way traffic controls lingered through 1938.[11] For a shorter time, the new Wawona Road closed too. The old

Wawona Road, which until then had remained passable for cars up to Inspiration Point, washed out for good. (It subsequently became a horse trail.)

The extreme weather of the late 1930s produced one of the most tragic stories in Yosemite history. The park superintendent's report to Washington for June 1938 announced that nine bodies had been discovered in the backcountry, victims of a plane crash. Two of the dead were a sister and brother – Jay Dirlam, twenty-two, and Mary Louise Dirlam, nineteen, each a popular student at Stanford. The remains of the passengers and crew had been carried out by pack animals. At the bottom of the long trip down, coroner's ambulances were waiting.[12]

On March 1, 1938, a twin-engine Transcontinental & Western Air (TWA)[13] passenger plane with the Dirlams aboard had been crossing the Sierra at night, in a storm, when it crashed into Buena Vista Peak. At 9,709 feet, Buena Vista is one of the highest points in the south-central part of the park, and also among the most remote. This was still the era before radar. John Graves, the pilot, had radioed that, flying at ten thousand feet, he was unsure of his location. Then the radio went silent. Searchers set out the following morning, but no one could find a sign of the sleek Douglas DC-2. Pilots and ground teams had to cope with terrible weather; in fact, the downed plane had gotten caught in the worst storm system on the West Coast in two-thirds of a century, producing seventy-seven inches of new snow at high elevations. The snowpack in the high country that winter exceeded all prior park records.

Once the weather cleared after a few days, more than fifty search planes took to the sky, combing a hundred square miles. Unfortunately, the designated search area was far to the south of the crash, off by more than thirty miles. The boundaries did not include the area around Buena Vista Peak, which in any case was concealing the plane under snow. More than four hundred searchers, three hundred of them from the CCC, scoured the foothills above Fresno, completely in vain.

A twenty-three-year-old Fresno man named H. O. Collier, who belonged to the CCC in Wawona, resolved to hunt for the plane inside Yosemite National Park. Carrying a few supplies, he would regularly hike out in his free time, methodically following his own search pattern. Nothing materialized. The misdirected larger search was finally called off, and in time Collier may have been hunting completely on his own. On Sunday afternoon, June 12 – on what would have been his last try, as he later recounted – he spotted the wreckage of the sixty-two-foot-long aircraft looming out of melting snow. It rested two hundred feet below the Buena Vista summit. Crash investigators later concluded that, peering into the gloom, Graves had probably been banking to try to get his bearings when he hit the peak.[14] Yosemite has never seen another fatal crash of a commercial aircraft. Nor has the park again experienced such loss of life in a single incident.

On July 15, 1938, a month after the plane crash discovery, Franklin D. Roosevelt arrived in Yosemite, the first sitting president to visit the park since Theodore Roosevelt thirty-five years before.[15] FDR had ridden the Presidential Special as far as El Portal on the now-reconstructed rail line along the Merced River. He was in the midst of a cross-country barnstorming trip, backing New Dealers up for reelection to Congress; with him were Senator William Gibbs McAdoo of California and his wife, Doris. Planning for the visit had been elaborate, involving collaboration between park rangers, the CCC, and the state highway patrol. Summoned out of retirement, Billy Nelson, who had provided Eleanor Roosevelt with the hot-water bottle for inside her sleeping bag, wore his old ranger uniform as a special presidential guest.

Roosevelt and the McAdoos toured the valley in the back seat of an open car. A parade of autos and buses followed. Press photographers scurried around – one of them, young Al Monteverde. Secret Service men kept watch. Rangers controlled intersections. Roosevelt, wearing a summer fedora, gestured up at Yosemite Falls, which, thanks to the hard winter, flowed abundantly that July. The party enjoyed a trout lunch in the Mariposa Grove. Then they headed back down to meet the train. Their time driving to the park, experiencing it, and driving back totaled a mere nine hours. FDR's visit to Yosemite had been a lot less strenuous than Theodore's backcountry expedition with John Muir in 1903, or Eleanor's with Lorena Hickok in 1934. Apart from the time limits imposed by a crowded political schedule, it had to be that way; because of his disability, Roosevelt could only have seen Yosemite by road.

Franklin D. Roosevelt visits Yosemite, 1938

By the time of FDR's visit, the national CCC was changing its structure, its educational mission, and, to some degree, the kind of work it did. In 1937, education-job training was upgraded to an equal priority with physical labor. Having transitioned early on from active-duty army officers to reserve officers, camp leadership changed again in 1939, when Roosevelt signed an executive order putting the camps under civilian direction. The overwhelming majority of camp leaders remained reserve officers, though, serving now out of uniform in their civilian capacity. And the army still remained in overall control.

Meantime, the expense of the program was on Roosevelt's mind. The annual cost of a CCC man to the taxpayers was $1,004, equivalent to $19,000 today. Each individual performed work whose value far exceeded the cost.[16] Adding the multiplier – that five out of every six dollars in pay went to support the rest of the enrollee's family – the value received per dollar spent was remarkable.

Leery of running persistent federal deficits, though, and confident the economy would continue recovering even if government spending fell, in 1937 Roosevelt ordered broad cutbacks in outlays for emergency relief and public works. This included shrinking expenditures for the CCC; the authorized size of the Corps would drop from 300,000 to 260,000. A hundred camps would have to close.[17] What followed the president's turn toward fiscal orthodoxy, though, was the recession of 1937-1938. The unemployment rate shot up again. Back in 1935, the CCC had labored unsuccessfully in trying to fill all its available slots; enrollment peaked at half a million men. Now, reverting to the pattern of 1933, the Corps again had more applicants than it could handle. The president decided to pump money back into the program.

The same year he experimented with cutting its budget, FDR launched a campaign to make the Civilian Conservation Corps a permanent feature of American life. At the outset of 1937, he asked Congress to transform the CCC into a federal agency enrolling some three hundred thousand men. Roosevelt made this request at a time when the bipartisan popularity of the Corps had reached its zenith. But the program, despite its striking popularity, had always had a pack of enemies doggedly snapping at its heels. Some attacked it, as we have seen, as a nascent paramilitary force. Others attacked it for the very act of lowering unemployment, which, so the complaint went, drove up private sector wages. One ironic obstacle to permanence was that the CCC from beginning to end had an *image* of temporariness. It was originally conceived, organized, and budgeted as an emergency program – Emergency Conservation Work – to cope with the Depression so long as the unemployment situation warranted.[18] The proposal for permanence also got tangled up with Roosevelt's failing attempt to expand the Supreme Court, which produced an epic political battle that left him weakened. In any case – after enough bickering to prove that congressional dysfunctionality does not belong exclusively to the twenty-first century – Congress could reach agreement only on an extension of three years.

Given its popularity, and despite the obstacles at the time, the 1937 failure to secure a permanent CCC came as a genuine surprise. In 1939, the idea arose again. All that resulted was renewal of the program from year to year. People who today ask, "Why don't we have a Civilian Conservation Corps now?" can look back to the late 1930s and early 1940s, when the Corps actually existed, for the germ of an answer. Roosevelt was a political genius; he had created the Corps; he retained a Democratic Congress; the CCC was the New Deal's most popular program; yet even in those ideal-seeming circumstances, the drive for permanence failed.

***

On the evidence that survives, during the New Deal's early phase, CCC men returned in overwhelming numbers to the unemployment rolls once they left the Corps.[19] Even Al Monteverde, who genuinely enjoyed the experience, wrote: "If I was *sure* of getting a job I *sure* would quit the C.C.'s."[20] What would he do next, though? Pursue photography some way? Join the army? – in 1935, Al considered that.[21] After John Ricci left the Corps in 1936, he struggled to find steady work. He and a buddy from the CCC hopped a freight train across the country, all the way to Seattle. Nothing. They hitchhiked south to Los Angeles. Still nothing. Down to their last few dollars, in the end they hopped freight cars all the way back to New Jersey.[22]

With Help Wanted signs few to nonexistent, a great many men understandably stayed on in the Corps for as long as they possibly could. Between 1933 and 1937, the unemployment rate did drop from 25 percent to 14 percent. The downturn of 1937-1938, though, spiked the rate back to 19 percent. After that, jobs in the private sector began to multiply again as the country started gearing up for war.

With federal resources being reallocated toward national defense, funding for the CCC fell once again after 1939. The 1940 recruitment quota failed to be met even so, and desertion rates were high. By the end of 1941, nationwide enrollment had dropped below 120,000 and the number of camps had shrunk considerably The dwindling number of camps in the national parks dramatically compromised new and ongoing projects.[23] The pain this caused was intense because the National Park Service had long since come to depend on the program – not only as a massive shot in the arm for desirable projects, but even to maintain existing essential services. By as early as 1935, the park service had more than doubled its own personnel just to meet its assigned responsibilities connected with CCC operations.[24]

That same year, 1935, NPS officials estimated that both forestry and development inside the parks had already advanced by one to two decades thanks to the Civilian Conservation Corps. In retrospect, we can see that this early appraisal only suggested what the final impact would turn out to be. The CCC, as John C. Paige has put it, "was in large part responsible" for the national and state parks as we know them today.[25] By the late 'thirties, though, the pre-New Deal age of austerity was starting to return.

Yet still the work went on. During 1938, CCC men planted tens of thousands of willow cuttings along the Wawona Road. A report from spring 1940 recorded seventy-three thousand more willow cuttings having gone into the ground along the Wawona and Big Oak Flat roads, with tens of thousands more to come. The plants both stabilized and beautified the roadsides. They could not just be stuck in the ground and abandoned, though. They had to be watered until they took hold, which involved tank trucks assisting a great deal of follow-up labor.[26]

In late 1938, much of Yosemite's CCC energy went into gathering trees and shrubs for display at the Golden Gate International Exposition of 1939-1940 – a world's fair staged on San Francisco's Treasure Island. The specimens included a thirty-eight-foot, twelve-ton Yellow pine.[27] Jack Gilpin, a heavy equipment operator based at Camp Cascades, recalled trenching around manzanitas so as to preserve their root systems. The specimens were then boxed and craned onto flatbed trucks.[28] One can only imagine what went into extracting and hauling a twelve-ton pine.

On through 1940 and into 1941, new undertakings continued – residential construction, landscaping, trail building, insect eradication, campground projects (including stone fire circles and a new restroom in Camp 14), preparation and planting of cuttings, minor infrastructure, demolition – all entirely familiar by now. In 1940, following precedent in the Tuolumne campground, the CCC began to set off and individualize campsites in Yosemite Valley so as to provide a break for the vegetation and control campers' impulse to crowd together cheek by jowl, what Charles Thomson had called tenement camping.

***

By now, Camp Wawona had long since become a sort of Dixie outpost, belting out Carter Family tunes. The men of Company 2548, stationed there in 1936-1937, had been quite diverse in their states of origin. In October 1937, though, Company 487 – originally from Bessemer, Alabama, a steel town – arrived. The new men called themselves Wabamans. The camp band was the Wabama Wythm Wascals. The newspaper got renamed the *Wabama News*. Full of joshing y'alls, it referred to the place as "this li'l bit of Alabama at Wawona."[29] As time went on, newly arriving rookies continued to overwhelmingly hail from the South – Alabama, smatterings from Mississippi, Georgia, and Florida, a few from Tennessee. Toward the end of its life, though, a notable number of Hispanic names appeared on the company rosters alongside all the Anglo southern ones.

In CCC camps around the country, one might sometimes have thought the Civil War had never ended. Northerners would get into fights with Southerners in camp. This kind of tension appears to have led John Ricci's company to be moved from Vicksburg, Mississippi – site of one of Grant's greatest Union victories – to California. Because so many members of Company 487 came from the South, the Civil War-Reconstruction movie saga *Gone with the Wind* made an especially big hit with them after its 1939 release. Whole groups of men went to see it.[30] The prior year, some men had been lucky enough to get tickets to the Rose Bowl game – the California Golden Bears vs. the Alabama Crimson Tide. Sadly for the Wabamans, Cal shut out Alabama 13-0.

Two years later, Eleanor Roosevelt made a second visit to Yosemite. Accompanied by Malvina "Tommy" Thompson, the First Lady was in the park April 5-8, 1940. Tommy Thompson was one of the New Deal's numerous characters. Indispensable as ER's scheduler and travel assistant, she smoked incessantly, drank Scotch, and had a fine sense of humor. Together, they traveled up to forty thousand miles a year inspecting New Deal relief projects.

On April 6, they spent the afternoon with Company 487. Camp Wawona had earned recognition as a particularly outstanding one, making it a fitting place to visit. Since the CCC was observing its seventh anniversary, everyone celebrated. In her regular newspaper column, My Day, ER recorded that Captain Rockwell (born in Savannah) and most of his men were Southerners.[31] The camp paper also recorded the occasion, noting that the First Lady showed an interest in the men and the camp that "was not the polite and perfunctory interest of a guest. She inspected the camp with the keenest enthusiasm." Omnivorously curious as always, she inquired about any possible problems, the education program, the economic prospects of the men, vocational placement, and a good deal more. In a camp paper editorial, enrollee John Doyle described ER as someone "who has an unswerving and dynamic faith in youth. One who knows American youth of all social levels, in all walks of life." He lauded the way she "goes to bat" for young people, and noted how his campmates felt at ease with her.[32]

***

Eleanor Roosevelt visits Camp Wawona, 1940

By the time of Eleanor Roosevelt's 1940 visit, change was in the offing for the CCC. Despite all the early efforts to douse the military connotation it aroused in nervous minds on the political right and especially the left, Douglas MacArthur did propose to Congress in 1935 that the Corps be used for direct military recruiting. Franklin D. Roosevelt considered the power-craving MacArthur to be one of the very most dangerous men in America.[33] CCC director Fechner jumped in to denounce the idea. Although the proposal was shot down, the concept never went away. Once the country began gearing up for war, the CCC was integrated into the defense program. Thus, by the fall of 1940 – though not given combat training – men were receiving other forms of training and education that would be useful in wartime; some were being transferred to defense work as such. Eventually, basic drill became universal in the CCC. Well before Pearl Harbor, a good many Corps projects had begun to focus on war preparation.

For Yosemite, the falling CCC budget in 1940-1941 and a dwindling number of men spelled the closure of the park's two summer-occupied camps, Crane Flat and Middle Fork, after they had already gotten up and running in 1941. Two others, Empire Meadow and Tamarack Flat, had not been reopened at all. Diminished numbers of men set back projects of all kinds, from forestry work to sewerage excavation. The park service had to hire regular laborers from the outlying area for Ribes eradication and other jobs. The remaining men at Cascades and Wawona were put to work battling infestations of a different invasive plant – exotic thistle, foreign to the North American continent. Crews had taken out one hundred twenty-three thousand thistle plants by that July.[34]

By September 1941, the Cascades camp was down to one hundred-eight men, Wawona down to ninety-one. Each had once hosted twice this number. Superintendent Kittredge reported that "low strength at both camps has drastically limited all activities." That month, stub camps at Tenaya and Ostrander lakes were evacuated. For want of men, work on the ski jump at Badger Pass that had been proceeding well came to a halt. The human shortage brought the park administration's remaining priorities for the Corps into high relief. These included the continuing battle against thistles; lesser work at Badger Pass; and splitting rustic-architecture roof shakes from reclaimed beetle-infested wood. By October, the number of men had further dwindled to eighty-six at Cascades and forty-eight at Wawona, a total of one hundred thirty-four. That month, both camps devoted themselves entirely to fighting a terrific fire in Merced Canyon, ignited when a tree falling in high wind near Arch Rock brought down a power line. By the time it ended, the fire had consumed 1,335 acres.[35]

Something else happened that October that foretold the direction things were headed. Close to two thousand army and navy personnel visited Yosemite. It was not the first occasion members of the armed forces had come to the park in numbers, but the trend was underlined this time when artillerymen posed at Tunnel View with two howitzers.[36]

In late November 1941, Camp Wawona was abandoned. Only Cascades remained occupied. Local labor was now being hired to finish off multiple projects that the CCC, due to dwindling manpower, had left hanging. The Corps stuck to what projects it could still carry out, but things kept getting harder; in December, Cascades fell to sixty-six men.[37]

That month, immediately on the heels of declaring war on the Axis powers, Roosevelt backed a bill to merge the CCC and the National Youth Administration – a big program set up in 1935 that employed teenagers and young adults regardless of gender – into a new Civilian Youth Administration. The man who introduced the bill in the House of Representatives was Texas congressman Lyndon Johnson. As presidents, FDR and Johnson were the two greatest legislative masters of the twentieth century. But with the Civilian Youth Administration, they failed. Congress gave the National Youth Administration one additional year, while voting to terminate the CCC straightaway. Had FDR lived, he might have tried yet again. In 1964, the Johnson Administration established the Job Corps. A clear descendant of the CCC, it benefited two million young people over the following six decades, albeit far fewer than the Civilian Conservation Corps had in just nine years.[38]

In Yosemite, the CCC had a staccato ending. As early as the beginning of 1941, men were being honorably discharged to join the army. That January, Cascades saw two of its foremen called up. Work continued as always, but everything was off-kilter. Five supervisors oversaw just sixty-two men, and the loss of the foremen signaled the beginning of additional transfers. As CCC crews labored on utilities work in a residential section of the valley, their numbers kept on dwindling. By April 1942, thirty-two remained at Cascades – about enough to fill a high school classroom. Many times that number of military personnel visited the park the same month, whether for rest and recreation or possibly scouting facilities and terrain for such needs as testing tanks at high altitude.[39]

Still the men kept at it, taking up a construction project on the museum, starting work on a new valley campground comfort station, excavating, doing cleanup – in other words, carrying out Yosemite CCC work. If the Corps was going down, it was going down with the flags up. In fact, in June, Camp Wawona was reoccupied by a company of a hundred men from Oklahoma. When a 36,000-acre fire erupted outside the park that month, Yosemite's CCC crews rolled out just as they always had to take it on.[40]

In July, the congressional thumbs-down at last caught up with the Civilian Conservation Corps in Yosemite. The Cascades and Wawona camps had revived their numbers to a remarkable combined total of two hundred forty-five men, overseen by a meager five supervisors. But it was the end. By early August 1942, the CCC had passed into Yosemite history.[41]

[9]
WHAT CAME AFTERWARD

Though many decades have passed, and we now live in another century, what transpired in Yosemite during the 1930s retains an ability to astonish. It astonishes us, first, because so many of the pressing issues then remain pressing issues now. Yosemite was originally set aside out of a conviction that it was simply too grand to destroy. During the New Deal, Yosemite became a focal point for confronting three questions: How can a place this precious be accessible to the public *without* being destroyed? How can it be protected from the forces of nature itself (and where should that stop)? And what should a national park actually *be?*

In wrestling with these questions, answers materialized both from Washington (especially FDR and Harold Ickes) and from inside the park itself (especially Charles Thomson). Resolution of the issues depended then, as it does now, upon ongoing human decisions. Meantime another great, related question has arisen out of that era which still remains ominously open in the twenty-first century. Can an ecosystem be permanently stabilized and preserved – the aspiration of the 1930s – and to what degree in an era of climate change?

The historic answer to yet another question – what does the federal government owe to the American people? – was turned on its head by the New Deal. The thousands of poor men and women who passed through Yosemite, constructing everything from campgrounds to bridges paid for by a surge of federal dollars, made the point. No subsequent president has ever shown the sheer audacity in an economic crisis that Roosevelt did; but the COVID-19 pandemic which took down the American economy in 2020 revealed that the impulse to provide relief has now become bipartisan. The remaining debate is no longer about whether, but about how much and to whom.

More than any other program in Yosemite, the Civilian Conservation Corps proved how much priorities had altered under the New Deal. The core mission of the CCC was to conserve young men and to conserve forests. Judging from the later lives of the men this book has followed, the program succeeded superbly.

For most enrollees, their next milestone following the Great Depression was World War II. We look back on them today as part of what we now call, with a generous measure of awe, the Greatest Generation.

As it turned out, CCC life – group existence, hard work, discipline, taking orders, physical fitness – translated well into military service. As an army major, Mark Clark helped oversee CCC operations during the 1930s. By the end of the war, he commanded Allied forces in Italy. Clark later said of the CCC: "Though we did not realize it at the time, we were training Non-Commissioned Officers."[1] In running the camps, a good many reserve officers learned leadership skills that served them well during the war.

John Ricci joined the army in March 1941. He later recalled that his CCC training translated exceedingly well to military duty, and he was quickly promoted to sergeant. He served initially stateside as a drill and training instructor. Transferred to Europe with the 71st Infantry Division, John saw a good deal of action during the final two months of the war and in mopping-up operations afterward. As it advanced, the 71st liberated a sequence of concentration camps. In later years, he never spoke about the war.

Afterward, John returned to civilian life, initially doing metallurgical work. Later, he became a port security guard in New York and New Jersey for Holland America and the Maersk Line, retiring at sixty-six in 1980. Looking back, he considered his CCC years to have been the best of his life. Taken with the beauty of Yosemite, he had had a wonderful time as a fire warden there. He stayed in touch with CCC buddies, and would speak "lovingly," as his son recalls, of their days together. John enjoyed travel, horse races and collecting coins. A quiet man for the most part, he relished big family gatherings, which would draw him out. He died in 1986, in the midst of a conversation with some of his nieces and nephews.[2]

Following twenty months in the CCC, Al Monteverde returned to Los Angeles, where he landed a darkroom job with International News Photos. He quickly moved up to photographing major news stories. Volunteering for military duty during World War II, Al distinguished himself as a Marine combat photographer in the South Pacific, where he headed the photo section of the 1st Marine Division. He was awarded the Purple Heart. After the war, he became a news photographer for a sequence of papers that included the *Los Angeles Times* – a career so noteworthy that it led to numerous awards and nomination for a Pulitzer Prize. In his spare time, Al cut and polished stones, made fine jewelry, and read a great deal of history.

In 1987, Al sat down with a pad of yellow paper and began to write a memoir of his days in the CCC, integrating many of his photos from the 1930s with the text. Well-written, straightforward, and witty, it is a classic account of the CCC experience in and around Yosemite. Al visited every national park in the United States. Yosemite always held a unique place, though, as it still does for his family on down to his great-grandchildren – a love of the park spanning five generations. A black-and-white photo of the fire lookout tower he had worked on, which still stands today, always hung in his home. As his daughter writes, "it all began because Albert F. Monteverde joined the Civilian Conservation Corps and, as a result, was blessed enough to call Yosemite home for twenty months."[3] Al died at eighty-one in 1996.

In 1941, Joe Bryan returned to Sanderson, Florida. Thanks to classes he had taken in the CCC, he was able to graduate that year with his high school class. While sending home twenty-five dollars each month, he had been saving the other five, and when he returned home he bought a used 1936 Plymouth. This made him one of just a few in the region who owned a car.

Like John Ricci, Joe recalled that CCC life made the transition to wartime military duty easy; he already knew a lot of the expectations and routines. The practical skills he had learned in the Corps helped too, such that he first found a job on a Florida military base as a civilian. He served in the army from 1943 to 1945. During the last stages of the European war, he drove trucks carrying portable bridges that could quickly be thrown across rivers as Allied units moved forward. After the war, Joe briefly returned to farming, then enlisted in the Air Force and later the Air Force Reserve. He had a long career as a senior master sergeant, retiring in 1983. Joe loved to talk about the CCC, calling those times "Happy Days." Always a Floridian, he lived until 1991.[4]

During World War II, Alf Bergly served as an army cook, a job for which his time in the CCC had helped prepare him. Before and then again after the war, he worked in Yosemite, including at The Ahwahnee and Badger Pass. Before he was finished, he had risen from general kitchen staff to baker. It was after returning from Europe to Yosemite following the war that he met his future wife, Ethel, who was also a park employee; they married in 1946. The couple moved to Washington State, where Alf's father (who had relocated there from North Dakota) trained him to be a brick and stone mason. Alf was highly skilled at the trade. Among other things, he had a quick mind for geometric calculations.

Alf had left school after eighth grade, which seems to have later affected his self-esteem; but he continued to learn on his own. He was a reader, with a curiosity about history. The family settled on a farm out in the country. While rebuilding the farmhouse, an almost unending project, Alf pursued other interests that included an avid love of fishing. He always enjoyed a good party, and, like a lot of men and women of his generation, was a fine dancer. As he had during his time in the CCC, he carried on with photography. Alf Bergy died at ninety-four in 2014. He left a bequest to the Lutheran church in Reynolds, North Dakota, which had helped his family get through his mother's untimely death so many years before.[5]

The later story of a CCC man we have only brushed with is well worth recounting, if only because the twists and turns would have delighted FDR. Clair Nelsen left the Corps, after a couple of years he had enjoyed, to take a job offered by the Forest Service. Having learned to drive a truck in the Corps – "a long sought honor" – he made a living for a time operating a dump truck. In the CCC, he had picked up enough knowledge of explosives to be rated as a demolition expert when he went into the Marine Corps in 1942. Later, Nelsen would earn a Ph.D. from Stanford, go on to a career as a professor of history at Fresno State, and be named a Fulbright Scholar.[6]

What became of the others whose stories make up this book? Heart attacks cut short the lives of many. During the early twentieth century, heart attacks claimed victims all the time, to a degree that amazes us in the twenty-first century world of aortic valve replacements, bypass surgery, and heart transplants (not to mention awareness of diet and the hazards of smoking). Charles Thomson's fatal heart attack had been the first. He was followed by Robert Fechner, sixty-three, on the last day of 1939, and Arno Cammerer, fifty-seven, in 1941. A heart attack took Forest Townsley, sixty, in 1943, while on a fishing trip to Townsley Lake. He had been a favorite of Eleanor Roosevelt's. That same year, Don Tresidder was named the fourth president of Stanford University. He guided the school out of the aftereffects of the Great Depression, through the student deficit of World War II, and into the postwar flood of returning GIs. He died of a heart attack at age fifty-three in 1948. Tresidder Memorial Union is today a hub of campus life at Stanford. Tresidder Peak memorializes him in Tuolumne Meadows.

Franklin D. Roosevelt is recognized by historians as the pivotal president of the twentieth century and as one of the three authentically great presidents in American history (with Washington and Lincoln). Following the political stalemate that stymied his administration in the late 1930s, he won an unprecedented third term in 1940 and a fourth in 1944. His reputation for leadership rests upon two massive pillars – as the transformative domestic president of the New Deal, and as America's wartime leader in the greatest conflict ever fought. He did not live to see its end. Roosevelt died at sixty-three of a cerebral hemorrhage on April 12, 1945.

Eleanor Roosevelt carried on the legacy – his and her own – until her passing in 1962 at age seventy-eight, following a health collapse brought on by a complex of causes. There had never been another First Lady like her, nor has there since. Traditionalists groused that FDR could not "keep his missus at home," but on the road, through the airwaves, and in her daily column, she was a critically important ambassador for the New Deal. ER's influence on her husband made him a better president. Her advocacy of social justice for African Americans and women – and for the downtrodden in general – was far ahead of public attitudes. It won her widespread admiration and widespread disdain; she was one of the most polarizing figures of her time. Appointed as an American delegate to the fledgling United Nations after World War II, she steered through the landmark 1948 Universal Declaration of Human Rights. The declaration stands as a memorial to her life.

Harold Ickes continued on as Secretary of the Interior until 1946, playing a vital part in wartime administration. Combative as ever, he got into a scrap with Roosevelt's successor, Harry Truman. Ickes submitted a scalding letter of resignation.

Every bit as prickly as Ickes, Truman accepted it with gusto. Ickes's difficult marriage to his first wife, Anna, had ended tragically when she died in a car crash in 1935. Three years later, at sixty-four, he married Jane Dahlman, then in her mid-twenties. One of their children, also named Harold, became Deputy Chief of Staff to President Bill Clinton. The senior Harold Ickes died of a heart attack in 1952.

***

Yosemite benefited immeasurably from the New Deal. Nothing of comparable scale has happened since. In retrospect, it is also obvious that much of what was done then would never be done today. The transformation Roosevelt's programs brought about originated in the conservation philosophy of the late nineteenth and early twentieth centuries – that conservation meant protecting a resource while also using it. Conservation included roads and dams and fish-planting and skiing. We have watched that philosophy start to tip by the mid-1930s toward today's greater focus on Yosemite as an unadorned resource in itself, a vast and unique natural wonder.[7] We have seen change take place in the minds of Harold Ickes, Charles Thomson, and the wilderness advocates. The tipping *point* was there, but the change itself would take many more years. In fact, it still continues, as do the old disagreements over degrees and methods.

While much that it achieved in Yosemite proved fleeting, and some of it misguided in today's thinking, the New Deal's legacies – roads, bridges, buildings, beautification projects – still serve millions of visitors each year. Stephen Mather might be stunned that four and a half million people came to Yosemite in 2019, or that five million did in 2016. During his era, the park struggled to accommodate just half a million. New Deal infrastructure was built to last, though, and now handles numbers unimagined in the 1930s. The democratic ideal for the national parks – FDR's great goal – was for the American people to be able to visit and enjoy the unique places that they own in common. At a time when travel from a widening array of states was news, Don Tresidder wanted to welcome visitors from around world. Now Yosemite does. The more democratic and welcoming it became, though, the more crowded Yosemite became, and the greater the pressure on its resources.

With the onrush of visitors, the democratic ideal changed somewhat. One of my most indelible memories of Yosemite is of an incident that occurred around

1949 or 1950. In a very untraveled place, my mother and I stumbled across the most astonishing large American Indian relic I have ever seen in the park. What immediately followed was spooky. Out of nowhere, a park official of some sort rode up on horseback. He said, "Now that you've found it, don't tell anyone else." Then he rode off. (Having promised, I cannot elaborate further.)

Up to that time, and for long afterwards, the spirit of the park was permissive. You spotted an arrowhead, you collected it. You noticed a rusting shovel inside a decaying sheepherder's cabin, you took it. A quartz crystal attached to a rock? Break it off; if you didn't, somebody else would. Campers in Tuolumne Meadows spotted an osprey – also known as a fish hawk – snatching trout out of a favorite lake. The bird disappeared; I recall hearing that rangers had taken care of the "problem."

Such practices have of course changed. The park, it turns out, can be *too* open, *too* welcoming. The balance between resource use and resource preservation has had to be recalibrated. Just as free-form camping came to an end in Tuolumne Meadows in the 'thirties because it could not continue, a new ethic materialized in which the resources must be protected against human onslaught, wear and tear, and ordinary vandalism. The battle to protect the Grizzly Giant, using anything from shrub barriers to barbed wire, was a precursor. The same for human artifacts. Decades after finding them, I donated the collection of arrowheads I had gathered in the park to the Yosemite Museum.

Fish are no longer planted in Yosemite. From the late nineteenth century up to the late twentieth, an estimated thirty-three million nonnative fish were stocked within today's park boundaries. During the early 'fifties, planting by mule gave way to stocking by plane. The Happy Isles hatchery closed in 1956 and was turned into a nature center. In Tuolumne Meadows, a time limit on camping imposed during the 1960s broke up the old fishing culture there. The park was no longer the fishing mecca it had once been anyway. As the joke went at the time, it really did seem as though there were more fishers than fish. Planting in the park came to an end in 1990.

The war against infestations like bark beetle that attacked the forests has changed, too. The demise of the CCC left a gaping deficit of people to do things in Yosemite like digging up Ribes or stripping off tree bark. In 1944, initial experiments took place within the park using a new insecticide, DDT. In the long history of chemical warfare against tree-destroying organisms, DDT offered the possibility of a transformative weapon, the atomic bomb of forestry. During the postwar era, the weapon was used. Starting in 1947, crews attacked an epidemic of needle-miner in the high country by spraying DDT from hand pumps. Fixed-wing aircraft sprayed from overhead in 1948 and 1953. I recall what were likely repurposed World War II bombers roaring over the Tuolumne campground. It was an exciting, unearthly experience to see the planes, but the DDT was just a familiar chemical compound. It was freely available for household use. I sprayed it myself. As an insecticide, it worked wonders. Then, in 1962, Rachel Carson published one of the most important books ever written about the environment, *Silent Spring.*[8] She showed that DDT worked too well; it threatened fish and birds, and also, on the evidence, humans.

I can remember encountering blister rust crews ripping out currant and gooseberry as late as the 1950s, but in the 1960s the crews, too, vanished. Blister rust, it turned out, was somewhat less threatening than had been feared in the 1930s; and so instead, it began to be surveyed and monitored.[9] But if it was not quite the equivalent of Dutch elm disease or chestnut blight, that did not make it benign. Today, blister rust has spread all across the United States and Canada. It had infected thirty-eight states by 2020, and is still spreading. In Yosemite, the hallmark timberline tree is the Whitebark pine, a member of the five-needle White pine family. Anxiety has risen about the future survival of Whitebarks. Blister rust, beetles, and drought have attacked them across the West, to the point that by 2018 more than half of all Whitebarks were estimated to be dead. Trying to figure out how to defeat blister rust, scientists gravitated toward planting replacement trees raised from Whitebark seeds harvested from fungus-resistant adults.[10] In the meantime, the forest pandemic that scientists and CCC crews struggled with through the early twentieth century goes on.

There is a stunning twist to the story which, in hindsight, is ironic enough to make one wince. Charles Thomson, as we have seen, held deep reservations about uprooting currant and gooseberry bushes all around Yosemite. Instead, he recommended research into the interaction between Ribes and the park's other plant and animal communities. What was known in the 1930s was that the complex life cycle of blister rust required two hosts – a White pine and a Ribes plant. Recently, two additional, alternate hosts have been identified: snapdragon and Indian paintbrush.[11] Indian paintbrush is an attractive, innocent-looking plant with a red flower. It is everywhere in Yosemite, with a range from two thousand to eleven thousand feet. As early as the CCC's first summer in the park, while many enrollees were methodically uprooting currant and gooseberry, other men were collecting Indian paintbrush seeds for propagation as a desirable variety of wildflower.

While various non-chemical methods are used to control it elsewhere, nothing is done in Yosemite about blister rust today, and the same is true of bark beetle. How best to cope with the beetle is still debated, while, thanks to climate change and related drought, the problem only grows worse. There is a general sense that forests go through phases; that, as in Yosemite, they can easily grow too dense; and that they thin themselves, often with the aid of "pests." We can view all this in two different ways. On one hand, without blister rust crews scouring the woods and planes rumbling overhead raining spray, Yosemite is a far less tended and more natural place than it was decades ago. On the other hand, blister rust and drought brought on by human-induced climate change are as unnatural to that setting as can be.

The big exception to today's more laissez-faire, less labor-intensive world of forest management is fire. In keeping with theories of forestry prevalent at the time, the CCC fought fires with a fervor. That commonsensical approach has led to overgrowth that has made forests more vulnerable to fire, and on an even more disastrous scale. John Bingaman, one of the most prominent Yosemite rangers of his era, published a classic memoir in 1961 about the history of the park and his own experiences from the nineteen-teens to the 'fifties. "The Indians," he observed, "used to set fires to clear out the underbrush so it was made easier for their hunting. Who knows? They may have had the answer." Right around the time Bingaman published his book, fire theory was beginning to change. Today, controlled burns are routinely used to thin growth in Yosemite. Bingaman also paid a powerful, heartfelt tribute to the CCC crews that fought forest fires.[12] Those crews would surely be welcome now, in the age of climate change. The fire that erupted near Arch Rock in October 1941 – described at the time as the biggest anyone could remember – consumed 1,335 acres.[13] The Creek Fire of 2020, which threatened Wawona, consumed 379,895 acres.

With the effects of climate change altering Yosemite along with the rest of the planet, the park provides a case study of the broader phenomenon. My wife, Kathy, a former rock climber, began noting the ongoing shrinkage of the Lyell Glacier during her girlhood in the 1950s; today it no longer qualifies as a glacier at all. Rattlesnakes and poison oak now appear in places and at elevations where they weren't before. In January 2012, it was possible to drive clear across the park in dead of winter. On New Year's Day 2014, Kathy and I set off to see how far we could hike up the Yosemite Falls trail before getting blocked by ice and snow. We just kept ascending; nothing stopped us at all, and, once we reached the top of the upper fall, we continued still farther. The experience was disorienting. On the return, another hiker gave us a knowing look and remarked, "Guilty pleasure."

The National Park Service has always been dedicated to preserving America's natural heritage. Change in some degree is innate in the natural world. Even so, policies, including those of the New Deal era, have been grounded on the assumption that environmental transitions will take place within relatively narrow, historically defined boundaries. Climate change has upended this assumption.

By the early twenty-first century, the National Park Service was conceding that, in an age of warming, conservation grounded on old historical models must quickly and urgently give way to new management techniques triaging what could be saved and determining how. Particular attention fell on forests, so dear to the New Deal generation. Now, fire was burning away huge swaths of trees already killed or weakened by drought and insects.[14] Yosemite National Park has always been perceived as a microcosm of the broader natural world – a laboratory for studying everything from geologic forces to small patches of ground, the way the ranger that Al Monteverde photographed for did. Humans use Yosemite to try to read the future, because the future arrives so intensely there. Today the park serves as a laboratory for studying climate change.

In some important ways, though, Yosemite's environment has improved over the decades. Since the 1930s, for instance, Wawona Meadow has come full circle. The diversion canals dug by the CCC to improve the meadow for livestock grazing and agriculture included more than fifty concrete check dams.[15] These controlled the rate at which water flowed. But check dams are generally built for temporary use, and, if for the longer term, must be regularly maintained in order to avert disintegration, washout, and debris backup. As the dams broke down over the decades, the channels deepened. Water flowed more swiftly, leading to further erosion. When the underlying water table dropped, the meadow dried out and began playing host to invasive non-native plants that were suited to the altered environment. This in turn degraded the habitat for wildlife.

Finally, beginning in 2010 as part of a massive project to restore Wawona Meadow, the park service filled in the ditches and reestablished native flora. The original model for meadow restoration, from the 1930s, was erased by a newer model that turned the clock back as much as possible to how things had been before human habitation. The golf course and decaying rail fences remained as reminders of all that had transpired since. What was referred to in the 1930s as the Meadow Loop Road is now commonly called the Meadow Loop Trail or just the Meadow Loop. The old paving is steadily rotting away.

The modern road network that spans the park had largely reached completion by the end of the New Deal era, but not quite all of it. The twenty-one miles from McSwain Meadows to Cathedral Creek remained to be done. A possible "High Line" route that Charles Thomson originally favored due to its spectacular scenery would have run past Mount Hoffmann and on to the remote Ten Lakes Basin and Tuolumne Canyon. The New Deal built iconic high-elevation summit routes like these in various national parks, most famously Skyline Drive in Shenandoah National Park and Glacier's Going to the Sun Highway. In the end, though, after a great deal of reflection, Thomson changed his mind; the High Line would simply inflict too much damage on the park's backcountry wilderness to justify a stunning travel experience. The High Line was also opposed by the Bureau of Public Roads and the Sierra Club, and was rejected by the National Park Service.[16] Instead, the decision was made for a highway passing along the northern side of Tenaya Lake, and from there in the direction of Yosemite Valley across a great deal of exposed granite. Preliminary plans were laid, but not totally finalized. Completion of the project was expected by the late 'thirties. It kept being pushed back, though. Federal funding never came through, and so the whole thing was delayed not just for the remainder of the 1930s, but through the 1940s and well into the 1950s.[17]

With gasoline rationed during World War II, Yosemite tourism plunged. So did the annual budget of the National Park Service. Between 1940 and 1945, it plummeted from $35,000,000 to under $5,000,000.[18] At a time when the national parks were stretched even to cover basic firefighting, the war spelled the suspension of roadbuilding. or even road master planning. Landscape engineering dissipated. With the New Deal's funding and labor supply just a memory, park budgets no longer supported the rustic architectural theme. Pressure even arose to raze rustic buildings because of the cost of maintaining them.[19] The new prevailing trend favored a genre that might be called low-budget utilitarian. At one of the most prominent road intersections in the Tuolumne campground, for instance, a restroom went up during the 1950s that resembles something you might find in a poor town's public park. It remains in use today.

Tuolumne Meadows campground restroom construction, 1930s (above) vs. 1950s (below)

In time, the priorities of the 1950s superseded those of the 1930s in ways that are perfectly visible today. The 1950s – the Eisenhower Era – was a far different time from the 1930s. While it is looked back on today as a golden age of economic expansion, there was also a general sense of cheapening. People complained that new cars were "tinny." Houses built one-at-a-time gave way to mass-produced suburbs. Objects like toys, once made of sturdy metal or wood, were now manufactured out of breakable plastic. Family dinners became TV dinners. Social critics lamented the decline of authenticity. In essence, the spirit of the 1950s was, *just get it done.* By the time that road construction finally restarted in Yosemite, the priority of harmonizing roadways with landscapes had declined dramatically.[20] How dramatically would soon be demonstrated.

Throughout the park, the new roads built during the FDR years had become choked with traffic by the 1950s. I recall it well, because from 1959 to 1964 I had a summer job working at gasoline stations in the valley and at Tuolumne Meadows. It wasn't hard to fill up during those years. The valley had three stations; Tuolumne got a brand-new one to replace a station left over from the Roosevelt era. (I helped mix the concrete.) In Yosemite Valley, which had already smelled of petroleum back in the 1920s, the air during the 1950s and '60s was thick with smog. I contributed my personal quota (and likewise to global warming), especially while horsing a roaring tow truck around on rescue missions. The park was accommodating levels of auto travel that had once seemed unimaginable – except perhaps in the worried mind of Charles Thomson. Accommodating auto travel, that is, except at one long choke point – the unfinished twenty-one miles of the Tioga Road between McSwain Meadows and Cathedral Creek.

Within the Sierra Club, some members began to take another look at the organization's support for completing the unfinished stretch of the Tioga Road. One argument held that the serpentine old route, with its speed limit of twenty-five miles per hour, should remain in place with only marginal improvements. Likewise, many old-time campers in Tuolumne who prized the isolation of the high country feared completion of a trans-Sierra highway that would provide a through route between California and Nevada. Of Yosemite's one million annual visitors in the mid-1950s, scarcely more than thirty thousand drove across the Tioga Road. But if it was modernized, the campers and some in the Sierra Club feared, people would take the highway not to enjoy the park, but simply to get from point A to point B.

Work on the final leg of the route was initiated under the Mission 66 program. Since the end of the CCC, hardly any development had occurred in Yosemite. After years of shoestring national park budgets, the situation around the country had grown desperate. The goal of Mission 66 was to make investments in the parks over a ten-year span climaxing in 1966, the fiftieth anniversary of the National Park Service. Visitor and camping accommodations would be improved, as would infrastructure and roads. The design philosophy that would guide development under Mission 66 represented what has been called "a radical departure from the Rustic-style heritage of the National Park Service."[21] It was functional; it was technological; it was modern. In 1956, the new Yosemite Lodge complex opened for guests, and soon as well the "mall" housing the Village Store and other concessions. In both places, tedious mid-twentieth century modernist architecture superseded rustic.

Like the architecture, cars too had changed. Instead of the sedans of the 1930s, the autos of the mid- and late-1950s were ornate fantasy creations, some resembling jet planes or, like the Cadillacs of the era, rockets. Depending on the engine, the descendant of a conventional Chevrolet family sedan of the mid-1930s might easily have twice the horsepower twenty years later, along with an automatic transmission. In 1962 you could buy a Corvette with a 362-horsepower engine, more than four times the power of a standard 1930s sedan. People clamored for speed, and highway designers insisted that the new Tioga Road must be engineered straight enough and wide enough for forty-five miles an hour.

The designated route for the finished twenty-one miles would rise from Tenaya Lake to Olmsted Point across a great gleaming escarpment – one of the finest glaciated granite faces in the park. It is hard to imagine this route getting greenlighted back in the 1930s,[22] given, among other considerations, Harold Ickes's stated opposition to fast highways in the national parks. Ickes had laid down a rule that no additional park roads could be built without his explicit permission. Charles Thomson had warned against letting unalloyed utilitarian instincts dominate road development in Yosemite – what he denounced as the philosophy of "engineering parks to death." He had halted construction along the Wawona Road on account of slipshod practices that included excess blasting, and compelled the contractor to repair the damage.[23]

If the Tenaya-Olmsted Point route had somehow gotten approval in the 1930s, one can only contemplate the cantilevering and other techniques engineers would have called upon to minimize the damage. But this was the 1950s, and now the method of choice was the same, cheaper one that had been used on the original wagon road in the 1880s – dynamite. Having voiced concerns about the Tioga route since 1933 – but then divided and basically dithered over the issue – the Sierra Club finally overcame its internal division sufficiently to stall the destruction in 1958, one year into the project.[24] But it had delayed too long: the reprieve was soon lifted. After that, you could hear the blasting as far away as Tuolumne Meadows. Ansel Adams damned it the way John Muir had condemned Hetch Hetchy.[25]

Blasted route between Olmsted Point and Tenaya Lake, late 1950s – early 1960s

The boiling controversy attracted national attention. Carl Sharsmith and a small corps of other genuinely gifted summer ranger naturalists had played a pivotal part in developing the principles used by the park service for interpreting the natural world to the public. Their campfire programs, hikes, and walks influenced entire generations of Yosemite visitors. At campfire programs in Tuolumne, Sharsmith and his charismatic colleague Will Neely would exhibit glacially polished slabs of the exploded granite as they denounced what was taking place. Their term for Olmsted Point was Desecration Point.

Exploded granite shards (at right)

In 1960, I first met my wife Kathy in Tuolumne Meadows. She needed a ride back to make the morning shift of her summer job at the Glacier Point Hotel. Since we had to drive across the park at night, and the Twenty-One Miles remained slow going, we had plenty of time to get acquainted. A few years later, we tied the knot. In 2021, Kathy spotted remnants of several granite slabs that she had last seen back when Sharsmith and Neely were displaying them – still there after six decades, in Tuolumne's Dana Campfire Circle. In her mind's eye she could still see the rangers unloading the slabs from the back of a truck as if performing a rite, holding them aloft for the assembled audience to see, and then – standing on them – using them as a platform from which to condemn the visual and spiritual carnage being inflicted on Yosemite.

The new stretch of blasted-out highway opened in 1961. To complete the overall modernization project east of the park, the California highway department realigned Lee Vining Grade later in the decade, widening the one-way section at the top and cancelling out the switchbacks. Following the familiar cycle, a better road meant more visitors. The Tuolumne campers had been right about trans-Sierra traffic passing through in a rush. "How many miles to Reno?" became a standard tourist question in Tuolumne Meadows.

I last spent time with Carl Sharsmith in 1983. He was in summer residence at the Ostrander Ski Hut that year, and groups (my family among them) would stay for a week or so to join him on botanical walks. Now and again, he would spontaneously drop to his knees to study a specimen. The hut was just as solid as when the CCC had finished it. Carl, too, remained the same, a delightful raconteur who would, occasionally, return inside himself. A few years later, I asked him how much longer he wanted to work in the park. He smiled and pointed skyward; only heaven knew. He still owned his old Ford. His final season as a summer ranger was 1994. He was the oldest active ranger in the National Park Service. A few weeks after the season ended, he died at ninety-one. An obituary was published in the *New York Times.*[26]

Carl's career had spanned a time when the number of visitors to Yosemite had risen into the millions. Yet, in speaking with a group out in a meadow during that final summer, he said he didn't think Tuolumne had "changed a bit in sixty years."[27] I would offer this, with which he might have agreed: Yosemite is a more *natural* place now than it was in the 1930s. Today, 94 percent of the park is designated wilderness, amounting to over seven hundred thousand acres. In Yosemite Valley, the firefall, bear feeding, and the movies of the 1930s are long gone. Yosemite Valley has no gas stations anymore, nor does Tuolumne Meadows. The rustic style is making a return; at places like Yosemite Falls and Glacier Point, the old style is new again. I expect that CCC men returning to Yosemite today would find the park a little dull compared to the New Deal era. They might also take surprise at the chaos of down timber, snags, brush, and trees encroaching on meadows. Nature can appear disorderly. But it is no longer necessary to attract visitors to the park by making Yosemite more attractive or entertaining. The challenge now is how to cope with their love of the place.

This brings us to a final observation about the contrast between Yosemite during the New Deal era and Yosemite now: that the transition from the earlier park to the one of today climaxed then. As we have seen, the conflict over a more natural park or a more artificial one started to be resolved. So did the problem of striking some balance within the park service's ambiguous mission between protecting the resource and welcoming people to experience it. The Civilian Conservation Corps, the Bureau of Public Roads, and the Public Works Administration surely opened up Yosemite so that more could share the space. That was Franklin Roosevelt's great vision. The remote isolation that Eleanor Roosevelt relished on her trip into the high country in 1934 has also endured. If we sometimes become impatient with today's crowds, we might remind ourselves how many of the things we happily take for granted – roads, campgrounds, trails, buildings – emerged out of the New Deal. We can also be thankful for things not built that could well have been.

We can consider, too, how much a stint of a few months or maybe a year in the park meant to destitute people, most of them young men. On the verge of leaving Camp Wawona in 1941, enrollee Frank Almeda wrote: "I believe I have done myself some good mentally, as well as physically." Frank had taken classes in journalism, typing, and auto mechanics, and had belonged to the drama group. "As time went on we became 'Old Boys.' I made friends and saw them complete their enlistments and leave. I knew some day I too, would leave, but I have not thought much of it until now when it is so close. Somehow, the mountains have gotten into my blood and I'm going to be sorry when I board that train."[28]

In 1936, during the very final months of his hitch in the CCC, Paul Monteverde, Al's brother, was transferred from Santa Barbara to Camp Cascades. Their sister Catalina urged him to return home to Los Angeles. "The beauty of this place has got me!" Paul replied.[29]

As Al wrote late in life, "I thank God we had the CCC's during a time of hardship for so many. I feel I'm a better man for it."[30] Serving a hitch in the CCC at Crane Flat, John Burgess later recalled, "was quite an awakening into the 'real' world at 17 years of age."[31] "Yes, I would do it all over again," Darrel Stover reflected. "I, like so many of the others, inlisted as a teenager and came out a man. And it happened in the most beautiful place in the world, YOSEMITE."[32]

Yosemite National Park captures us today exactly the way it captured these young men then. Like Frank Almeda, we discover that it gets into our blood. If we allow it to, the park can help us become better people. Its ageless glories challenge our culture's preoccupation with status and wealth. Yosemite puts our lives into a different perspective, just as it did for Eleanor Roosevelt and Harold Ickes. The park casts judgment on us, too, for the ways we respond to it and treat it. How *should* humans relate to a unique natural wonder? The question accompanies every single visit to Yosemite, whether or not the visitor is aware. And it is, in microcosm, the greater question of how we should relate to the broader planet.

NOTES

All online sources were accessible as of 2024.

Introduction

1. *Yosemite: The Park and Its Resources; A History of the Discovery, Management, and Physical Development of Yosemite National Park, California, vol. 2, Historical Narrative* (1987; repr., Delhi, India: Facsimile Publisher, [2021]), 735.
2. A manuscript about that era to which I contributed, "Tuolumne Meadows, Barely Discovered: The 1930s through the 1950s" (1986), may be found in the Yosemite Archives.
3. Kim Slowey, "By the Numbers: Women in Construction," https://www.constructiondive.com/news/by-the-numbers-women-in-construction/549359/.
4. For a brief but comprehensive treatment of the New Deal's approach to diverse racial and ethnic groups, see Paul J. Baicich and Richard A. Walker, "How FDR's Original Green New Deal Challenged Jim Crow," https://www.jacobinmag.com/2021/09/fdr-new-deal-racial-equality-jim-crow-america-civilian-conservation-corps.
5. Carl "Mel" Melvin, interview by the author.
6. John C. Paige, *The Civilian Conservation Corps and the National Park Service, 1933-1942: An Administrative History* (Washington, D.C.: National Park Service, 1985), 128.
7. calflora.org.

Driving Across the Park in the Mid-1930s

1. I have employed the term "fall" for ones with a single drop, and "falls" for those with multiple drops. Common usage varies, such that one will see Bridalveil Fall sometimes referenced as Bridalveil Falls.

Chapter I: Yosemite Takes Off in the 1920s

1. New York: 1921, 1928. *Terry* is quoted below from the Kindle edition.
2. Alfred Runte, *Yosemite: The Embattled Wilderness* (Lincoln: University of Nebraska Press, 1990), 184.
3. "An Act Authorizing a Grant to the State of California...," June 30, 1864, https://www.nps.gov/parkhistory/online_books/anps/anps_1a.htm.
4. John Broesamle and Anthony Arthur, *Clashes of Will: Great Confrontations That Have Shaped Modern America* (New York: Pearson Longman, c. 2005), 89.
5. "Report of Yosemite Park Commission," December 5, 1904, https://calisphere.org/item/bb957843227bf4e5299979a140f2229a.
6. Also clumsily but conventionally termed the South Fork Merced River. I similarly refer in this book to the South Fork *of the* Tuolumne River.
7. "An Act Authorizing a Grant to the State of California."
8. "Act to Establish a National Park Service (Organic Act)," August 25, 1916, https://www.nps.gov/grba/learn/management/organic-act-of-1916.htm.
9. H. B. Magill, *Motoring thru the Yosemite* (San Francisco: Yosemite Publishing Co., c. 1926).
10. Runte, *Embattled Wilderness,* 143-44.
11. Horace M. Albright and Robert Cahn, *The Birth of the National Park Service: The Founding Years, 1913-33* (Salt Lake City: Howe Brothers, 1985), 62.
12. Ibid., 264-65.
13. Runte, *Embattled Wilderness,* 94.
14. Ibid., 96.
15. Shirley Sargent, *Yosemite's Innkeepers: The Story of a Great Park and Its Chief Concessionaires,* 2nd rev. ed. (Yosemite, CA: Ponderosa Press, 2000), 55.

16. Monthly Report of the Superintendent, Yosemite National Park, to the Director, National Park Service, U.S. Department of the Interior, Washington, D.C., February 1937, January 1938. Further cited as SMR (superintendent's monthly report).
17. Fernando Peñalosa, *Yosemite in the 1930s: A Remembrance* (Rancho Palos Verdes, CA: Quaking Aspen Books, 2002), 188.
18. The following account of bears is taken from: ibid., 172; SMR, March 1934, September 1936, August 1937; Greene, *Historical Narrative,* 624; Runte, *Embattled Wilderness,* 142, 149, 150; Douglas Brinkley, *Rightful Heritage: Franklin D. Roosevelt and the Land of America* (New York: Harper, c. 2016), 249; Elizabeth Stone O'Neill, *Mountain Sage: The Life Story of Carl Sharsmith, Yosemite Ranger/Naturalist* (Yosemite National Park, CA: Yosemite Association, c. 1988), 139.
19. SMR, August 1934.
20. Albright and Cahn, *Birth of the National Park Service,* 200-02; John W. Bingaman, *Guardians of the Yosemite: A Story of the First Rangers* (Lodi, CA: END-KIAN Publishing, 1970), 50-51; Department of the Interior, *Yosemite National Park, California* (Washington: United States Government Printing Office, 1936), 20.
21. Technically a char not a trout, though commonly thought of as one.
22. SMR, April 1938.
23. Ibid., May 1934, August 1935, April 1937, April 1938.
24. "100 Years of the Rangers' Club,". https://yosemite.org/rangers-club-centennial/.
25. *Seed of the Future: Yosemite and the Evolution of the National Park Idea* (Yosemite National Park: Yosemite Conservancy, c. 2013), 169.
26. National Park Service, *Yosemite National Park Roads and Bridges,* by Richard H. Quin, Historic American Engineering Record CA-117 (Washington: National Park Service, 1991), 67, 69.
27. Ibid., 9; Sargent, *Yosemite's Innkeepers,* 107. Today's Badger Pass Ski Area, developed in the 1930s, was actually constructed at Monroe Meadows, about half a mile from Badger Pass itself.
28. NPS, *Roads and Bridges,* 38, 60-61, 94; Timothy Davis, *National Park*

Roads: A Legacy in the American Landscape (Charlottesville: University of Virginia Press, 2016), 172.

29. NPS, *Roads and Bridges,* 77.
30. One of its members was Frederick Law Olmsted, Jr., like his father a renowned landscape architect.
31. Ibid., 94; Davis, *National Park Roads,* 172-73.
32. Sargent, *Yosemite's Innkeepers,* 101.
33. SMR, September 1937; July, September 1940.
34. *Yosemite in the 1930s,* 45.
35. SMR, July 1933.
36. Now most commonly referred to as "interpretive park rangers."
37. It is true, though, that ranger naturalist positions provided summer jobs for a good many college and high school educators. For many years, the great majority of seasonal naturalists came from the teaching world.
38. O'Neill, *Mountain Sage,* 107, 139; Peñalosa, *Yosemite in the 1930s,* 61.
39. The following paragraphs draw upon: Mark Spence, "Dispossessing the Wilderness: Yosemite Indians and the National Park Ideal, 1864-1930," *Pacific Historical Review* 65, no. 1 (February 1996): 27-59 passim, quotations 52-54; Mark David Spence, *Dispossessing the Wilderness: Indian Removal and the Making of the National Parks* (New York: Oxford University Press, 1999), chs. 7-8 passim; SMR, September 1929; and Rebecca Solnit, *Savage Dreams: A Journey Into the Landscape Wars of the American West* (Berkeley: University of California Press, 1999), 287-88. The Thomson quotes are taken from Spence, "Dispossessing the Wilderness," 52-54.

Chapter 2: FDR and the New Deal

1. Brinkley, Rightful Heritage, 218
2. Centrally on account of an affair FDR had had with ER's social secretary, Lucy Mercer, during World War I, when Roosevelt was Assistant Secretary of the Navy. ER learned of the affair in 1918. The marriage, however, survived.
3. Broesamle and Arthur, *Clashes of Will,* 142, 144.

4. Later called the Work Projects Administration.
5. *Rightful Heritage,* 46-48.
6. William E. Leuchtenburg, *Franklin D. Roosevelt and the New Deal: 1932-1940* (New York: Harper Torchbooks, 1963), 136.
7. At first the CCC program was referred to by its official title, Emergency Conservation Work, or "ECW." Neither appellation became popular, but "CCC" caught on as the prevailing acronym. In 1937, the name was officially changed to Civilian Conservation Corps. We will stick with that or CCC throughout this book.
8. Ren Davis and Helen Davis, *Our Mark on This Land: A Guide to the Legacy of the Civilian Conservation Corps in America's Parks* (Granville, OH: McDonald & Woodward, 2011), 12-13; "Franklin Delano Roosevelt: Greetings to the CCC, July 1933," https://www.parks.ca.gov/?page_id=24917.
9. Second fireside chat, May 7, 1933, https://www.presidency.ucsb.edu/documents/second-fireside-chat.
10. John Broesamle, *Reform and Reaction in Twentieth Century American Politics* (Westport, CT: Greenwood Press, 1990), 117.
11. Thomas Parrish, "Harry Hopkins's Continuing Relevance," https://historynewsnetwork.org/article/86318.
12. July 7, 1941, 52-53.
13. Roosevelt agreed with Hoover, though, that the bonus itself should not be paid early, as the Bonus Army demanded. Instead, Roosevelt pushed for work relief. Some World War I veterans served in Yosemite, but information about them is exceedingly scarce.
14. T. H. Watkins, *Righteous Pilgrim: The Life and Times of Harold L. Ickes; 1874-1952* (New York: Henry Holt, 1990), 648-49; Terence Young, "'A Contradiction in Democratic Government': W. J. Trent, Jr., and the Struggle to Desegregate National Park Campgrounds, https://www.jstor.org/stable/40608542.
15. Benjamin F. Alexander, *The New Deal's Forest Army: How the Civilian Conservation Corps Worked* (Baltimore: Johns Hopkins University Press, 2018), 52-60.

16. On the last point, see John A. Salmond, *The Civilian Conservation Corps, 1933-1942: A New Deal Case Study* (1967; repr., Washington, D.C.: National Park Service, n.d.), https://www.nps.gov/parkhistory/online_books/ccc/salmond/index.htm.
17. Tracy Campbell, The Year of Peril: America in 1942 (New Haven, CT: Yale University Press, c. 2020), 5.
18. Eric Rauchway, *Why the New Deal Matters* (New Haven, CT: Yale University Press, c. 2021), 32-33.
19. Neil M. Maher, *Nature's New Deal: The Civilian Conservation Corps and the Roots of the American Environmental Movement* (New York: Oxford University Press, 2008), 92, 99.
20. *Happy Days,* February 22, 1936.
21. Donald D. Deignan, *The Shadow of Sacrifice: The True Story of a Pearl Harbor Survivor and His Nephew and Namesake* (Parker, CO: Outskirts Press, c. 2017), 153.
22. Salmond, *Civilian Conservation Corps.*

Chapter 3: The CCC Arrives

1. Albert F. Monteverde, *My CCC's: 1933* (written, 1987; privately printed, 2021), in the author's possession; copy also in Yosemite Archives.
2. Jack Ricci, correspondence with the author.
3. Andrea Miller, correspondence with the author.
4. Sue Fouke, correspondence with, interview by the author.
5. Paige, *Civilian Conservation Corps and the National Park Service,* 78.
6. In 1937, conditioning camps were discontinued, and men began reporting directly to their work sites.
7. *My CCC's.*
8. *"Your CCC": A Handbook for Enrollees,* rev. ed. (repr., Edinburg, VA: Civilian Conservation Corps Legacy, 2011), 73.
9. *My CCC's.*
10. SMR, June 1933.
11. *Wabama News,* April 15, 1938.
12. *My CCC's.*

13. Ibid.
14. Ibid.
15. *Wabama News,* October 17, 1938.
16. *Valley Scavenger,* March 23, April 5, 1939.
17. SMR, March, May 1935.
18. When these camps went up on the Wawona Meadow, they took the name A. E. Wood 1 and 2, after the park's first acting superintendent during the era of army administration, Abraham Epperson Wood. The name was changed to Wawona 1 and 2 in order to quell complaints that the A. E. Wood title sounded too military. Yosemite National Park and the United States Department of the Interior/National Park Service identified camps using different numerical systems. In the USDI scheme, these were NP 15 and 16.
19. "Biography of Howard L. Cox," James F. Justin Civilian Conservation Corps Museum.
20. Al Monteverde to Paul Monteverde, June[?] 1935, copy in the author's possession.
21. SMR, August, October 1933.
22. Ibid., August 1933; October 1934; February 1935.
23. Runte, *Embattled Wilderness,* 164-65.
24. SMR, October, November 1938.
25. Ibid., September, November 1933; Runte, *Embattled Wilderness,* 165.
26. SMR, December 1933; January, February, December 1934; March, July 1936.
27. *My CCC's.*
28. SMR, October 1933, September 1935.
29. Kate Morgan, "Once upon a Tree: The Demise and Potential Revival of the American Chestnut," *Sierra Magazine,* March/April 2021, 31 ff; "The American Chestnut," https://tacf.org/the-american-chestnut/history-american-chestnut/.
30. Elizabeth Kolbert, "Life Hacks," *New Yorker,* January 18, 2021, 32-39; "Dutch Elm Disease," https://www.britannica.com/science/Dutch-elm-disease.

31. Greene, *Historical Narrative,* 980.
32. SMR, November 1938.
33. Paige, *Civilian Conservation Corps and the National Park Service,* 102.
34. Maher, *Nature's New Deal,* 168.
35. Salmond, *Civilian Conservation Corps;* SMR, August, September, October 1934; November 1938; May 1940; February 1941.
36. Ibid., March, May 1935.
37. Ibid., December 1933; February, March, July, September 1934; April 1940; John Newcomb, "Experiences I Recall," undated, Civilian Conservation Corps Collection, National Museum of American History, Smithsonian Institution.
38. SMR, July 1935, May 1936.
39. Paige, *Civilian Conservation Corps and the National Park Service,* 98-99.
40. Bingaman, *Guardians of the Yosemite,* 28.
41. "Climate Change: Temperature Change; 1895-2016," https://www.nps.gov/yose/learn/nature/climate-change.htm
42. SMR, October 1935.
43. Ibid., September 1933.
44. Clair E. Nelsen, "Remembering the CCC: Buck Meadows, California, 1933-1934," *Journal of Forest History* 26, no. 4 (October 1982), https://www.jstor.org/stable/4004683.
45. *Wawona Bear Claws,* January 19, 1935.
46. SMR, July 1934.
47. Bingaman, *Guardians of the Yosemite,* 57.
48. Salmond, *Civilian Conservation Corps.*
49. SMR, August 1934.
50. "Experiences I Recall."
51. Darrel E. Stover memoir, undated, Civilian Conservation Corps file, Yosemite Research Library.
52. *My CCC's.*
53. Stover memoir.
54. *Healdsburg Tribune,* December 4, 1935; "Ponderosa Way – CA," https://livingnewdeal.org/sites/ponderosa-way-ca/.

Chapter 4: Twisting Roads

1. Betsy Gaines Quammen, *American Zion: Cliven Bundy, God & Public Lands in the West* (Salt Lake City: Torrey House Press, 2020),101-02.
2. NPS, *Roads and Bridges,* 20.
3. Davis, *National Park Roads,* 37.
4. NPS, *Roads and Bridges,* 47.
5. Sargent, *Yosemite's Innkeepers,* 12.
6. NPS, *Roads and Bridges,* 48.
7. Davis, *National Park Roads,* 66.
8. Ibid., 62, 66.
9. Sargent, *Yosemite's Innkeepers,* 32.
10. NPS, *Roads and Bridges,* 48.
11. Ibid., 69.
12. Ibid., 72-75. The remainder still arrived via the automobile's fading competitors, train, old-style stagecoach, and motor stage.
13. Davis, *National Park Roads,* 142.
14. Albright and Cahn, *Birth of the National Park Service,* 19-21; "Tioga Road (HAER No. CA-149) Written Historical and Descriptive Data," https://tinyurl.com/e2ky5pu5.
15. Albright and Cahn, Birth of the National Park Service, 264-65.
16. Davis, *National Park Roads,* 171.
17. NPS, *Roads and Bridges,* 77.
18. Davis, *National Park Roads,* 171.
19. Greene, *Historical Narrative,* 769.
20. NPS, *Roads and Bridges,* 91.
21. Greene, *Historical Narrative,* 768-69.
22. Today's Federal Highway Administration.
23. Davis, *National Park Roads,* 6-9.
24. Ibid., 174.
25. SMR, April 1934.
26. NPS, *Roads and Bridges,* 103.
27. Ibid., 98.
28. SMR, August 1933.

29. Annie Reynolds and Albert Gordon, *Stage to Yosemite: Recollections of Wawona's Albert Gordon* (El Portal, CA: Big Tree Books, c. 1994), 24.
30. SMR, December 1933, March 1934.
31. Ibid., March 1934.

Chapter 5: The Pivotal Year: 1934

1. T. H. Watkins, *Righteous Pilgrim: The Life and Times of Harold L. Ickes; 1874-1952* (New York: Henry Holt, 1990).
2. Brinkley, *Rightful Heritage,* 245.
3. Paige, *Civilian Conservation Corps and the National Park Service,* 105-06.
4. *The Secret Diary of Harold L. Ickes,* vol. 2, *The First Thousand Days: 1933-1936* (New York: Simon and Schuster, c. 1953), 176.
5. Ibid., 177.
6. Peñalosa, *Yosemite in the 1930s,* 1; Sargent, *Yosemite's Innkeepers,* 112.
7. The following account is taken from Nancy Newhall, *Ansel Adams: The Eloquent Light; His Photographs and the Classic Biography* (New York: Aperture, c. 1980), 114-17.
8. Watkins, *Righteous Pilgrim,* 550.
9. Sargent, *Yosemite's Innkeepers,* 118-19.
10. Watkins, *Righteous Pilgrim,* 552-53, 579.
11. Ibid., 575.
12. Brinkley, *Rightful Heritage,* 265.
13. Maher, *Nature's New Deal,* 171, 177, 178.
14. Greene, *Historical Narrative,* 734.
15. National Park Service, *Cultural Landscapes Inventory: Tuolumne Meadows Historic District; Yosemite National Park* (2007), https://www.nps.gov/yose/learn/management/upload/Final-TMDistrict-CLI-09-13-07.pdf
16. SMR, July 1933.
17. Ibid. The Sierra Club had an inholding at the site of Parsons Memorial Lodge, where the NPS lacked authority. There camping continued – well off the river – over the ensuing decades. Thus, a private campground

coexisted with the new public one.

18. Inspired by its resident landscape architect, John Wosky, Yosemite's master plan was completed in 1934, though in Tuolumne its overall goals were being acted upon far earlier.
19. National Park Service, *A Sense of Place: Design Guidelines for Yosemite National Park* (n.d. [2011?]), https://tinyurl.com/4vm3tay6.
20. Albert H. Good, *Patterns from the Golden Age of Rustic Design: Park and Recreation Structures from the 1930s* (1938; repr., Lanham, MD: Roberts Rinehart, 2003).
21. NPS, *Tuolumne Meadows Historic District.*
22. *Wawona Wolverine,* October 1940.
23. The following year, CCC men tore down the now-disused mess hall and cookhouse at Ranger Camp.
24. Benjamin Alexander, "85 Years Ago: FDR's Forest Army Planted 3 Billion Trees . . . ," https://treesource.org/news/lands/ccc-tree-planting/; "Shelterbelt Project (1934)," https://livingnewdeal.org/glossary/shelterbelt-project-1934/; "6 Projects the Civilian Conservation Corps Accomplished," https://www.history.com/news/civilian-conservation-corps-projects; *The National Parks: America's Best Idea,* episode 5, "Great Nature," PBS, 2009.
25. SMR, January 1934.
26. Ibid., February 1934.
27. NPS, *Roads and Bridges,* 77, 80, 87.
28. SMR, October 1934. Further details do not appear to have survived.
29. Ibid., August 1934.
30. Ibid., January 1935, July 1936, April 1937; NPS, *Roads and Bridges,* 101.
31. NPS, *Tuolumne Meadows Historic District.*
32. Peñalosa, *Yosemite in the 1930s,* 16.
33. SMR, January 1934.
34. Ickes, *First Thousand Days,* 177. Here as elsewhere, sources conflict on the details of ER's 1934 Yosemite trip. For differing accounts, see Blanche Wiesen Cook, *Eleanor Roosevelt,* vol. 2, *1933-1938* (New York: Viking, 1999), 206-08; and Brinkley, *Rightful Heritage,* 255.

35. Eleanor Roosevelt, *This I Remember* (New York: Harper & Brothers, c. 1949), 120.
36. Cook, *Eleanor Roosevelt,* 205.
37. Brinkley, *Rightful Heritage,* 254.
38. Sargent, *Yosemite's Innkeepers,* 85.
39. Lorena A. Hickok, *Eleanor Roosevelt: Reluctant First Lady* (New York: Dodd, Mead, 1980), 165.
40. The following paragraphs detailing the trip are drawn from: ibid., 166; Roosevelt, *This I Remember,* 142-43; Bingaman, *Guardians of the Yosemite,* 17, 40; Shirley Sargent, *Yosemite's Famous Guests* (Yosemite, CA: Flying Spur Press, c. 1970); Cook, *Eleanor Roosevelt,* 205-06; Elizabeth Stone O'Neill, *Meadow in the Sky: A History of Yosemite's Tuolumne Meadows Region,* rev. ed. (Fresno, CA: Panorama West Books, 1986), 116; Peter Browning, *Place Names of the Sierra Nevada: From Abbot to Zumwalt,* 2nd ed. (Berkeley, CA: Wilderness Press, 1991), 158.
41. Lake Eleanor was not named for ER. It was named instead during the 1860s for the daughter of the geologist Josiah Whitney, for whom Mount Whitney is named. During the early twenty-first century, Roosevelt Lake was returned to a fishless state.
42. Doris Kearns Goodwin, *No Ordinary Time: Franklin and Eleanor Roosevelt; The Home Front in World War II* (New York: Simon and Schuster, 1994), 219.
43. See, for instance, ibid., 219-25; and Cook, *Eleanor Roosevelt,* passim.
44. *No Ordinary Time,* 221.
45. Ibid., 223-24; Roosevelt, *This I Remember,* 142-43; Hickok, *Reluctant First Lady,* 167; Cook, *Eleanor Roosevelt,* 207.
46. Hickok, *Reluctant First Lady,* 168-69.
47. Cook, *Eleanor Roosevelt,* 207-08.
48. John F. Burgess memoir, undated, Civilian Conservation Corps file, Yosemite Research Library.
49. O'Neill, *Mountain Sage,* 140.

Chapter 6: Life in the CCC

1. February 15, 1937, 9.
2. Numbers vary from a very precise 6,816 to over 8,000. See Lois Orr, "The Civilian Conservation Corps (CCC) in Yosemite," *Yosemite,* Fall 2005, 3 (lower number), and Davis and Davis, *Our Mark on This Land,* 278 (higher number). Despite the attempt at scrupulous record-keeping, I have not seen a number I would bet on; likely none exists.
3. *Wabama News,* October 17, 1938.
4. "Biography of Herbert S. Lake," James F. Justin Civilian Conservation Corps Museum.
5. *Wawona Wolverine,* November 1941.
6. Al Monteverde to Paul Monteverde, March 4, 1936, copy in the author's possession.
7. Davis and Davis, *Our Mark on This Land,* v (writer unnamed).
8. Sue Fouke, correspondence with the author.
9. *Wawona Wolverine,* October 1940.
10. Cox biography.
11. Ray Hoyt, *"We Can Take It": A Short Story of the C.C.C.* (1935; repr., Edinburg, VA: Civilian Conservation Corps Legacy, 2015), 34; Nelsen, "Remembering the CCC."
12. *Wabama News,* April 6, 1938.
13. Ibid., April 15, 1938.
14. Jack Ricci, correspondence with the author.
15. Melvin interview. Mel Melvin was not stationed in Yosemite.
16. *Wawona Wolverine,* October 1940.
17. Yosemite Research Library.
18. Alexander, *Forest Army,* 97.
19. Nelsen, "Remembering the CCC"; Salmond, *Civilian Conservation Corps.*
20. Jack Rettinhouse memoir, May 19, 1989, Civilian Conservation Corps file, Yosemite Research Library.
21. Al Monteverde to Paul Monteverde, April[?] 1935, copy in the author's possession.

22. Stover memoir.
23. Alexander, *Forest Army,* 104, 106.
24. Salmond, *Civilian Conservation Corps.*
25. For example, *Pow-Wawonian,* December 24, 1936.
26. *Wawona Bear Claws,* March 29, 1935.
27. *"Your CCC": A Handbook for Enrollees,* 42.
28. Stover memoir.
29. *Wawona Bear Claws,* November 28, 1934.
30. "Remembering the CCC."
31. *Wawona Wolverine,* February 1941.
32. Ibid., January 1941.
33. Salmond, *Civilian Conservation Corps.*
34. Stover memoir.
35. *Wawona Bear Claws,* January 19, 1935.
36. O'Neill, *Mountain Sage,* 132.
37. *Wabama News,* September 22, 1938.
38. *Pow-Wawonian,* December 24, 1936.
39. Stover memoir.
40. *Wawona Bear Claws,* February 16, 1935.
41. Ibid., March 29, 1935.
42. *My CCC's.*
43. *Wawona Bear Claws,* random page, undated.
44. *My CCC's.*
45. Al Monteverde to Paul Monteverde, February [?] 1935, copy in the author's possession.
46. *My CCC's.*
47. Ibid.
48. Jack Ricci, correspondence with the author.
49. Maher, *Nature's New Deal,* 11, 14.
50. U.S. Census Bureau, "Highest Educational Attainment Levels Since 1940," https://rb.gy/m37sg1; "What Percent of Americans Graduate from High School?" https://www.winginstitute.org/what-percent-of-americans.

51. Salmond, *Civilian Conservation Corps.*
52. Catalina Monteverde to Paul Monteverde, May 21, 1935, copy in the author's possession. Original in caps.
53. Alexander, *Forest Army,* 24, 83, 89, 113. John C. Paige indicates that park superintendents in general were not enthusiastic about the CCC education program, though not exactly why, or how Thomson or his successors felt. (*Civilian Conservation Corps and the National Park Service,* 83 ff.)
54. *Pow-Wawonian,* June 23, 1937.
55. *"We Can Take It,"* 91.
56. Salmond, *Civilian Conservation Corps.*
57. Alexander, *Forest Army,* 86; Davis and Davis, *Our Mark on This Land,* 26.
58. *Wawona Wolverine,* April, September 1941.
59. SMR, January 1934.
60. *Pow-Wawonian,* August 29, 1936.
61. *Wawona Bear Claws,* February 16, 1935.
62. *"Your CCC": A Handbook for Enrollees,* 32.
63. Arnold Seibel to Alice and Maurice, August 1, 1933, Seibel-Murphy Archives.
64. *Pow-Wawonian,* September 14, 1936; *Wawona Wolverine,* October 1940.
65. 1937-1940.
66. *Cascade News,* May 18, 1936; *Wabama News,* January 17, June 13, August 29, 1938; *Wawona Wolverine,* November 1940, July 1941.
67. *My CCC's*; Nona Monteverde Rafferty and Gary Rafferty, correspondence with the author.
68. *Oakland Tribune,* April 4, 1978.
69. Roger G. Kennedy and David Larkin, *When Art Worked: The New Deal, Art, and Democracy* (New York: Rizzoli, 2009), 26.
70. *Wawona Bear Claws,* November 28, 1934.
71. Another CCC art project entailed producing large relief maps of the Sierra range for the Yosemite Museum. The maps were molded by CCC

men in Berkeley, then painted by enrollees inside the museum under the supervision of park naturalists.

72. *Oakland Tribune,* April 4, 1978.
73. Several can easily be found at the following: "Historical Civilian Conservation Corps (CCC) Newspapers Online," https://rb.gy/esm4vw/.
74. January 19, 1935.
75. June 22, 1939.
76. *Wawona Bear Claws,* January 19, 1935.
77. March 16, 1935.
78. April 5, 1939.
79. Cox biography.
80. Alexander, *Forest Army,* 105, 110.
81. SMR, May, July 1935.
82. Stover memoir.
83. John Sharsmith and Allan Sbields, eds., *Climb Every Mountain: A Portrait of Carl Sharsmith* (Mariposa, CA: Jerseydale Ranch Press, c. 1996), 53.
84. As of 1938, for instance, gates at the south entrance and Arch Rock were open 6:00 AM-10:00 PM.
85. Stover memoir.
86. SMR, January 1937.
87. *Wawona Bear Claws,* May 3, 1935.
88. *My CCC's.*
89. Salmond, *Civilian Conservation Corps;* Paige, *Civilian Conservation Corps and the National Park Service,* 88. By the late 'thirties, concerns developed over the fact that potentially eligible recruits were opting for better-paying jobs in the private sector, and also, it seems, about the caliber and morale of many of the men who were newly enrolling. In 1938, the eligibility age was lowered to seventeen and the conditioning camps were scrubbed; now men went directly to their company worksites. In 1941, the \$30.00/\$5.00 formula underwent change as well, and the number of leader positions was raised.
90. O'Neill, *Mountain Sage,* 135-36; Sharsmith and Shields, *Climb Every*

Mountain, 56 ff.

91. Alexander, *Forest Army,* 78-79.
92. SMR, July 1934, May 1941; *Cascade News,* May 18, 1936; Monteverde, *My CCC's*; *Valley Scavenger,* February 24, 1940.
93. Al Monteverde to Paul Monteverde, March 4, 1936, and undated letter, copies in the author's possession; *Wawona Bear Claws,* April 5, 1935; SMR, August 1939.
94. *Wabama News,* September 22, 1938. Meantime, a dentist was making regular tours of the camps.
95. SMR, November 1934, May 1939; Michael P. Ghiglieri and Charles R. "Butch" Farabee, Jr., *Off the Wall: Death in Yosemite* (Flagstaff, AZ: Puma Press, c. 2007), 110, 219, 227.
96. Ibid., 109-10, 186, 257-58; SMR, May 1935, June 1937, January 1938.
97. Stover memoir. Mention must also be made of the lives lost expanding the dam at Hetch Hetchy. The first phase of construction (1921-1923) had been a bloodbath; eighteen workers died, a conspicuous number of them from sickening falls. Phase two (1935-1938), when more safety precautions were taken, cost an additional four lives. (Ghiglieri and Farabee, *Off the Wall,* 107-09.)
98. Salmond, *Civilian Conservation Corps.*

Chapter 7: Big New Initiatives: The Mid-1930s

1. Maher, *Nature's New Deal,* 71.
2. Richard P. Ditton and Donald E. McHenry, "Self-Guiding Auto Tour of Yosemite National Park" (1956), https://t.ly/SI0Jj.
3. SMR, September 1940; Runte, Embattled Wilderness, 174.
4. *The Dreamt Land: Chasing Water and Dust across California* (New York: Alfred A. Knopf, 2019), 247.
5. SMR, October, December 1934; September 1935; January, March, April 1936.
6. Maher, *Nature's New Deal,* 70, 73, 161-62.
7. Ibid., 73.
8. "A Ranger Talk with Dr. Carl Sharsmith," video by Tom Bopp, August

29, 1994.

9. Greene, *Historical Narrative,* 758.
10. SMR, November 1933, October 1934; Jim Snyder, interview and correspondence with the author; NPS, *Roads and Bridges,* 94; Peñalosa, *Yosemite in the 1930s,* 146.
11. *Pow-Wawonian,* August 29, 1936.
12. Jim Snyder, correspondence with the author.
13. SMR, March 1935.
14. Ibid., November 1935.
15. Ibid., March 1936.
16. Ibid., February 1937, February 1940.
17. In the late 1920s, development of ski huts had commenced in Yosemite, either as new buildings or by opening existing cabins as high as Tuolumne Meadows for winter use. This was done in anticipation of ski touring becoming a major winter sport. YP&CCo pioneered cross-country ski tours in the U.S., lasting two to six days. But unlike downhill skiing, ski touring never really took off in the park. (Sargent, *Yosemite's Innkeepers,* 109-10; Greene, *Historical Narrative,* 670-71.)
18. SMR, August, October 1940; *Wawona Wolverine,* September 1941. The hut was set up to accommodate two dozen skiers. It even had a registration desk. Guests could rent beds and buy meals prepared by YP&CCo staff, or else carry in their own food and sleeping bags. There were two kitchens, one to accommodate each type of guest. A dinner menu from the early 1940s featured a choice of salmon or veal. (Undated menu provided to the author by Andrea Miller.)
19. SMR, February 1941.
20. *Yosemite Sentinel,* November 6, 1941.
21. At this point, the PWA was absorbed into the new Federal Works Agency, as was the Works Progress Administration, now renamed the Work Projects Administration. Joining them was the Public Roads Administration, successor to the Bureau of Public Roads.
22. Sargent, *Yosemite's Innkeepers,* 23, 28, 30.
23. SMR, July, August 1937.

24. Greene, *Historical Narrative,* 785.
25. SMR, January 1935.
26. Ibid., June 1936; NPS, *Roads and Bridges,* 108.
27. NPS, *Roads and Bridges,* 110; SMR, June 1940.
28. SMR., January 1936.
29. Ibid., September 1936, June 1937.
30. Ibid., September, October 1937.
31. Ibid., October 1938, October 1939.

Chapter 8: The End

1. Kittredge had been named chief engineer of the NPS in 1927.
2. NPS, *Roads and Bridges,* 107.
3. Greene, *Historical Narrative,* 968, 971.
4. *The Wild Muir: Twenty-Two of John Muir's Greatest Adventures,* ed. Lee Stetson (Yosemite National Park: Yosemite Association; Berkeley, CA: Heyday Books, c. 1994), 73-81.
5. "The Yosemite Rock Fall of July 10, 1996," https://seismo.berkeley.edu/blog/1996/07/10/the-yosemite-rock-fall-of-july-10-1996.html.
6. *Cascade News,* May 18, 1936.
7. Greene, *Historical Narrative,* 852, 969; SMR, December 1937; NPS, *Roads and Bridges,* 107-08.
8. SMR, December 1937.
9. Jim Snyder, correspondence with the author; *Wabama News,* December 18, 1937; Greene, *Historical Narrative,* 853.
10. SMR, December 1937.
11. When the All Year Highway did finally reopen, cars had to proceed for miles in convoys under a control system. Restoration of the route continued until at least 1939. Pumps cleared the water out of the long tunnel on the Big Oak Flat Road. All of this – the storm, the snow, the road carnage – depressed annual visitation for 1938.

    The National Park Service had not even existed when the last big flood hit in 1907, and the 1937 flood shocked the NPS. Camp Cascades had been situated in an excellent setting, barring the river's unexpected rise. The flood was categorized as a freak event, an outlier. In retrospect, it was instead a harbinger of more big floods to come. The next one occurred just thirteen years later. (Jim Snyder, correspondence with the author.)

12. The following account is based upon: SMR, April, June 1938; *New York Times,* June 14, 1938; Ghiglieri and Farabee, *Off the Wall,* 115-19; Bingaman, *Guardians of the Yosemite,* 33. Sources on the disaster tend to contain widely conflicting information as well as factual errors.
13. The predecessor of Trans World Airlines.
14. TWA had offered a reward of $1,000 to anyone who found the plane, which Collier had. Meanwhile, Collier had just received an honorable discharge from the CCC. Being out of government service made him eligible to claim the reward. Rumors circulated that he had found the wreck earlier, but waited until mid-June to report it. Whether this was true or not has never been resolved, and is likely unknowable. The wreck, revealed by snowmelt, had certainly not been visible for long. Collier died in 2005, at the age of ninety.
15. The following paragraphs detailing the visit are drawn from: SMR, July 1938; Bingaman, *Guardians of the Yosemite,* 38; Sargent, *Yosemite's Famous Guests,* 35; Al Monteverde, draft résumé, copy in the author's possession.
16. Salmond, *Civilian Conservation Corps.*
17. Ibid.; Alexander, *Forest Army,* 122.
18. Salmond, *Civilian Conservation Corps.*
19. Alexander, *Forest Army,* 93.
20. Al Monteverde to Paul Monteverde, undated, copy in the author's possession.
21. Al Monteverde to Paul Monteverde, June [?] 1935, copy in the author's possession.
22. Jack Ricci, correspondence with the author.
23. Paige, *Civilian Conservation Corps and the National Park Service,* 31, 88.
24. NPS, *Tuolumne Meadows Historic District.*
25. Paige, *Civilian Conservation Corps and the National Park Service,* 129.
26. SMR, July, August 1936; May, June 1938; March, April 1940.

27. Ibid., December 1938.
28. Jack C. Gilpin memoir, undated, Civilian Conservation Corps file, Yosemite Research Library.
29. *Wabama News,* January 24, 1938.
30. *Valley Scavenger,* February 24, 1940. The film portrays a version of history that historians have roundly discredited.
31. April 9, 1940.
32. *Valley Scavenger,* April 1940.
33. David M. Kennedy, *Freedom from Fear: The American People in Depression and War, 1929-1945* (New York: Oxford University Press, 1999), 237.
34. SMR, July, September 1941.
35. Ibid., September, October 1941; *Wawona Wolverine,* November 1941.
36. SMR., October 1941.
37. Ibid., December 1941.
38. Other legacy organizations include the California Conservation Corps.
39. Ibid., January, February, April 1942.
40. Ibid., May, June 1942.
41. Ibid., July, August 1942.

Chapter 9: What Came Afterward

1. Alexander, *Forest Army,* 137.
2. Jack Ricci, correspondence with the author.
3. Nona Monteverde Rafferty, introduction to *My CCC's.* The portrait of Al's life after the CCC draws on correspondence and interviews with Nona Monteverde Rafferty and Gary Rafferty.
4. Sue Fouke, correspondence with, interview by the author.
5. Andrea Miller, correspondence with the author.
6. Nelsen, "Remembering the CCC."
7. For a broadly concurring judgment in an important book that takes a somewhat different perspective from this one, see Runte, *Embattled Wilderness,* 160. The rethinking, indeed, went back to the 1920s – for instance, with establishment of the new Advisory Board and the beginning of the

elimination of the Old Village in order to consolidate the footprint of services and open up scenery. The 1920s did not represent the tipping point, but did anticipate it. For the first time, during that decade the conflict between preservation and use in Yosemite came to be recognized. See Greene, vol. 3, *Discussion of Historical Resources . . . ,* 1014 ff.

8. (Boston: Houghton Mifflin.)
9. Greene, *Historical Narrative,* 981.
10. Matthew Brown, "Mountain Pine Tree That Feeds Grizzlies Is Threatened," https://www.khon2.com/news/national/us-mountain-pine-tree-that-feeds-grizzlies-is-threatened/.
11. "White Pine Blister Rust," https://www.fs.usda.gov/rm/highelevation whitepines/Threats/blister-rust-threat.htm.
12. *Guardians of the Yosemite,* 28, 30.
13. SMR, October 1941.
14. *New York Times,* May 18, 2021; "Planning for a Changing Climate . . . in the National Park Service," https://rb.gy/jwdmz5.
15. Wawona Wolverine, November 1941.
16. For the details of this convoluted story, see Davis, National Park Roads, 174-75.
17. SMR, October 1935; June, September 1936; "Tioga Road (HAER No. CA-149) Written Historical and Descriptive Data."
18. Greene, Historical Narrative, 749.
19. Peñalosa, Yosemite in the 1930s, 28.
20. NPS, Roads and Bridges, 111.
21. NPS, A Sense of Place.
22. As of 1935, according to the monthly report of the park superintendent (October 1935), planning envisioned some route that would include the spectacular views in the vicinity of Tenaya Canyon. We have seen, though, that details had not been finalized by the end of the New Deal era.
23. Davis, *National Park Roads,* 145, 155-56, 184.
24. The dispute played a role in terminating the longstanding alliance between the club and the park service. William E. Colby – a leading

advocate of roads in the park who had delivered the keynote address for the Big Oak Flat Road opening in 1940, and who backed the Tioga Road alignment as proposed by the government – was so stung by the club's opposition that he resigned from the board of directors. (Various points in the Sierra bear his name, and the club's library is named in his memory.) Ansel Adams, who took the opposite position, had his own resignation from the board rejected by its other members. (Ibid., 238-39; Greene, *Historical Narrative,* 797; NPS, *Roads and Bridges,* 103.)

25. Robert Turnage, "Ansel Adams: The Role of the Artist in the Environmental Movement," https://www.anseladams.com/ansel-adams-the-role-of-the-artist-in-the-environmental-movement/.
26. October 16, 1994.
27. "A Ranger Talk with Dr. Carl Sharsmith."
28. *Wawona Wolverine,* February 1941.
29. Paul Monteverde to "My Dear Beloved People," July 4, 1936, copy in the author's possession.
30. *My CCC's.*
31. Burgess memoir.
32. Stover memoir.

PHOTO CREDITS

Cover credit

Front Nona Monteverde Rafferty

Interior credits

p. 9 Yosemite Archives
12 Yosemite Archives
16 Superintendent's annual report, 1937; Yosemite Archives
30 The Living New Deal; Yosemite Archives
32 Franklin D. Roosevelt Presidential Library and Museum
35 Yosemite Archives
36 *Al Monteverde*, Nona Monteverde Rafferty
36 *John Ricci*, Jack Ricci
37 Andrea Miller
38 Sue Fouke
43 Superintendent's monthly report, June 1933; Yosemite Archives
44 Nona Monteverde Rafferty; photographer Al Monteverde
45 Carolyn Vondriska
46 Yosemite Archives
60 Carolyn Vondriska
70 Yosemite Archives
71 Smithsonian National Postal Museum
76 Yosemite Archives; photographer Ralph Anderson

77	Yosemite Archives; photographer Ralph Anderson
82	Carolyn Vondriska
87	Franklin D. Roosevelt Presidential Library and Museum
96	Yosemite Research Library
100	Nona Monteverde Rafferty; photographer Al Monteverde
103	Nona Monteverde Rafferty; photographer Al Monteverde
110	Superintendent's monthly report, August 1936; Yosemite Archives
128	Carolyn Vondriska
129	Carolyn Vondriska
134	John Broesamle
136	Yosemite Archives; photographer Ralph Anderson
137	Carolyn Vondriska
140	*Yosemite Falls view*, AP
140	*From tunnel view*, AP
145	Yosemite Archives
160	*1930s restrooms*, Carolyn Vondriska
160	*1950s restrooms*, Carolyn Vondriska
163	Carolyn Vondriska
164	Carolyn Vondriska
203	Carolyn Vondriska

INDEX

Note: Italicized page numbers refer to images. Page numbers followed by an "n" denote endnotes.

ABOUT THE AUTHOR

Author John Broesamle was professor emeritus of History at California State University, Northridge, where he taught for thirty-two years. He held a Ph.D. in history from Columbia University. A political and social historian of modern America, he also wrote about and taught environmental history. Broesamle was a prolific and passionate author, and *Transforming Paradise* was his tenth and final book. He died on June 17, 2023, after a five-year battle with pancreatic cancer. The Press at California State University, Fresno accepted the manuscript for publication just weeks before his death, and it is being published posthumously in partnership with his family.

Broesamle had a lifelong association with Yosemite. As visitor for more than 80 years and as trained historian, he provides a living link between Yosemite during the New Deal era and the Yosemite of today. His family was one of the original Tuolumne Meadows "old-timers," a community of teachers who spent entire summers there. His parents taught him to fly fish, a lifelong calling he fostered in his children and grandchildren. He also saw it as a vehicle for imparting values and ethics; the fly-fishing life became the perfect symbol of his abiding commitment to tread lightly and humanely on the planet. He met his wife, Kathy, during one of the many college summers they both worked in the park.

Broesamle's other "home" was the Ojai Valley, where his decades of nonprofit environmental leadership resulted in the creation and restoration of large open space preserves, as well as a community chest of more than a million dollars to protect and sustain the environmental quality of the valley. Broesamle's environmental work over the decades earned him the reputation as "conservation giant." His hands-on work evokes the very spirit of much of what the New Deal accomplished in Yosemite.

In many ways, this is a tale that only John Broesamle could tell.

John Broesamle – beloved husband, father, grandfather, professor, and friend
February 10, 1941 – June 17, 2023
(pictured here at new Camp Cascades, mess hall stone fireplace)

Made in the USA
Monee, IL
23 August 2024

64361333R00125